Make every Web page look like a masterpiece!

Easy
web graphics

Microsoft

Julie Adair King

PUBLISHED BY
Microsoft Press
A Division of Microsoft Corporation
One Microsoft Way
Redmond, Washington 98052-6399

Library of Congress Cataloging-in-Publication Data
King, Julie Adair.
    Easy Web Graphics / Julie Adair King.
        p. cm.
    ISBN 0-7356-1192-0
    1. Computer Graphics.   2. Web sites--Design.   I. Title.

    T385.K48817   2001
    006.6--dc21

                                                            00-053302

Printed and bound in the United States of America.

1 2 3 4 5 6 7 8 9   QWT   6 5 4 3 2 1

Distributed in Canada by Penguin Books Canada Limited.

A CIP catalogue record for this book is available from the British Library.

Microsoft Press books are available through booksellers and distributors worldwide. For further information about international editions, contact your local Microsoft Corporation office or contact Microsoft Press International directly at fax (425) 936-7329. Visit our Web site at mspress.microsoft.com. Send comments to *mspinput@microsoft.com*.

FrontPage, Microsoft, Microsoft Press, PhotoDraw, Picture It!, PowerPoint, and Windows are either registered trademarks or trademarks of Microsoft Corporation in the United States and/or other countries. Other product and company names mentioned herein may be the trademarks of their respective owners.

Unless otherwise noted, the example companies, organizations, products, people, and events depicted herein are fictitious. No association with any real company, organization, product, person, or event is intended or should be inferred.

Acquisitions Editor: Casey Doyle
Project Editor: Sally Stickney
Technical Editor: Robert Lyon

TABLE OF contents

Part One: Image Is Everything

What's the easiest way to turn a so-so Web site into a great place to visit? A design makeover! Add a picture here, change a font there, and you can not only improve the look of your site but also make pages easier to navigate. The chapters in Part One show you how.

Part Two: The Fine Print

The chapters in Part Two will help you achieve a balance between style and sensibility on your Web pages. First you'll walk through the process of adding and formatting your regular body text in Microsoft FrontPage—a task that's surprisingly more complex than formatting text for print documents. Then you'll learn how to create some cool text effects that you can use for banner heads and other large type elements.

Part Three: Picture This

In Part Three, you'll learn how to use the drawing, painting, and photo editing tools in PhotoDraw 2000 to create custom logos and illustrations, enhance and retouch digital photos, and create rollover buttons and animated images. You'll also walk through the process of adding all the elements you've created in earlier chapters to your Web pages in FrontPage.

acknowledgments

I would like to express my sincere appreciation to the wonderful folks at Microsoft Press who lent their considerable talents to this book. Many, many thanks to Sally Stickney, for her astute and patient editorial guidance; to Shawn Peck, for his thoughtful and thorough manuscript edit; to Robert Lyon, for his keen technical insights; and to Rob Nance, Elizabeth Hansford, William Teel, and the rest of the production staff for their design and layout artistry.

I am also grateful to Casey Doyle for inviting me to be part of this project, and to Chris Van Buren of the Waterside Productions agency for all his efforts on my behalf.

Finally, I am indebted to Hew Hamilton, who helped design some of the Web pages and graphics you see in this book and graciously shared his knowledge and experience with me.

All of you improved this book immeasurably, and I consider myself incredibly lucky to have had you in my corner.

introduction

Perhaps you're developing a Web site for a business, school, or community organization. Or maybe you're creating an online meeting place for your family or for people who share your interest in a particular subject. Whatever the case, I assume that you picked up this book for one reason: you want simple, quick ways to make your site more visually appealing. That's exactly what you'll find in *Easy Web Graphics*.

This book is packed with easy, no-experience-required techniques that you can use to enhance the appearance of your Web pages. Along with plenty of examples for inspiration, you'll find fully illustrated, step-by-step instructions for creating your own logos and other custom art, shooting and editing digital photographs, and working with clip-art graphics. Even if this is your first foray into computer graphics or Web design, you'll be able to produce eye-catching backgrounds, navigation buttons, banner text, product shots, and more.

Of course, developing great-looking Web pages requires more than creating bucketloads of graphics. You need to blend all those graphics, along with the text portions of your pages, into an overall design. To that end, this book explains the basics of effective design so that you can analyze your site and make it more attractive—and more convenient for people who visit it. I'll also break down the technical side of Web design into easy-to-understand language to help you avoid problems that can cause your site to load slowly or to be displayed incorrectly in some browsers.

In short, this book tells you everything you need to know to create dynamic Web pages—fast!

A Quick Look Ahead

Having just promised to help you get your Web site design—or redesign—projects done quickly, I won't waste your time with a lengthy preview of all the topics covered in this book. Instead, here's a quick rundown of which chapters cover what subject so you can easily locate the one that may be first on your agenda.

If you want to know how to . . .	Look here
Develop an attractive, functional page design	Chapters 1 and 4
Put together a Web graphics studio	Chapter 2
Ensure that graphics display at the right size	Chapters 3, 9, and 10
Select "Web-safe" colors for your graphics and text	Chapter 3
Use tables to control page layout	Chapter 4
Create cool page backgrounds using image tiles and other tricks	Chapter 5
Choose the right fonts, type sizes, and other text attributes	Chapter 6
Design and create banner text and graphical bullets	Chapter 7
Draw and paint logos, buttons, and other custom artwork	Chapter 8
Locate and use clip-art graphics	Chapter 8
Improve the photos on your Web site	Chapter 9
Save pictures in the JPEG or GIF formats	Chapter 9
Insert and position graphics in your Web pages	Chapter 10
Create image maps and other graphical links	Chapter 10
Avoid technical pitfalls related to graphics and design	All chapters!

Note that this list represents just a sampling of what you'll find in the pages to come. For a more detailed look, scan the Table of Contents or the index at the back of the book.

Software Requirements

The examples and instructions in *Easy Web Graphics* feature the following software:

- Microsoft PhotoDraw 2000 Version 2
- Microsoft FrontPage 2000

PhotoDraw 2000 enables you to create and edit graphics and photos, and FrontPage 2000 is a Web design and site-building program. Included in Microsoft Office 2000 Premium Edition, PhotoDraw and FrontPage are designed to work together to simplify your Web projects. PhotoDraw 2000 Version 2 is an updated version of the original release of PhotoDraw 2000 Version 1. This book features capabilities available in Version 2 that are not available in Version 1. However, even if you're using Version 1 or some other program, you'll be able to easily adapt many of the concepts in this book to your software.

If you *are* working with PhotoDraw and FrontPage, I suggest that you visit the Office Update Web site (*http://officeupdate.microsoft.com*) to see whether you need to download and install any files to update your software to the most current version. You should also make sure that your computer system meets the minimum requirements for running these two programs, which are accessible on the Microsoft Office Web site:

http://www.microsoft.com/office/

Most of All, Have Fun!

I want to add one final word of advice and encouragement before you start exploring the rest of this book. As you may already be aware, some aspects of creating Web graphics can be a little confusing. You have to deal with pixels, color palettes, and other technical issues that tax even the most capable brain. But don't worry if the Web's technical side seems overwhelming at first. *Easy Web Graphics* will get you up to speed quickly so that you can stop struggling with the technical questions and start experiencing the joy of the creative process.

Whatever the purpose of your Web site—whether you want to add just a few new graphics touches or do a complete design makeover—this book will provide you with the ideas and information you need to be successful. So fire up your computer, flip to a chapter that piques your interest, and have fun!

Support

Every effort has been made to ensure the accuracy of this book. Microsoft Press provides corrections for books at the following address:

http://mspress.microsoft.com/support/

If you have comments, questions, or ideas regarding this book, please send them to Microsoft Press via e-mail to:

mspinput@microsoft.com

or via postal mail to:

Microsoft Press
Attn: *Easy Web Graphics* Editor
One Microsoft Way
Redmond, WA 98052-6399

Please note that product support is not offered through the above addresses.

PART

one

IMAGE IS everything

What's the easiest way to turn a so-so Web site into a great place to visit? A design makeover! Add a picture here, change a font there, and you can not only improve the look of your site but also make pages easier to navigate.

But how do you decide what should go and what should stay? What tools do you need to spruce up your site? The chapters in this part offer answers to these questions as well as ideas to inspire your creative side. In addition, you'll find step-by-step instructions for laying out a basic design framework and creating backgrounds that enhance the text and graphics on your site.

Good Web design isn't all about outward appearances, though—you also need to understand the technical nature of the Web. If you don't, you can cause yourself all sorts of problems, from pages that aren't displayed properly in some browsers to download times so excessive that your audience may click away before your site even finishes loading. To help you avoid these pitfalls, the chapters in this part also give you the firm technical footing you need to make your design projects a success.

seeing

1

with a
DESIGNER'S EYE

All you need to know about . . .

- Evaluating your site from your audience's perspective

- Avoiding visual overload

- Focusing the visitor's eye on critical information

- Giving the eye a "resting place"

- Eliminating time-wasting design features

- Tailoring the look of your page to your audience

- Designing around the Web's technical hazards

In the early years of the World Wide Web, you didn't need to worry much about the appearance of your site because the programming code used to create and display Web pages limited you to plain gray backgrounds and text-only pages. Your site looked just like all the others—which is to say, boring.

Today's Web browsers and Web site–building programs make possible a much broader range of design possibilities. You can give your pages a colorful background, add fancy text and graphics, and even use animated buttons as page links. And with programs such as Microsoft FrontPage and Microsoft PhotoDraw, you no longer have to mess with lots of complicated programming code to add these design elements to your site. You just click a button or choose a menu command, and the software does the rest.

That's the good news. The bad news is that most people don't understand how to blend all these newfound design options into an attractive, well-functioning site. As a result, they create pages that look unprofessional, take forever to download, or make visitors work too hard to locate the information they came to find—and, too often, all of the above.

In this chapter, you'll get a crash course in good Web design so that you can better assess your own site and draw up a plan for a design makeover. In addition to showing you examples of well-designed pages, I'll assault your eyes with examples of design gone horribly wrong so that you don't make similar missteps. You'll also find tips to help you avoid technical hazards as you improve the look of your site.

Weed Out the Clutter

One of the biggest mistakes people make when creating their Web pages is cramming too much content onto a page. Figure 1-1, an online version of a small newspaper, is a clutter case in point. It's filled with so many graphics and ads that the news—which is presumably what people come to the site to find—gets lost in the mess. The headlines aren't even visible in the first screen that loads onto the page. (The figure shows where the page breaks when viewed on a monitor running at a screen resolution of 800 by 600 pixels.) The lack of any clear organizational structure adds to the confusion. Worst of all, the ad for the scuba store dominates the page. Most people look first at the largest, most colorful element on the page, so the visitor's first impression may be that this is a site for a dive shop, not a newspaper!

note

All the Web pages in this book feature made-up companies or organizations. I've elected not to show real Web sites because (a) my lawyer turned frighteningly pale when I suggested it and (b) I didn't want anyone to be embarrassed if I picked their site as an example of awful design. But although the content of the pages is imaginary, I based all the examples on real-life eyesores. If your site happens to share some common characteristics with these pages, don't feel bad—even some sites related to improving Web design make many of the same mistakes discussed here. And unlike the people who put those sites together, you're just a few minutes away from understanding how to make the Web's new design flexibility work *for* you instead of against you.

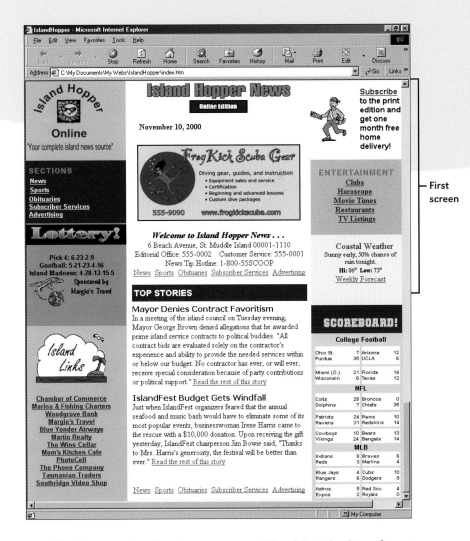

The first step in cleaning up a page like this is looking for extraneous content that you can send to the digital dumpster. If a graphic or a block of text doesn't contribute significantly to the page design or information flow, out it goes. For example, notice the dueling *Island Hopper* logos at the top of the original newspaper page. What's the purpose of having two identifiers so close together? Are visitors to this site so thick that they won't know where they've landed if they see only one logo?

As for the tag line in the leftmost logo—*Your complete island news source*—it's an example of corporate ego overruling the interests of the customer. Fluffy, feel-good tag lines like this may be important to the marketing department or to the company owners, but customers couldn't care less. If you're designing a site for a client or boss who insists on keeping this kind of stuff, at least make it as unintrusive as possible.

Remember, every byte of data adds to download time and increases the chances that visitors will get impatient and move on. So if you really want people to see your site as a friendly haven, be ruthless about cleaning it out. In addition to enabling people to download your pages in less time, you'll add emphasis to the content that's really important.

Figure 1-2 shows the post-makeover *Island Hopper News* site. A single logo takes center stage, and the layout, which resembles that of a traditional

Figure 1-2
The redesigned site returns the focus to the paper and makes important news easily accessible.

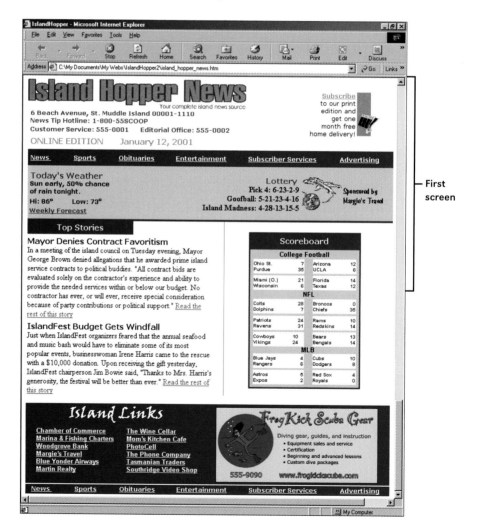

newspaper, leaves no doubt as to the purpose of this site. In addition, the news that's of most interest—the day's top story, the weather, and, of course, lottery results and sports scores—are all within easy reach. Links to other parts of the site are provided at both the top and bottom of the page so that people can jump to another page without scrolling. I also chose to consolidate all the entertainment links (found in the column on the right in the original site) under one main link. Having two distinct and differently formatted blocks of links, as in the original, is confusing and wastes space. If you decided that having any of the individual entertainment links on the home page was important, you could easily blend it into the list of links in the lower-left corner of the page.

Guide the Eye to Important Content

As I mentioned earlier, most people look first at the largest or boldest element on a page. Then they scan the page quickly, this time noticing the general design created by the text and graphics. Finally, they begin to read the actual words on the page.

You can take advantage of this typical reading pattern by laying out the page in a way that directs the reader's eye to critical content. In the redesigned *Island Hopper News* page, the eye goes first to the paper's logo because it has the most visual impact on the part of the page that appears on-screen when the user arrives at the site. Next, the eye is pulled to the second-most prominent elements: the gray band containing the weather and lottery information and the *Top Stories* and *Scoreboard* headline bars. The red vertical line provides an additional organizational clue by clearly separating the news and sports content. It also helps direct the eye downward, which encourages the reader to scroll to see the rest of the page.

Be Smart About Ad Placement

For some Web sites, paid advertising is a fact of life; without the advertiser's dollars, these sites wouldn't be able to offer free or discounted services to customers. However, if you accept paid advertisements, don't allow them to be so large, so gaudy, or so prominently placed that they overwhelm *your* content. After all, if visitors ignore your message in favor of the ads, why bother having a site at all?

Giving your own content preferential treatment doesn't mean that you need to bury ads, however. In the redesigned *Island Hopper News* site, the scuba shop's ad appears underneath the sports scores, for example. That's a good placement for this advertiser because its customer base likely includes sports enthusiasts. When readers scroll the page to see all the box scores, they see the ad. You can similarly group your ads with content related to the advertiser's target audience.

Spice Up Text-Heavy Pages

While the original newspaper site shown in Figure 1-1 is so graphically loaded that it looks like a crazy quilt—only not as attractive as a real crazy quilt—the library site shown in Figure 1-3 suffers from the opposite problem: not *enough* visual interest. This page looks more like a school research paper than a Web site. You can almost hear the librarian whispering, "*Please*, the library is a place for our *quiet* voices!"

Figure 1-3
Virtually devoid of visual interest, this library Web site is about as appealing as a legal contract. Who'd want to visit a place this boring?

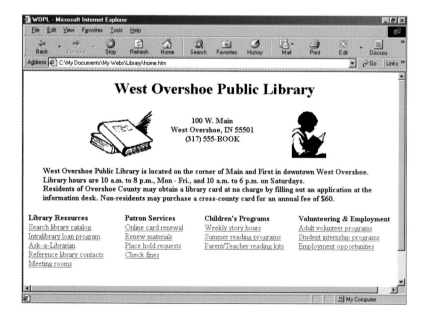

The two clip-art graphics at the top of the page aren't enough to offset the snore-inducing appearance of the rest of the page. To make matters worse, the graphics feature two different artistic styles, creating a disjointed look. The graphic on the left is feathery and free-form, while the one on the right is formal and blocky.

As Figure 1-4 proves, you can create a more polished, lively presence by making just a few small changes. A roomier layout, some variations in type, and swapping out the black-and-white clip art for two-color graphics give the site a more modern, inviting look.

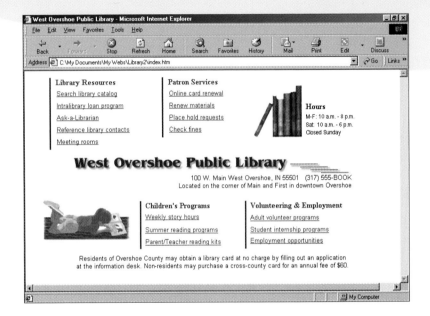

Figure 1-4
Simply rearranging the content into a contemporary layout, mixing up the typefaces, and adding two colorful graphics turn the library's image from dull to dynamic.

see also — Artist Hew Hamilton created the book graphic in Figure 1-4 in PhotoDraw; the other image is a clip-art graphic that I tweaked to match the artistic style and color theme of the rest of the site. Chapter 8 explains how to create your own graphics and use the clip-art provided in the Microsoft Clip Gallery.

Create Visual Rest Stops

Long, unbroken masses of text like those in Figure 1-3 are more than ugly—they're tiring on the eye. And tired eyes, as you know if you've ever tried to wade through a novel at the end of a long day, aren't likely to keep reading, no matter how intriguing the content.

Research tells us that one way to ease eyestrain is to include plenty of "white space"—empty areas where the eye can take a break as it scans a page. In the new library page in Figure 1-4, the columnar layout and some changes to the information flow create a nice balance between content and white space. The only change made to the actual content was replacing the long sentence about the library hours with the abbreviated block in the upper-right corner of the page.

Note that "white space" doesn't literally have to be white, as it is in the example; if the page background were pale yellow, for instance, the eye could still nap in the empty areas. But vividly colored or boldly patterned backgrounds don't provide the same restful quality, so limit your use of such backgrounds to small areas of your page, and set your most vital text and graphics against a plainer backdrop.

Dump the Splash Screen

Your goal as a Web designer is to provide the highest-quality content in the least amount of download time. Unfortunately, some popular design tactics work against that purpose. Figure 1-5 shows one of the biggest time-wasters: the use of a design-heavy, content-light "welcome screen" as a home page.

Figure 1-5
This "welcome screen" takes forever to download and provides the site visitor with no useful information.

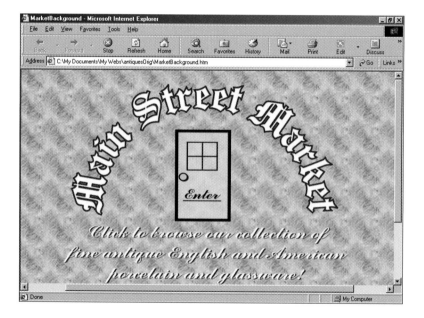

This page takes nearly 2½ minutes to download, thanks to the large graphics. In regular time, that sounds like nothing. But in Web time, even a 10-second wait seems like forever. And if you do hang around long enough to load the page, what do you get for your reward? An invitation to download *another* page to see what the shop is selling.

Many Web designers love welcome screens—known as *splash screens* in the trade. In my opinion, that's because splash screens give designers a chance to show off their artistic skills without worrying about fitting actual content into the mix. But art for art's sake belongs in a museum or on a living room wall, not on a Web page. People don't come to the Web to sit on their hands and wait while pretty pictures load on their computer screens. They log on to get or share information, period. Adding a few small graphics to give your site some visual appeal is fine, but don't make people click through hoops to get to the meat of your site. Let them get in and get out as quickly as possible.

The redesigned home page for the antiques shop, shown in Figure 1-6, provides visitors with a more direct route to browsing the shop's goods. Visitors also get clear instructions on how to view and buy items and contact the shop, which is critical for helping newcomers feel comfortable with online buying. And even though this page includes four quality product images, it takes only 26 seconds to download on a 28.8 Kbps modem—less than 20 percent of the time needed to load the original home page. *That's* the kind of welcome people appreciate.

Figure 1-6
The revamped home page includes higher-quality product shots and useful buying information, yet it loads significantly faster than the original.

see also | One reason for the shortened download time of this site is that the background is created using a very small image that gets tiled (repeated) to fill the page, whereas the background in Figure 1-5 is a full-page image. Chapter 5 explains how to create and use tiled backgrounds.

Make Text Easily Readable

As if the whole idea of a splash screen weren't annoying enough—sorry, not quite done with that rant—the thin, ornate, type used in Figure 1-5 is all but impossible to decipher against the textured background. Using light type against a darker background (typically known as *reverse type*) adds to the legibility problem.

Reverse text may *look* great. But if you want people to actually *read* your text, dark type on a plain, light-colored background is the way to go. And reserve fancy fonts and other high-design type treatments for short headlines. They should never be used for longer blocks of text. I know, that sounds pretty dull, especially when you're browsing through all the cool fonts that you've installed on your system over the years. But favoring form over function defeats your ultimate purpose—communication.

see also | *Chapters 6 and 7 show you how to create text that's both visually interesting and highly readable. You'll also find information about the technical side of type on the Web, which is a stickier issue than you might expect.*

Create Identity Through Design

Before you change a single graphic or block of text, take some time to think about the purpose of your site and the audience you hope to reach. People base their opinion of you or your organization in part on the overall "feel" of your site, so you need to make sure that the design you choose creates the right impression.

For example, if you're trying to attract a traditional, conservative audience, you'll have better luck if your pages have a simple, elegant layout rather than a trendy, free-form look. If you're developing a site for teenagers, on the other hand, the trendier, the better. (And if you're older than, er, 30, like me, don't assume that you know what today's youth consider hip, or *phat,* or *da bomb,* or whatever the term is now. Trust me, you'll be way off base, so ask your local teenager for guidance.)

Figures 1-7 and 1-8 illustrate how the same content can take on two entirely different personalities based solely on design. The first page has a formal, classic look, designed to appeal to the serious wine enthusiast—someone who knows a Pinot Noir from a Petite Sirah and would never dream of sipping a Cabernet from a water goblet. The second page is whimsical and unstructured, giving the site a casual, fun attitude that would appeal to people who feel intimidated by wine stewards and see no harm in toasting one another with paper cups if all the wine glasses are in the dishwasher.

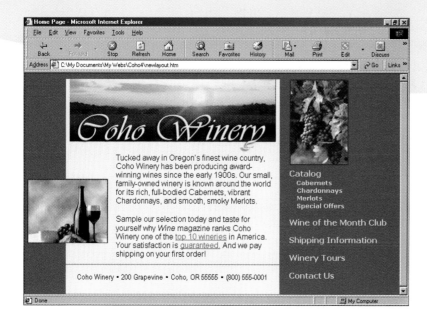

Figure 1-7
With its elegant, sophisticated design, this winery page is geared toward the serious wine enthusiast.

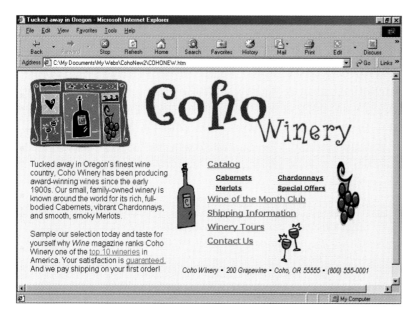

Figure 1-8
The more relaxed, contemporary version of the winery site is geared to a more casual audience.

If you're working on a Web site for a business, of course, your design needs to mesh with the established corporate identity. In that case, your pages should contain at least some, if not all, of the same design elements as the company's brochures, ads, and other print pieces. And if other people are contributing to the site as well, make sure that everyone agrees on a basic design template and sticks to it. Consistency throughout all your marketing pieces helps reinforce whatever image the business wants to project and also reassures Web customers that they've found the site for your company and not some similarly named business.

Be Aware of Technical Traps

Despite all the new goodies added to the Web designer's toolbox in the past few years, some design limitations still exist. As you no doubt know if you've been making Web pages for very long, certain design elements can lead to "broken" pages—pages that refuse to load or load incorrectly in some browsers. In addition, when users set their monitors to certain display settings, your pages may not appear with the right colors or at the size you expect.

Although the length and scope of this book prevent me from listing all the possible problems that can arise, I can steer you away from the major danger zones. If you keep the following guidelines in mind, you'll greatly improve the odds that everyone who comes to your site is impressed by what they see.

- **Don't use sophisticated effects.** Resist the temptation to incorporate the hottest new animations, audio effects, and other fancy multimedia elements into your page. First, they increase download time. Second, not everyone who visits your site will be using a browser that supports these elements or be willing to download whatever plug-in or software is required to display them. Third, although whirling graphics, gyrating text, silly sound effects, and the like may be mildly amusing on first encounter, they get old quickly.

- **Get a grip on graphics.** Although advertisers would have you believe that creating digital photos and other graphics is a no-brainer, the reality is that properly preparing your artwork for the Web is one of the more confusing aspects of designing a site. The abundance of blurry, jagged images proves just how many people don't have a clue about the technical side of Web graphics.

| see also | To help you get on the right graphics road, Chapters 8 and 9 give you a crash course in creating simple drawings, using clip art, and editing digital photo art. You'll have to engage a few brain cells, but I'll try to make things as painless as possible. |

■ **Limit yourself to basic HTML.** The newest versions of FrontPage and other site-building programs support new HTML technologies that were developed to provide enhanced design options. (For the uninitiated, HTML, or Hypertext Markup Language, is the programming language used to create Web pages.) For example, you can use Cascading Style Sheets, or CSS, to apply the same kind of paragraph formatting that you can generate in a word processing program and to place elements on the page using specific horizontal and vertical coordinates.

The problem is, only the latest browsers can make sense of some of the new technologies. In older browsers, positioning goes haywire, text doesn't appear as it should, or the page may not load at all. So unless you know what browsers your audience uses— for example, if you're designing pages for a corporate intranet— stick with the tried and true. And don't make the mistake of thinking that just because you and some of your technologically savvy friends always work with the latest browser, the majority of people visiting your site will do likewise. Ask around your neighborhood, office, or school, and you'll be surprised at how many people use outdated browsers. Browsers may be free for the taking, but that doesn't mean that people feel comfortable downloading and installing them or want to take the time to learn a new browser interface.

To create the examples for this chapter, I used only features supported by both Microsoft Internet Explorer and Netscape Navigator versions 3.0 and later. I did the same in the rest of the book except in Chapter 10, which shows you some of the design tricks that newer Web technologies make possible. Yes, this approach complicates your design challenge a little, but if you're going to spend time making your site look good, you want as many people as possible to be able to view it properly.

see also | *Chapter 4 offers some tips and tricks for creating sophisticated page layouts using the most basic of HTML features.*

■ **Test your site in a variety of browsers.** To double-check your pages for browser compatibility, preview your site in the major browsers: Internet Explorer, Netscape Navigator, the AOL browser, and the WebTV browser.

■ **Preview pages at various screen resolutions and color depths.** The monitor settings that people use when viewing your pages control how accurately the colors in your graphics appear and how much of your page is visible without scrolling. You can eliminate most

Browser Compatibility In FrontPage 2000, you can tell the program to disable any features not supported by certain browsers and Web servers. Choose Page Options from the Tools menu to display the Page Options dialog box, and then click the Compatibility tab to reveal the options shown here:

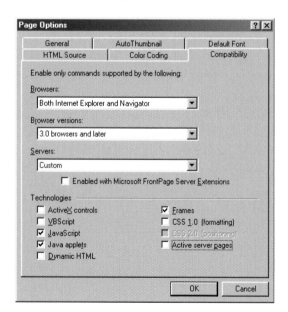

FrontPage will enable only the options supported by the browsers and the server you select from the first three drop-down lists in the dialog box. You can also clear the check boxes at the bottom of the dialog box to disable specific technologies. (A check mark in the box indicates that the option is enabled.)

potential problems in this area by following some special color and sizing rules that I explain in Chapter 3.

■ **Test your pages at default browser color and type settings too.** Some browsers enable users to override the colors in your pages and use their own colors or the browser's default colors. To complicate matters further, most browsers enable the user to override your type specifications and display the page using other fonts and type sizes.

see also | *Chapter 5 explains how to preview your page at the common browser-default color settings. Chapter 6 shows you how to format text in a way that increases the chances that it will appear as you planned.*

■ **Be aware of platform differences.**   Add a preflight check of your site on the major computer platforms too. You may be surprised about some of the differences that can affect your site display. For example, the same-size text looks smaller on a Macintosh computer than on a computer running Microsoft Windows, and pictures appear lighter on a Macintosh than on a computer running Windows.

see also | *Again, see Chapter 6 for rules of safe text handling; Chapter 9 shows you how to adjust image brightness.*

Of course, this list focuses only on design trouble spots. If your page "breaks," your site may have a technical flaw unrelated to your layout, graphics, or text. You may be able to discover the answer by going to the Web site of the company that makes your site-building software or the browser that can't display your pages. You may also want to pick up a copy of *Easy Web Page Creation,* by Mary Millhollon with Jeff Castrina (Microsoft Press, 2001), which will help you understand the more technical aspects of building a Web site.

Online Resources for Web Designers

Where do you look for details about browser compatibility issues and answers to other thorny technical questions? The Web, naturally. Here are some of my favorite sites related to Web design:

- ■ *www.webtv.net* Follow the Developers links for tips related to the browser used by people who subscribe to WebTV. You can even download the WebTV viewer to see how your site will look on the "big screen."

- ■ *www.aol.com* Download the latest AOL browser here.

- ■ *www.w3.org* This is the official Web site of the World Wide Web Consortium (W3C), an international group dedicated to developing technical standards for the Web. Look here for help with any technical aspect of site design.

- ■ *www.howdesign.com* This is the online arm of *How* magazine, an excellent publication geared toward professional print and Web designers. Tip: The annual Self-Promotion Awards and Digital Design issues are loaded with examples of inspired, effective promotional design. If you miss them on the newsstand, follow the Back Issues links to buy them online.

- ■ *www.webdevelopersjournal.com* A great online magazine devoted to all aspects of Web design, this site also offers mailing-list discussion groups related to various Web technologies and tools, including FrontPage.

- ■ *www.webdeveloper.com* Another treasure trove of information, this site offers still more forums, how-to articles, and hardware and software reviews.

- ■ *www.webmonkey.com* Ignore the goofy name—this site is packed with good information, including charts that show which design features are supported by which browsers. There's even a Webmonkey for Kids section offering lessons and projects for kids who want to build Web sites.

- ■ *www.officeupdate.com* Last but not least, visit the Microsoft Office Update site for tips on using FrontPage, PhotoDraw, and other Office programs. You'll also find technical support articles and additional program design templates and themes here.

fast and

2

easy
DESIGN TOOLS

All you need to know about . . .

- Checking your system capabilities

- Sorting out digital cameras, scanners, and other graphics hardware

- Finding storage space for all your files

- Picking drawing and photo editing programs

- Keeping track of your graphics with cataloging software

In my office, I have four computers, three printers, two digital cameras, a scanner, a CD recorder, a drawing tablet, about 30 graphics programs that I've collected over the years, and, most important, a little electric coaster that keeps my coffee warm. Truth be told, though, I could get along fine with just 25 percent of this stuff. (The coffee warmer stays.) I use the rest only for occasional special projects.

The point is, creating Web graphics requires just a few vital hardware and software components, which we'll explore in this chapter. I'll also introduce you to a few goodies that aren't absolutely necessary but will make your graphics work easier and more enjoyable.

Hardware: Is Your Computer Up to the Job?

Working with graphics puts a significant strain on a computer's resources. If your system doesn't have much muscle, your graphics software will run very slowly and may even cause the computer to freeze up on occasion.

The system components that affect graphics work the most are the processor, RAM (*random access memory,* or simply *memory*), the hard drive, and the video card. Here's a look at how each of these components factors into the graphics equation and my advice on the minimum requirements for speedy, reliable performance:

■ **Processor**   It's probably no secret to you that the processor plays a big role in how quickly the system carries out your commands. The good news is that if you bought a new computer in the past two years, you've probably got the processor power you need. At a minimum, I recommend a Pentium II 233 MHz chip (or its equivalent). Most new systems go well beyond that, especially if they're designed for computer gaming.

■ **RAM (memory)**   This is the category where the average system falls short. If your computer doesn't have adequate RAM, it may not be able to perform some high-level graphics tasks or allow you to keep more than one picture open at a time.

Most new graphics programs require a minimum of 32 MB of RAM, but trust me, you won't be happy with anything less than 64 MB, especially for photo editing and creating 3D artwork. More RAM is definitely better; go for 96 MB or 128 MB if your budget allows.

■ **Hard drive**   When it comes to your system's hard drive, it's not overall size that counts but the amount of *empty* storage space. Your hard drive is the location where you will typically store your graphics and other personal files, but your computer frequently uses it too. When you work on your computer, data typically gets stored temporarily in RAM. If the RAM supply gets low, your computer may use your hard drive as additional storage. So you should always keep some empty space on your hard drive.

If your hard drive is really cramped and you can't offload any files to a floppy disk, CD-ROM, or some other secondary storage device, do yourself a favor and invest in a bigger hard drive or add a second drive to your system. Some programs allow you to specify a removable-media drive, such as a Zip drive or a CD-ROM drive, for your temporary storage space, but these drives typically are too slow for this purpose.

lingo

We techno-weenies sometimes refer to the drive space that the system uses as a temporary data-storage area as a *swap file* or a *scratch disk.*

■ **Video card**   The speed at which images are displayed on your monitor is determined in part by the video card, sometimes called the *graphics card* or *display adapter.* Equally important, the video card also controls the maximum screen resolution and the number of colors your monitor can display at each of the resolution settings the card offers.

Evaluating video cards requires an advanced degree in geekology because so many designs exist. But for graphics work, one critical spec is the amount of video RAM on the card. You need a card with at least 2 MB of video RAM to display 24-bit color (about 16.7 million colors) at a screen resolution of 800 by 600 pixels and a card with 4 MB video RAM to get 24-bit color at a screen resolution of 1024 by 768 pixels. Especially for digital photography work, I think that 24-bit color—also known as *true color*—is a must, but everyone's not as picky as I am. (Note that the actual video RAM requirements for these examples are about 1.4 MB and 2.3 MB, respectively, but cards come in configurations of 1 MB, 2 MB, 4 MB, and up.)

Again, if you're using a relatively new computer, your system likely meets all these qualifications. If your computer isn't up to snuff and a new one isn't in the cards, you can improve performance by cleaning out your hard drive to free up more scratch disk space. Investing in additional RAM also offers a good return, although memory isn't as cheap as it used to be. As for upgrading your video card or processor, neither option is simple or inexpensive, so be sure to weigh the cost/benefit ratio of upgrading to buying a new system.

see also | *See Chapter 3 for additional information about screen resolution and color depth.*

Scanner or Digital Camera—or Both?

Once owned only by graphics professionals, scanners and digital cameras are now mainstream, thanks mostly to more affordable prices. The fact that people think these gadgets make good gifts for fathers and other

Graphics Storage: What's the Best Option?
If you work on a computer that's part of a large corporate hive, you may never have to worry about finding storage space for all your graphics files. But if you're flying solo—doing your work on a laptop, at home, or in a small office system—you'll eventually reach the point where you can't stuff one more file onto your hard drive. You can always add a second hard drive, of course, but you should also think about investing in an auxiliary device that stores files on some type of removable medium. This option not only enables you to reserve your hard drive space for files that you use regularly but also protects you from losing important files if your hard drive goes wacko.

There are many storage options, but my top pick at the moment is a CD recorder, which costs around $150 to $400, depending on the model's speed and whether you buy an internal or external unit. When CD recorders were first introduced on the consumer market, I considered them too complicated and too prone to problems to recommend to anyone but experienced computer gurus. But now they're as easy to use as a floppy drive. Using special recording software, you can simply drag and drop files to the CD drive's icon, just as you do when copying or moving files to a floppy.

For the best deal, get a CD recorder that offers both CD-R and CD-RW capabilities. (In case you're wondering, the *R* stands for *recordable* and the *RW* stands for *rewritable*.) With CD-R, you can record your files to a CD, but you can't erase any files from the CD once they're on it. CD-RW enables you to add and delete files as necessary. Some older CD drives can't read CD-RW disks, however, so you'll need to stick with CD-R for files that you need to access on those drives. Also, CD-R is best for archiving files that you want to keep for a long time; data on CD-R disks is less likely to degrade over time, and you can't accidentally overwrite an important file. Best of all, CD-R disks are cheap, cheap, cheap—about 30 cents apiece if you watch the sale ads. A CD-RW disk costs a little more—about $1.00 on sale—but of course, you can reuse a CD-RW disk over and over, whereas a CD-R disk is a one-shot deal.

hard-to-buy-for relatives probably has something to do with steadily increasing sales as well, but that's another discussion altogether.

Scanners and digital cameras both produce the same end result—a digital image. But they each serve different digital imaging needs, and the option that makes the most sense for your Web projects depends on your budget as well as how quickly you need to put pictures on your Web site after you shoot them.

Scanners definitely have the edge when it comes to cost. You can buy a decent scanner for less than $100. Although you can buy sub-$100 digital cameras, they produce only low-resolution images and usually lack some of the features that make digital photography so convenient, such as a small on-camera monitor for reviewing your pictures. True, you don't need high-resolution pictures for Web use, but you do if you want to print good-quality copies of your pictures. To get that kind of resolution from a digital camera, you'll pay a minimum of $200. By contrast, even an entry-level scanner can create images suitable for printing.

see also | *If you need help understanding image resolution, check out Chapter 3.*

On the other side of the coin, digital cameras win out in terms of efficiency. If you use a scanner, you have to shoot a roll of film, wait for the film to be developed, and then scan the image. With a digital camera, you just shoot the picture and then download the image to your computer. In addition, you don't have to pay for film and film processing, so if you're a prolific photographer, a digital camera can save you money over the long run.

Both devices involve some system setup—and you *know* the chances of everything going smoothly the first time—plus a willingness to spend some time studying the user's manual to figure out which buttons to push when. Learning how to use a digital camera is definitely more complex than learning to use a scanner, but if you've mastered a standard point-and-shoot film camera, many digital camera features will be familiar to you.

To sum up, if your budget is tight and you want the highest resolution for your money, a scanner is the right choice. Go for a digital camera if being able to put a picture up on the Web as soon as you shoot it is important and you don't mind investing a little more time and money in exchange for the added speed and convenience.

Scanner Buying Guide

Scanners come in two basic forms: *flatbed* and *sheetfed*. A flatbed scanner has a horizontal scanning orientation—you place the item you want to scan face down on a glass bed, and a scanner head underneath the glass travels the length of the bed to make the scan. With a sheetfed scanner, you insert your picture into a roller mechanism, and the photo winds its way slowly past the scanner head. (Those all-in-one printer/scanner/fax machines incorporate sheetfed scanners.)

A flatbed scanner is the best choice for scanning photographic prints. You don't have to worry about your photo getting bent as it winds its way through a sheetfed scanner, and you can scan three-dimensional objects as well as flat pictures or documents. For example, if you need a picture of a pencil, you can put a pencil on the scanner glass and scan away.

After scanner type, the most important specification to consider is resolution. Scanner resolution is stated in terms of *dots per inch,* or *dpi,* but that's a bit of a misnomer because the value measures how many pixels—which are squares, not dots—your scanned images can contain. A resolution of 600 dpi means that you get 600 pixels for every linear inch of your original. For example, if you scan a 2-inch-square photo, your scanned image is 1200 pixels wide by 1200 pixels tall.

see also | *Not sure what I mean by* pixel? *Chapter 3 tells all.*

Most new consumer-level scanners offer a resolution of 600 dpi, but some offer 1200 dpi or more. Prices for 600-dpi models start at about $80; 1200-dpi models start at about $200. How high do you need to go? Well, for Web pictures, a 600-dpi scanner is more than enough. But if you move up to a 1200-dpi or higher model, you can print larger copies of your scanned images. For example, if you scan a snapshot at 600 dpi, you can

tip

You may be able to get by without *either* a scanner *or* a digital camera, thanks to new photofinishing services that process your undeveloped film and deliver both prints and scanned copies. Many local film labs offer this option, and you can find scores of online providers as well. If you need only the occasional digital image, this may be a good solution for you. However, you'll pay about $5 to $10 extra to add the digital copies to your film processing order, depending on the picture resolution and the delivery option you choose—CD-ROM, floppy disk, or online retrieval. So you can quickly reach the point where buying your own scanner or digital camera makes better economic sense.

output a high-quality print at twice the original size. Scan that same photo at 1200 dpi, and you can enlarge the print four times the original size. (I base this calculation on the fact that most printers do their best work with pictures that have an image resolution of 300 pixels per linear inch.)

If you need to scan film negatives or slides, you'll need either an adapter, available for some flatbeds, or a specialized photo scanner designed for these materials. These special-purpose scanners typically offer resolutions of 2400 dpi or higher, which is necessary because of the small size of the originals. Entry-level scanners in this category start at about $400.

Aside from resolution, scanner type, and price, the other critical factors to consider are how the scanner connects to your computer—USB port, parallel port, and so on—scanner speed, and, of course, image quality. You can't tell much about image quality from scanner specifications, but computer magazines publish reviews that will help in this regard.

Digital Camera Buying Guide

Shopping for a digital camera can be an incredibly confusing task. You can find models priced from $30 to $1300, all claiming to be the ideal digital photography solution. A thorough buying guide is beyond the scope of this book, but I can give you a general idea of what type of camera will work best for your needs. The following sections give you a look at the major categories of cameras.

Web cams

These small, low-resolution cameras, developed primarily for Internet videoconferencing, are really video cameras, but they can capture a single video frame to use as a still image. The left image in Figure 2-1 shows one Web cam, the Logitech QuickCam Pro, which costs about $80. Most Web cams are designed to perch atop your monitor and work only while tethered to your computer. Top resolution currently is 640 by 480 pixels, which is plenty for on-screen pictures but not enough to produce quality prints.

caution

Always focus on the *optical resolution* of a scanner. Most manufacturers state this value on the box but make more noise about *interpolated* or *enhanced resolution,* which may be double the optical resolution or more. That higher resolution is achieved through software manipulation, which actually can result in lower image quality. Also, optical resolution is typically stated using two numbers, such as 600 × 1200. Ignore the higher number; the lower one indicates the real story.

note

The prices I state throughout this chapter represent approximate retail prices at press time. But you may find some or all of these products available for less—the computer marketplace is one arena where prices tend to go down as time goes by. Also, the specific products I mention are simply representative of the types of equipment and software available; many other quality choices are available in each category. Again, browsing computer magazines and online buying guides can help you narrow the field to the products best suited to your projects and your budget.

Figure 2-1
Here you see two different styles of Web cams, the Logitech QuickCam Pro(left) and the Kodak EZ200 (right).

The key benefit of a Web cam is its low cost: bare-bones models cost as little as $30. But using a camera that's shackled to your computer restricts your photo-taking options, obviously. You have to bring whatever you want to shoot to the camera instead of the other way around. And most Web cams don't have a viewfinder; an on-screen preview is your sole guide to framing your shot. In addition, Web cams typically use lower-quality lenses, lack a flash, and have limited focus adjustment capabilities, all of which translates to lower image quality than you can get from a standard still digital camera.

If you move toward the top of the Web cam price range, though, you can find specialty Web cams that offer more mobility as well as better image quality. Kodak, for example, offers the EZ200 for about $150. The EZ200, shown on the right in Figure 2-1, is a cross between a Web cam and a stand-alone camera. You can either leave the camera hooked up to the computer or detach it for remote shooting.

My advice   A Web cam offers a cheap, easy-to-use option if your main need is to exchange visual information quickly, you need videoconferencing capabilities, or you don't require top image quality. Many people use these cameras to shoot pictures of goods they want to sell in online auctions, for example.

VGA still cameras

For about $100, you can buy a low-resolution stand-alone camera offering a maximum resolution of 640 by 480 pixels (referred to as *VGA resolution*). Because these cameras are geared to still photography, not video, they usually produce better images than their Web-cam cousins. They typically boast better lenses, flash capability, and focus adjustment. Some also include a liquid crystal display (LCD) for reviewing the pictures you just shot, which is one of the major benefits of digital photography. The trade-off is that you can't use these cameras to transmit live video, as you can a Web cam.

My advice   If putting pictures on your Web site is your *only* concern, a camera in this category makes sense. You get basic photography features, decent picture quality, and a low price. What you won't get is image resolution suitable for good-quality prints. Also, these cameras typically can store images only in their internal memory, which is rather limited. That means you can shoot only so many pictures before you have to stop and download them to your computer, usually via a cable-transfer process that can be maddeningly slow. More expensive cameras enable you to store pictures on removable media cards, so when you fill up one card, you just pop in another and keep shooting.

Megapixel cameras

If you want to be able to print decent pictures, you need a camera that can capture at least 1 million pixels—termed a *megapixel camera*. With a 1-megapixel model, you can output great snapshot-size prints and decent 5-by-7-inch prints. Two megapixels gives you sharp 5 × 7s and darned good 8 × 10s; 3-megapixel models can deliver high-quality 8 × 10s and even larger.

Of course, the more pixels, the higher the camera price. You can get a good 1-megapixel model for about $200, 2-megapixel cameras start at about $300, and 3-megapixel cameras start at approximately $700.

Aside from extra pixels, higher-priced models accept removable memory cards and also offer advanced photographic controls, such as manual focus and exposure controls like those available on a 35mm SLR (single-lens reflex) camera. Some cameras, such as the $999 Canon PowerShot G1, shown in the top image in Figure 2-2, can capture short video clips and provide internal guides that help you shoot a series of pictures that can later be "stitched" together into a panorama image. This 3-megapixel Canon model also offers a 3X zoom lens, a wireless remote controller, a choice of metering modes, the option to attach accessory lenses, and a variable-angle LCD monitor that rotates up to 270 degrees. (If you want video-recording capabilities but don't need 3-megapixel resolution, Casio and Sony offer the feature on lower-resolution cameras.)

Figure 2-2
The Canon PowerShot G1 offers 3-megapixel resolution in a small package; the 2-megapixel Kodak DC5000 features a tough, weatherproof body for shooting in rugged environments.

caution

Before you buy, check the retailer's return policy. Many stores charge a "restocking" fee, which means, "Sure, you can bring it back, but you'll pay 10 to 15 percent of your purchase price for the privilege." Excuse me? Why consumers put up with this practice, I don't know, but you don't have to accept it. If you're buying a stand-alone camera (as opposed to a Web cam), shop at a reputable camera store, even if you pay a few bucks more than you might at the megadiscount store down the street. The salespeople will be better equipped to help you find the right camera for your needs, and they won't try to gouge you if the product doesn't work out as promised. In addition, while camera stores usually focus on the current camera models, superstores often feature last year's products. Although the older cameras may be selling for less than they did when originally released, they often don't represent the best values. As the market for digital photography has grown, camera manufacturers have been upping their production, which means lower per-unit costs. Thus, you may get more features for the same money if you opt for this year's camera than a model that's been around for a year.

My advice   If you're a real photography enthusiast who wants sophisticated focus and exposure controls and resolution high enough to output very large images, save your pennies for a 3-megapixel model. Otherwise, go for either a 1-megapixel or 2-megapixel unit, depending on the size of prints you like to make. Then match camera features with your specific photography plans. For example, if you need to shoot lots of close-up pictures, compare the close-up ranges of different models (they vary widely), or if you want to be able to use accessory lenses—wide-angle, fish-eye, and the like—look for models that can accept them. (Not all do.)

Whether you go for 1, 2, or 3 megapixels, remember that digital cameras are tiny computers at heart, and water, dust, and dirt can damage them. So if you plan to shoot outdoors in all types of weather or in a heavy industrial environment, make sure that the model you choose is built to withstand the punishment. Some manufacturers, including Kodak, now offer cameras geared toward these special shooting situations. The Kodak DC5000, shown in the bottom half of Figure 2-2, for example, has a weatherproof outer shell, rubber handgrips, and oversized buttons that you can work even when wearing gloves.

Software: Do You Have What You Need?

If you own Microsoft Office 2000 Premium Edition, you're already well equipped in the software department. The suite includes Microsoft FrontPage 2000, which you can use to build your Web pages and handle other site-management chores, and Microsoft PhotoDraw 2000, a combination drawing and photo editing program. The examples you see in this book feature these two programs. (I used Version 2 of PhotoDraw instead of Version 1, which originally shipped with the Office 2000 suite.)

You may want to invest in additional specialty programs, however, to expand your graphics capabilities a little and handle a few tasks that neither FrontPage nor PhotoDraw is designed to do. As I mentioned at the start of this chapter, graphics software abounds; the following sections introduce you to a few of my favorites.

Photo Editing Software

Software for creating and editing computer graphics typically comes in two flavors: drawing programs and painting programs. Drawing programs create pictures using simple lines—*vectors,* in tech talk—that can be defined by mathematical equations. Painting programs create pictures with *pixels,* tiny squares of color arranged on a rectangular grid, much like tiles in a mosaic.

lingo

Digital artists refer to the process of converting a vector graphic to pixels as *rasterizing*.

Both types of programs have advantages and drawbacks. Drawing programs are great for logos, text banners, and other illustrations that feature simple shapes because you can enlarge or reduce a drawing as much as you want without degrading the image. The computer just adjusts the equation as necessary. But drawing programs can't reproduce the smooth, seamless color transitions found in photographs—for that type of picture, sometimes called a *continuous-tone image,* you need pixels. Pixel-based graphics can't be enlarged without a loss of image quality, however, for reasons that I'll explain in Chapter 3.

For creating Web graphics, the choice between a drawing program and a painting program is currently moot because the overwhelming majority of browsers display only pictures saved in JPEG or GIF format, and both formats are firmly rooted in pixels. Even if you create a drawing, it gets converted to pixels when you save it to JPEG or GIF. Vector-based formats may become a viable alternative for the Web in the next few years, but for now, pixels rule.

Until a few years ago, you needed one program to create drawings and another to work with pixel-based art. But now a few programs, including PhotoDraw, enable you to create both types of graphics. Again, the pictures that you create for your Web site will ultimately be converted to pixels, but the vector drawing features are great for your print projects and also make some aspects of creating complicated graphics much easier than they are in a painting program. In fact, although I own Adobe Photoshop, the top-of-the-line professional painting program, I sometimes turn to the automated tools in PhotoDraw for creating text effects, 3D Web buttons, and simple shapes filled with patterned designs. You can also import and customize clip art from the Microsoft Clip Gallery, and you can blend photos, clip art, and vector drawings into a single picture.

For photo editing, PhotoDraw offers the same basic tools found in most entry-level image editors. You can tweak colors, crop out unwanted portions of the picture, and apply sharpening to make pictures look a little more focused. You can also blend multiple pictures together into a photo collage. Many of the PhotoDraw image editing features are similar to those found in Microsoft Picture It! Photo, a program designed expressly for photo editing.

Although, PhotoDraw, Picture It!, and similar programs offer a great jumping-off point for novice photo editors, if you get really serious about digital photography, you may want to upgrade to a program that offers more sophisticated controls. Adobe Photoshop is undoubtedly the cream of the crop, but it's very expensive and includes many high-end features that most people will never use. Photoshop Limited Edition, or Photoshop LE, a "lite" version of Photoshop that retails for about $95, offers a good intermediate-level alternative. Photoshop LE is basically a stripped-down version of Photoshop, giving you the tools that most people need on a daily basis without the really advanced image manipulation tools that even professional image editors use only occasionally.

The biggest advantage offered by a program such as Photoshop LE is more advanced *selection tools*—tools you use to rope off the area of the image you want to edit. Selection tools in beginner-level programs tend to favor ease of use over flexibility, which makes sense but also can make creating a precise selection outline more difficult. Photoshop LE gives you many ways to create your initial selection outline and to fine-tune an existing outline. For example, you can use a regular paintbrush to "paint" a selection outline along the edges of an object, changing the size and shape of your brush as needed to work your way along tiny curves and angles with precision. Figure 2-3 shows the beginning of a selection outline that I'm building in this fashion; the red areas indicate deselected pixels. Advanced imaging programs also provide you with more sophisticated filters for tweaking image brightness, contrast, and color balance.

Figure 2-3
Intermediate-level image editors such as Adobe Photoshop LE offer sophisticated selection and image correction tools not found in beginner-level programs.

tip

Before buying, you can download demo versions of Photoshop LE (*www.adobe.com*), PhotoImpact (*www.ulead.com*), and Paint Shop Pro (*www.jasc.com*) to see which one you like best.

Other contenders in the intermediate photo editing category include Ulead Systems' PhotoImpact and Jasc Software's Paint Shop Pro, both of which retail for about $100. Ulead Systems also sells several *plug-ins,* which are miniprograms that add extra features to Photoshop, Photoshop LE, and many other imaging programs.

Trading Your Mouse for a Stylus
If someone *did* force me to get rid of 75 percent of my graphics equipment, which I boasted that I could do at the beginning of this chapter, one product that would definitely be a keeper (aside from the coffee warmer) is my drawing tablet. A *drawing tablet* enables you to do your drawing and photo editing by drawing on an electronic tablet, using a penlike stylus. You get better control over your software's drawing and editing tools, and you don't wind up with the hand pains you get from clawing at a mouse all day. Some editing and painting programs are compatible with certain models of drawing tablets, enabling you to vary the size or opacity of your painting and editing strokes simply by varying the stylus pressure. For example, you can press hard to paint a fat, opaque stroke and then let up on the pen a little to draw a narrower, more translucent stroke.

Although you can buy professional tables that sell for as much as $1000, you don't need to spend that much to enjoy the advantages of this device. Wacom Technologies, long the leader in this product group, is one of a few companies that sell a consumer-oriented tablet. The Wacom Graphire, shown below, has a 4-by-5-inch drawing surface and comes with both a pen stylus and a cordless mouse so that you can switch between the two input options. (Although a 4-by-5-inch drawing area may seem small, it's actually ideal. With larger tablets, you wind up moving your arm more to reach all areas of the tablet.) The Graphire costs about $100.

Graphics Cataloging/Management Software

As you create and acquire more and more graphics, keeping track of them can be a headache. Is the product shot that needs to go on your home page named ProductA or Product A1? Which of the 50 files in your My Pictures folder contains the most current image of your staff? An image cataloging program can not only help you manage a burgeoning graphics collection but can also enable you to view small thumbnail previews of your images as you scroll through a list of files.

In Microsoft Windows 98, Windows Me, and Windows 2000, you can view image thumbnails in Windows Explorer. To see thumbnails in Windows 98, click the View menu (or the Views button on the Standard Buttons toolbar), click As A Web Page, and then click the filename. Unfortunately, you can display only one thumbnail at a time. In Windows Me and Windows 2000, you can display thumbnails for all pictures in a folder, as shown in Figure 2-4, by clicking the View menu (or the Views button on the Standard Buttons toolbar) and then clicking Thumbnails. In addition, you can right-click a thumbnail and choose Properties from the shortcut menu to display details about the image, including the image resolution and color depth.

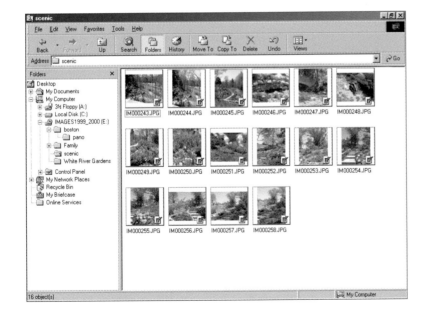

Figure 2-4
In Windows Me and Windows 2000, Windows Explorer can display thumbnails of all images in a folder at once. On the View menu, click Thumbnails to make it so.

PhotoDraw offers its own thumbnail browser to help you track down a file you want to open in the program. (Chapter 8 shows you how to use this browser.) Between the PhotoDraw browser and the thumbnail feature found in Windows Explorer, you might get along just fine if your image collection is small. But for large image collections, you should consider a full-fledged cataloging program such as ThumbsPlus, from Cerious Software (*www.cerious.com*), shown in Figure 2-5. ThumbsPlus costs about $80; you can download a demo version from the Cerious Software Web site.

Figure 2-5

If your image collection is large, a cataloging program such as ThumbsPlus makes finding and organizing your images easier.

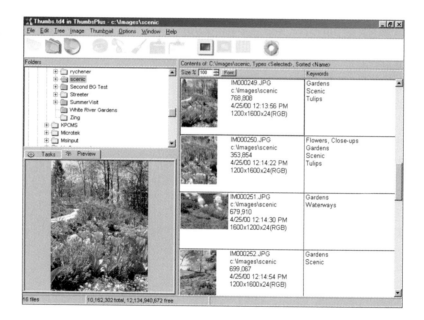

ThumbsPlus enables you to browse thumbnails of your images as well as add annotations that you can store along with the image file for future reference, search for images by keyword, assemble a group of images into a Web page, and perform a bunch of other file management and basic image correction operations. If you shoot with a digital camera that stores metadata (information about the settings you used to take the picture) in the image file, you can display that information as well, as shown in Figure 2-6.

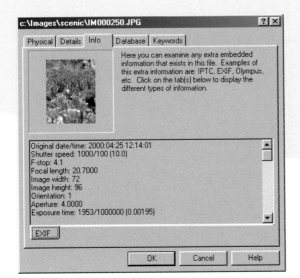

Figure 2-6
If your digital camera stores camera settings as metadata with a picture file, ThumbsPlus can read and display this information.

Other popular cataloging programs include ACDSee, from ACD Systems (*www.acdsystems.com*), which costs about $50; and Portfolio, from Extensis (*www.extensis.com*), which costs about $200. You can download a trial version of ACDSee from the ACD Systems Web site.

pixels,

Basic c...

...um colors:

Define Cu...

OK

3

palettes,

AND OTHER PESKY DETAILS

All you need to know about . . .

- ■ Working with pixels
- ■ Sizing pictures and other page elements
- ■ Designing your page for no-scroll viewing
- ■ Choosing "safe" colors
- ■ Matching colors from one page to another

Remember when your elementary-school teacher introduced you to finger painting? If you were like me, you were so thrilled with the chance to be messy that you slopped on as much paint as you could, realizing too late that such excess resulted in warped paper and colors that ran together. If you were lucky, your teacher gave you a second sheet of paper and showed you how to adapt your technique to better suit your artistic medium. More likely, though, you didn't get a chance for a redo, and when your teacher tacked everyone's pictures to the bulletin board, you were roundly mocked for your rumpled, runny mess.

You can suffer similar humiliation if you don't understand the properties of the digital canvas you use when creating Web pages. Because of the way monitors and browsers display graphics and text, you need to use some different techniques than when you design printed materials. Otherwise, your audience may see something entirely different than you had in mind.

In this chapter, we'll cover the two most misunderstood aspects of Web design: working with color and sizing graphics. I'll warn you up front that this stuff is fairly technical, which is a polite way of saying that you'll be tempted to wander off to chapters that look like more fun. But trust me, this information is essential if you want visitors to linger and admire your work instead of pointing and snickering, "My first-grader could do better!"

Think Pixels, Not Inches

Most of us are used to specifying the size of a picture or page in inches, millimeters, or picas. But designing for the screen calls for a different measuring stick: the pixel. In the next three sections, I'll introduce you to pixels and explain how to size your Web graphics correctly in this digital unit of measure.

Squaring Away Pixels

If you were to peer at your monitor's screen through a magnifying glass, you would see nothing more than row after row of tiny colored squares. These tiny blocks, known as *pixels,* are arranged on a rectangular grid that covers the viewable area of the screen. When you open a Web page in your browser, the computer colors each pixel as needed to reproduce the words and images on the page.

lingo

In case you were wondering, *pixel* is short for *picture element.* Pixel-based pictures are also known as *bitmap images, paintings,* or simply *images.*

To see pixels in action, take a look at Figure 3-1. In the upper-left image, the pixels are so small that you can't make out the individual squares, and your brain perceives a seamless image. The blocklike nature of the graphic doesn't reveal itself until you magnify the view, as I did to create the other two examples in the figure.

Figure 3-1
Everything you see on-screen is merely a collection of colored squares, called pixels.

Unfortunately, most people have trouble getting a good fix on how pixels work, which leads to some mistaken approaches to creating Web graphics. So perhaps an analogy will make the situation clear. Imagine drawing a picture by coloring the individual squares on a piece of graph paper. You're limited to one color per square—you can't fill half the square with blue and the other half with red, for example. And if you add color to a square, you must fill the square completely; you can't leave a portion of the square empty and dump color in another area.

Your computer uses this same approach to reproduce your Web pages. But whereas you can make a square lighter or darker by varying the pressure you use when you rub the crayon on paper, the computer simply adjusts the brightness of a pixel.

see also | *For a more in-depth look at creating pixel-based artwork, see Chapters 7 through 9.*

Comparing Screen Pixels and Image Pixels

Like monitors, digital cameras and scanners build pictures out of pixels. When you save a graphic in either of the two leading Web file formats, JPEG and GIF, you also create a pixel-based image.

It's important to differentiate between the pixels in your Web graphics and the pixels that your monitor uses to display your Web pages. Each image pixel contains data that describes the color and brightness of that particular area of the picture. When you load a Web page that contains an image, the computer reads the image data and then adjusts the screen pixels as necessary to render the picture on-screen.

At this point, you're no doubt saying to yourself, "Gad, why is she dragging me through this technical swamp? I don't care about this behind-the-scenes junk; I just want to be creative!" To which I'm forced to reply, "Sorry, but you really have to care, at least a little, if you want to create good-looking Web graphics." Understanding screen pixels and image pixels is key to sizing your page elements correctly and avoiding jaggedy, blurry pictures, as I'll explain in the next two sections.

Measuring page elements in pixels

All monitors can generate a finite number of screen pixels. Typically, the user can choose from several settings, each of which results in a different number of horizontal and vertical pixels. For example, I have a 19-inch monitor that offers a choice of five settings ranging from 640 by 480 pixels to 1600 by 1200 pixels. (The horizontal pixel count is always listed first.) My laptop computer, however, is limited to just two display options: 640 × 480 and 800 × 600. Naturally, as you raise the number of pixels, the pixels get smaller because you're cramming more pixels into the same space.

Regardless of the screen resolution or monitor size, a Web browser always uses one screen pixel to represent one image pixel. If you create a picture that's 400 pixels wide and 300 pixels tall, for example, the graphic consumes 400 horizontal screen pixels and 300 vertical screen pixels. If the user raises the screen resolution, the pixels—and your graphic—just appear smaller. Conversely, when the screen resolution goes down, pixels get bigger, which means that your graphic gets bigger.

Figures 3-2 and 3-3 illustrate this point. In Figure 3-2, you see a Web page displayed on a monitor running at a screen resolution of 640 × 480. The second figure shows the same page on a monitor running at a resolution of 800 × 600. In Figure 3-3, the screen pixels are smaller, which means that more of the page can be displayed in the browser window.

lingo

People commonly use the term *screen resolution* when referring to the number of pixels that a monitor can display. Really high-tech types refer to 640 × 480 pixels as VGA resolution, 800 × 600 as SVGA resolution, and 1024 × 768 as XGA resolution. I hate this use of the term *resolution* because technically, resolution means the number of pixels per inch, not the total number of pixels. And in this case, the number of pixels per inch depends on the physical size of the monitor. (If you set a 15-inch monitor to display 800 by 600 pixels, you get more pixels per inch than you do when running a 17-inch monitor at the same setting.) But I fear that if I deviate from the norm and use some other terminology, I'll only wind up adding to the confusion, so *screen resolution* it is.

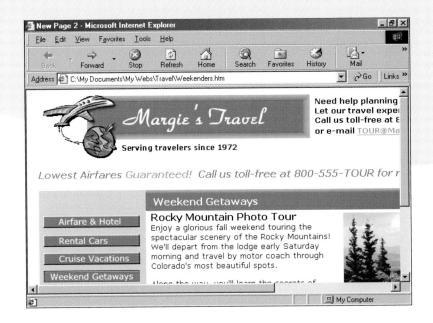

Figure 3-2
When displayed at the 640 × 480 screen resolution, this Web page doesn't fit within the browser window.

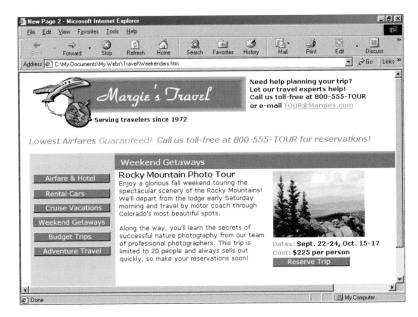

Figure 3-3
Changing the screen resolution to 800 × 600 reduces pixel size so that more of the page is visible.

Resampling vs. resizing graphics

While you're building your site in Microsoft FrontPage 2000, you can enlarge a selected graphic by dragging a corner handle, as I'm doing to the larger bird image in Figure 3-4. When you do this, you're not changing the number of pixels in the image but simply *magnifying* the image, which destroys that one-to-one relationship between image and screen pixels. The image pixels get bigger, which means the browser uses more screen pixels to reproduce each image pixel. If you enlarge the graphic significantly, the individual image pixels become noticeable, and the result is a blocky-looking—read "ugly"—picture. Compare the smaller bird image with its larger neighbor to get a better idea of the kind of quality loss you can expect.

Figure 3-4
Enlarging an image in FrontPage increases the size of the image pixels; the number of pixels remains constant unless you resample the picture.

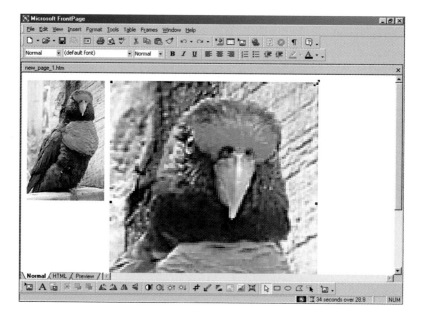

After stretching or shrinking an image in FrontPage, you can choose to *resample* the image by clicking the Resample button on the Pictures toolbar. (See Figure 3-5.) Resampling means to add or delete image pixels. FrontPage adjusts the pixel count as needed to match the new screen area that the picture occupies. For example, if you enlarge a 100-by-100-pixel image so that it occupies a 200-pixel square area of the screen, the software adds 100 pixels horizontally and 100 pixels vertically. Now the one-to-one screen pixel to image pixel ratio is restored. Unfortunately, your image probably looks even worse than it did before you resampled. The program has to guess at the color and brightness of the pixels it adds, and even for the most sophisticated software, that's a difficult proposition. Your images usually lose detail and become blurry. Figure 3-5 shows the enlarged image from Figure 3-4 after I resampled it in FrontPage.

Resample

Figure 3-5
Resampling the picture in FrontPage does even more damage.

Adding pixels not only degrades image quality but also adds to the size of the picture file because each pixel brings with it a certain amount of extra data. Deleting pixels usually does less visible damage and has the added benefit of reducing file size, which translates to shorter download times. But for the best results, don't enlarge or reduce your pictures in FrontPage. Instead, do this work in your image editing program, which is probably better equipped to handle the resampling work than FrontPage.

see also Chapters 8 and 9 provide more details about the right and wrong way to change the size of Web graphics. Chapter 10 explains more about inserting and sizing pictures in FrontPage.

Sizing graphics by percentage

Some Web design programs enable you to specify the size of graphics either in pixels or as a percentage of the visible browser window. For example, you can set a graphic to occupy 10 percent of the horizontal window space and 15 percent of the vertical space. When a user loads your page, the browser automatically adjusts the graphic as necessary so that it occupies the specified percentage of the window.

This option has its pros and cons. On the upside, you don't wind up with a graphic that's too big when displayed on a monitor running at a low screen resolution or too small on a monitor set to a high resolution. No matter what the screen resolution, the graphic occupies the same percentage of the browser window.

The downside is that if the browser has to enlarge the graphic substantially, the picture quality can suffer, as Figures 3-4 and 3-5 illustrate. Or if the browser dramatically reduces the graphic, users might not be able to see the details in the graphic clearly. For these reasons, I recommend that you stick with pixels when setting the size of important graphics. That's the only way to retain control over the quality of the image.

see also These sizing rules apply to text that you create as graphics as well as to ordinary pictures. But sizing regular type that you create in FrontPage or in a word processor involves some different issues, which I'll save for Chapter 6. For ideas on creating text-based graphics, see Chapter 7.

Designing for the Small Screen

Have you ever tried to read a newspaper while occupying the middle seat on an airplane? If there's someone sitting next to you, you can't open the paper fully to read interior pages—at least, not without encroaching on your fellow passenger's space and possibly getting an elbow jabbed in your side. So you fold the paper to a manageable size, read a story or two, and then unfold and refold to access another page. All that folding and unfolding gets tiresome pretty quickly—so much so that you just may decide to abandon your quest for last night's business section and opt to study the inside of your eyelids instead.

If you make your Web pages too wide or too long, you create a similarly cramped environment for visitors to your Web site. They have to keep scrolling up and down, back and forth, to find out what you're selling or saying. All that scrolling takes a toll on the user's patience, not to mention the strain on the finger that has to hold down the mouse button or flick the scrolling wheel.

So what's the perfect page dimension? The answer depends on whom you ask—the grandfather who sets his monitor to VGA resolution (640 × 480 pixels), the businesswoman with a laptop running at SVGA resolution (800 × 600), or the graphic designer who has a screen as big as a city block and works at a screen resolution of 1600 × 1200. (I believe that's called big-as-a-city-block resolution.) The page area that each user can display without scrolling is different, so each user will have different ideas about the dimensions of the perfect page.

You can't please everyone, so your best option is to design with the lowest common denominator in mind. Ideally, that means placing the vital elements of a page within the first 640 × 480 pixels of the page—in other words, the area that the user sees first when your page loads. Some people refer to this area as "above the fold," which is the lingo that newspaper designers use to refer to the top half of a newspaper page. Most people read the area above the fold first, so that's considered prime page space. People passing by a newspaper vending box see *only* the area above the

Debunking the Resolution Myth

If you explore some Web design sources or lurk in online discussion groups devoted to the subject, you'll no doubt be told that you should size your image in inches and then set the image resolution to 72 pixels per inch or 96 pixels per inch. Although this method is popular, it's not the best approach.

Pixels per inch—ppi, for short—applies only when you *print* pictures. Then the number of pixels per inch determines the print quality. The smaller the print size, the more pixels per inch, and the better the image looks on paper. You establish the resolution in your image editing program before sending the picture to the printer.

For screen display, all that matters is the number of horizontal and vertical pixels in the graphic. A computer screen pays no attention to the resolution value that you set in your image editor. It simply displays as many pixels as the user's screen resolution setting allows, as the earlier section "Measuring page elements in pixels" explains.

So where did the 72 ppi/96 ppi thing come from? Well, back in the early days of computers, most PC monitors left the factory set to a screen resolution that resulted in about 96 screen pixels per linear inch of viewable screen area. The default Macintosh screen resolution gave you approximately 72 pixels per inch. So if you set your image size to, say, 2 inches by 2 inches and set the image resolution to 96 ppi, you wound up with exactly the number of pixels you needed to fill 4 square inches of a PC screen; if you set the resolution to 72 ppi, you got enough pixels to consume 4 square inches of a Macintosh screen. But this didn't happen because the monitor paid attention to the image resolution—it still simply matched screen pixels to image pixels.

Today, the 72/96-ppi guideline is outdated because we have a much wider range of monitor sizes and therefore a broader range of default screen resolutions. For example, a 12-inch laptop screen typically leaves the factory set to 800 × 600 resolution, which indeed gives you an effective screen resolution of about 72 ppi. But a 19-inch desktop monitor also heads into the world set to 800 × 600, and that gives you a screen resolution of about 45 pixels per inch. (These are rough values based on actual screen area, which is slightly less than the actual monitor size.)

On a practical note, FrontPage and other Web design programs don't allow you to size elements in terms of pixels per inch—only in actual pixels or percentage of the total window area. So if you're building a table, for example, and want to create a graphic that fits perfectly inside a table cell, you won't find any measurement that gives you the cell size in inches. Cell dimensions are measured in pixels across by pixels down, and you simply set the pixel dimensions of your graphic to match.

To sum up: When people tell you to make your Web graphics 72 or 96 ppi, nod politely, but ignore them. Better yet, tell 'em what I just told you and make their lives a little easier.

fold on the front page and may make a buying decision based on that content. Similarly, people logging in to your site may decide to click away if what they see in that first browser window doesn't intrigue them.

Practically speaking, though, 640 × 480 is a very limiting size. And if you ask around, you'll likely find that most people these days surf the Web using a screen resolution of at least 800 × 600, if not higher. (Many people won't even know they can *change* the screen resolution to a lower setting than the factory default.)

Here's my advice: on your home page, try to keep important links and information in that above-the-fold zone, assuming an 800 × 600 screen resolution. If you can whittle it down for a 640 × 480 screen, so much the better. If you do extend your page beyond the viewable area, as most people do, duplicate vital links so that they're always within easy reach.

Remember too that the browser interface itself eats up part of the available screen area—the exact number of pixels you lose to the interface varies depending on the browser and which browser tools the user displays. In Microsoft Internet Explorer 4 and later, you have less screen space at your disposal when the History bar is displayed, as in Figure 3-6, than if it's hidden.

Figure 3-6
When sizing your pages, don't forget that the browser interface consumes some of the available screen area.

Of course, if you have a content-heavy site, limiting yourself to such a small design area means that you have to spread information over many pages. And having to navigate through a long series of linked pages to view related content can be just as irritating as being forced to scroll. So you just have to try to strike a balance that enables people to get everything they want from your site with as little effort as possible.

Choose "Safe" Colors

After pixels, color is one of the most confusing aspects of Web design. I know that sounds odd—blue is blue and red is red, right? Well, maybe, and maybe not. Depending on the colors in your graphics and the capabilities of the user's monitor, video card, and browser, blue and red may turn out to be purple and magenta, or teal and orange, or any number of other variations on the theme.

In the next few sections, I'll explain how color works on the Web and how you can make sure that what you see is what your users get.

Making Color with Light

Whereas a printer reproduces the colors on a page by mixing different shades of ink—usually, cyan, magenta, yellow, and black—digital cameras, scanners, monitors, and other digital devices create color by blending red, green, and blue light.

The amount of red, green, or blue light in a color is measured in values from 0 to 255, with 255 indicating full-intensity light and 0 indicating no light. So if the red, green, and blue values are each set to 0, you wind up with black—the absence of light, if you will. And if you crank up the light box and set all three values to 255, you get white, as you would if you aimed red, green, and blue spotlights at the same target. If you mix equal amounts of red, green, and blue light at any other value, you get a shade of gray.

Luckily for the math-haters in the audience (I consider myself your humble leader) you don't have to memorize a bunch of R, G, and B values to assign colors in today's graphics programs. You just click a color in the program's color picker, and the software takes it from there. When you're choosing colors for the Web, however, you may need to specify colors using hexadecimal values, which are based on RGB values, which is the whole reason I even bring up the subject. For details, see the upcoming section "Specifying colors with hexadecimal values."

lingo

People in the digital imaging business refer to a particular method of creating colors as a *color model* or, sometimes, *color space*. The traditional printing model is CMYK (for cyan, magenta, yellow, and black ink), and the light-based model is called RGB (for red, green, and blue light).

Keeping Colors in Bounds

If you were to display the same Web page on 10 different monitors, you'd very likely see 10 different takes on the colors on the page. How your pages are displayed depends on many factors, including the monitor, the computer's video card, and the browser software. Because so many different types of hardware and software exist, the colors you see on your monitor may change markedly when you display the page on someone else's computer.

First, let's consider the hardware side of the equation. Most systems enable you to set the monitor to display 16 colors, 256 colors, 65,536 colors, or 16.7 million colors. The more colors, the better things look on-screen. Figure 3-7 shows the same graphic captured at the three of these color settings. Although the image doesn't suffer much when trimmed from 16.7 million to 65,536 colors, backing off all the way to 256 colors results in a very mottled image.

24-bit color
(16.7 million colors)

16-bit color
(65,536 colors)

8-bit color
(256 colors)

Figure 3-7
Here you see the same graphic as it appears when displayed using 16.7 million colors (top), 65,536 colors (middle), and 256 colors (bottom).

lingo

Color capabilities are also sometimes stated in terms of *bit depth* because the number of colors determines how many bits of data are needed to create those colors. Each bit can represent two colors. At the lowest possible color depth, 1-bit color, you get just two colors, black and white. With 4 bits, you get 16 colors, and with 8-bits, you get 256 colors (2^8 equals 256). With 16 bits, you get 65,536 colors, and with 24 bits, you get roughly 16.7 million colors.

Given the impact on the screen display, you may be wondering why anyone would opt for fewer colors. In a word, speed. In another, memory. The computer needs more time and system memory for each additional color. So people working with less powerful systems can improve their computers' performance by working at a lower color depth.

The question for you, then, is how to create graphics that will look great—or at least, won't look *too* awful—no matter what the bit depth of the user's system. For the answer, keep reading.

The dithering dilemma

If you display a graphic that contains more colors than the monitor's chosen bit depth allows, the computer *dithers* the extra colors. That just means that it blends two available colors to create colors beyond the 256-color limit. Sometimes dithering works out fine, and other times, you get the kind of speckled appearance that you see in the bottom example in Figure 3-7.

How does the computer decide which 256 colors to keep and which to dither? On the Web, the browser software makes the call. If your page contains more colors than the user's selected bit depth can display, the browser consults an internal color palette, which we geeks refer to as a CLUT (*color look-up table*). Then it dithers any colors that aren't included in that palette.

Just to make things a little more difficult, the basic 256-color system palette varies depending on the hardware platform. The top two rows in Figure 3-8 show the Microsoft Windows system palette and the Apple Macintosh system palette, for example. Because the palettes don't contain exactly the same colors, an image may look one way when viewed on a Windows-based system and another when displayed on a Macintosh. It's enough to make you give up color altogether and stick to black-and-white pages!

If you're working with photographs, you really can't do much about this problem except hope that most of the people who view your site will be seeing it at a higher color depth. But for other page elements—text, borders, simple buttons, and so on—you can avoid the dithering uglies by choosing colors contained in a so-called *Web-safe palette*. This palette contains 216 colors that are included in all the major system and browser palettes, which means that a color should look the same on every computer. The bottom row in Figure 3-8 shows the Web-safe palette.

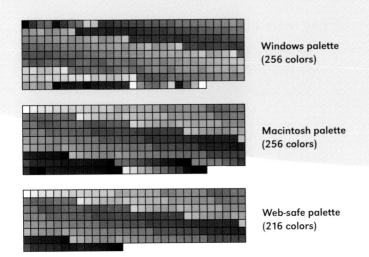

Windows palette
(256 colors)

Macintosh palette
(256 colors)

Web-safe palette
(216 colors)

Figure 3-8
You get a different base palette of colors in Windows (top) than on the Macintosh operating system (middle). Staying with the 216-color Web-safe palette (bottom) improves the chances that site visitors will see your graphics as you design them.

The next section explains how you can select a Web-safe color in FrontPage 2000 and Microsoft PhotoDraw 2000. But before you move on, let me add a word of caution. Don't expect perfect color consistency even from a Web-safe palette. The room lighting in which people view your site—as well as their eyes' own sense of color—can create variations in perceived color. So if color accuracy is a vital part of your business—for example, you're an interior designer selling slipcovers and draperies—you should add a disclaimer that explains that colors of actual products may not match those on-screen exactly. To make your customers even happier, offer to send actual samples or color swatches upon request.

Working with a Web-safe color palette

When you're building your Web pages in FrontPage or some other design program, stick with Web-safe colors for text and simple page elements, such as borders and rules. Ditto for graphics that you create in PhotoDraw or any other program. Sure, you're more limited in your color choices, but you don't have to worry about a cool graphic getting the dithering measles either.

Some programs enable you to customize your color picker (the dialog box or panel where you choose your colors). In PhotoDraw, for example, you can tell the program that you want to see Web-safe colors only in the color picker. The steps on the next page show you how.

Loading a Web-safe palette in PhotoDraw

1 The key to loading a Web-safe palette is the PhotoDraw color picker, which appears in the workpane whenever you're formatting an object using the solid-color Fill or Edge options or when you're working with a tool that applies color. In Figure 3-9, I selected a text object and then clicked Fill in the Text workpane to display the color picker.

Figure 3-9
To specify a Web-safe palette as the active palette, choose More Colors from the color picker menu.

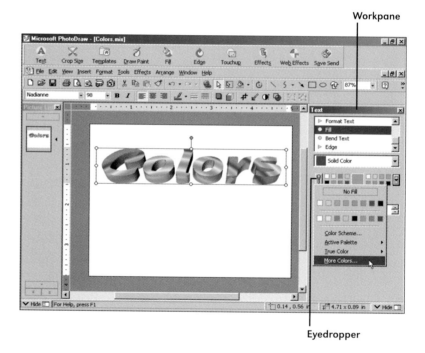

Workpane

Eyedropper

2 In the workpane, click the arrow button at the end of the row of color swatches to display the color picker menu, shown in the figure.

3 Choose More Colors to display the More Colors dialog box, which you can see in Figure 3-10.

4 Choose Web-Solid Colors from the Color Palette drop-down list.

5 Click OK.

6 Click the arrow button again, and point to Active Palette. PhotoDraw displays color swatches for the entire Web-safe palette. You can simply click a color to use it.

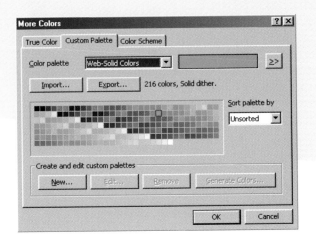

Figure 3-10
Choose Web-Solid Colors for the safest collection of colors.

If you're working in FrontPage, Microsoft Word, or some other software that doesn't allow you to load a Web-specific palette, you can specify colors in terms of hexadecimal values, as explained in the next section.

Specifying colors with hexadecimal values

As I mentioned a few sections ago, the color tags used in the HTML code that generates your Web page are based on RGB values. The color tags are designed around the hexadecimal number system, which I won't even try to explain because it makes me nauseous just thinking about it and doesn't matter anyway. All you need to know is that a color tag contains three pairs of letter or number combinations. The first pair indicates the amount of red light in the color, the second pair represents the amount of green light, and the third pair specifies the amount of blue light. Figure 3-11 highlights four color tags on a page of HTML code.

see also | *To see a chart of Web-safe colors with their hexadecimal equivalents, see the appendix of this book.*

If your Web design or graphics software enables you to specify colors using hexadecimal values, you can ensure that your page contains only the 216 Web-safe colors by using only certain pairs of characters. These character pairs are: 00, 33, 66, 99, CC, and FF.

Figure 3-11

In HTML code, colors are specified using a six-character hexadecimal value.

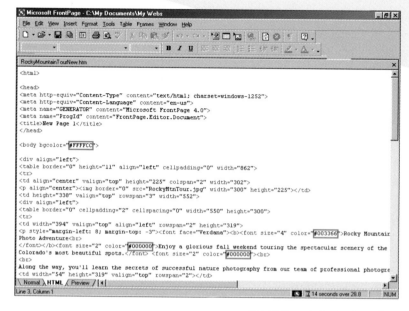

 Hexadecimal color values

The following steps show how to choose Web-safe colors using hexadecimal values in FrontPage.

Specifying Web-safe colors in FrontPage

1 From any color menu, choose More Colors. For example, to select a text color, click the down arrow to the right of the Font Color button on the Formatting toolbar, and then choose More Colors, as shown in Figure 3-12. Or choose Font from the Format menu to display the Font dialog box and then choose More Colors from the Color drop-down list.

Figure 3-12

Choose More Colors from the Font Color menu to display the More Colors dialog box and select a color by using hexadecimal values.

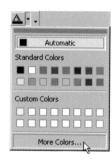

Either way, you get the More Colors dialog box, shown in Figure 3-13. The dialog box contains 127 color swatches. Most of these colors are Web-safe, but some are outside the 216-color palette.

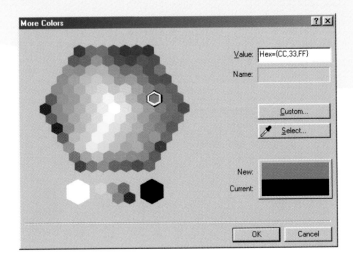

Figure 3-13
If you click a color swatch, check the hexadecimal value to see whether it uses any unsafe character pairs.

2 Enter the hexadecimal values for the color you want to use in the Value box. You also can click a color swatch and then check the value to see whether it uses any character pairs other than the six I mentioned earlier. If not, the color's safe.

3 Click OK to select the color.

After you select a color, it appears in the Document's Colors section of the various FrontPage color menus. You can then just click the swatch in the menu to apply the same color to another page element.

Calculating Web-safe RGB values

Moving right along from nerdy to incredibly nerdy, you can also specify Web-safe colors in terms of RGB values, an option that comes in handy if your software doesn't let you choose colors by hexadecimal values. Remember, hexadecimal values are based on the amount of red, green, and blue in the color. Almost every graphics program lets you pick colors by entering R, G, and B values. So all you need to know is how the six safe hexadecimal pairs translate to RGB values. Table 3-1 provides the secret decoder ring. As you can see, as long as you set the R, G, and B values to 0, 51, 102, 153, 204, or 255, you're Web-safe.

table 3-1

Web-safe color values

Hexadecimal value	RGB value
00	0
33	51
66	102
99	153
CC	204
FF	255

You can take advantage of this option in FrontPage, Word, and PhotoDraw. In FrontPage, click Custom in the More Colors dialog box, which opens the Windows color picker, shown in Figure 3-14. (If you don't see the right half of the window as shown in the figure, click Define Custom Colors to display it.) Enter the RGB values in the Red, Green, and Blue boxes. In the figure, I selected a Web-safe teal by setting the Green and Blue values to 153 and leaving the Red value at 0. In hexadecimal numbers, the value for this color is 009999.

Figure 3-14
You can specify Web-safe colors in the Windows color picker by limiting the Red, Green, and Blue values to any of six numbers: 0, 51, 102, 153, 204, 255.

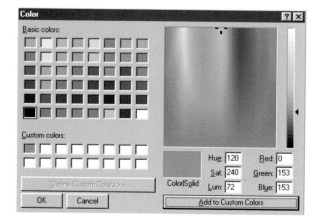

In PhotoDraw, you access the RGB options by clicking the True Color tab in the More Colors dialog box, shown back in Figure 3-10. In Word 2000, click the Color tab in the More Colors dialog box instead.

Matching an existing color

Suppose you want to match the color of some text on a page to color in an existing graphic. In many programs, including FrontPage and PhotoDraw, you can click the graphic with an eyedropper tool to "lift" the color and make it the active color. The eyedropper lives inside the More Colors dialog box in FrontPage; in PhotoDraw, the eyedropper appears with the color picker in the workpane. (See Figure 3-9.)

Another option is to match colors using hexadecimal values. You just look at the HTML code (you can do this in FrontPage by switching to HTML view), and jot down the hexadecimal number that's assigned in the color attribute. Then just enter that same value—or its RGB equivalent—when you select colors in your graphics program.

This technique is a great way to ensure color consistency when several people are creating pages for the same Web site. Just give everyone a list of the hexadecimal or RGB values for the colors you want to use for different elements on the page.

Preview, Adjust, and Preview Again!

As I mentioned in Chapter 1, testing your site in a variety of browsers is critical to making sure that your pages don't "break." In addition to viewing each page in various editions of the major browsers, preview your site at a low, medium, and high screen resolution to see whether you need to tweak your page layout or resize a particular element. Also, check the look of your graphics when displayed at a minimum color depth of 256 colors. In Windows, you typically adjust these settings on the Settings tab of the Display Properties dialog box. To open this dialog box, right-click the desktop and choose Properties from the shortcut menu. Your video card or monitor may also provide custom controls.

Also, remember that some browsers enable users to override the colors in your pages and use their own colors or the browser's default colors. Of course, you can't check for every possible combination of user-selected colors, but you should at least make sure that things look okay at the browser's defaults. Also, preview your page with the background color set to plain white because that's a popular option among people who customize their browser displays.

---

see also | *Chapter 5 includes additional information about color defaults, including tips on making your site more accessible to people who have difficulty perceiving colors accurately. Also pay a visit to Chapter 6, which discusses text-display defaults and how they can affect the size of your Web type.*

creating

4

your
DESIGN FRAMEWORK

All you need to know about . . .

- Choosing a design scheme

- Modifying colors, graphics, and text in Microsoft FrontPage themes

- Roughing out your plan

- Using tables to control layout

- Creating a custom design template

When you walk through the galleries of an art museum, you probably pay little attention to the design of the gallery itself. You focus on the art, which is just what you're supposed to do. But the fact that you don't notice the backdrop against which the exhibit is staged is actually a testament to the expertise of the museum staff. Curators and exhibit designers work for months in advance of a show's opening to choose just the right shade of paint for the gallery walls, arrange the individual works in some meaningful order, and tweak the gallery lighting so that it illuminates each piece perfectly. Even the height at which the works are hung and the placement of visitor benches are carefully orchestrated to make sure that the user experiences the art from the most powerful perspective—and with no distractions from anything in the background.

You should take the same approach when designing your Web pages. The page background, navigation buttons, and other basic elements should all serve to complement, not compete with, the main content of your site.

To that end, in this chapter and the one that follows, I'll offer ideas and instructions about building your site's overall design framework. In this chapter, you'll find information about choosing an artistic style and a color palette, using tables to control page layout, and taking advantage of Microsoft Office themes to improve design consistency. In Chapter 5, I'll share some recipes for creating backgrounds, sidebars, and other elements that provide the visual backdrop for your site.

Developing a Design Theme

The first step in creating a visually pleasing site is to decide on a design theme—the basic color palette, artistic style, and page layout that will be used throughout your Web site. Then you need to create or revamp all the elements on your page so that they fit within those design boundaries.

To get a better idea of what I mean, take a look at Figure 4-1. Lacking any design consistency, this page is a mishmash of contemporary and classic styles, bold and subdued colors, and free-form curves and sharp angles.

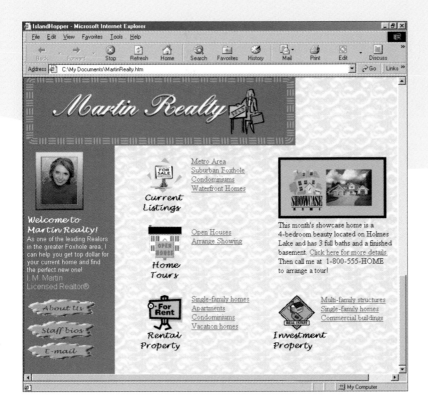

Figure 4-1
A jumble of mismatched styles and colors gives this page a disjointed, unprofessional appearance.

If you're new to design, you may not understand exactly what's broken here or how to fix it, although your eye may sense that something's not quite right. So here's a more specific breakdown of the design faux pas made throughout this page:

- The traditional script font used for the company logo clashes with the contemporary pattern that serves as the logo border.

- Speaking of that logo border, its rounded corners look odd set against the sharp angles of the blue bar behind. And the lines in the pattern don't blend well with the circular pattern of the page background. The organic look of the blue buttons in the lower-left corner creates still more visual disharmony.

- The logo uses a different script font than the one used for the welcome message, the buttons, and the section heads. One is classic, with precise letterforms, whereas the other has a modern, free-form look designed to resemble handwriting.

■ Some of the graphics are perfectly rectangular, whereas others have irregular shapes. Some feature a rough, hand-drawn quality, whereas others feature crisp edges. In addition, each of the four section graphics incorporates a different typeface.

■ Although all colors on the page are based on the same five hues—blue, green, orange, yellow, and red—some elements use bold, highly saturated versions, whereas others use less vivid, more pastel shades. And whereas some colors are warm tones, others are decidedly cool. ("Warm" tones have more orange, yellow, and red; "cool" shades have more blue, green, and violet.) For example, compare the green of the For Sale graphic with the green in the Showcase Homes graphic, and the blue of the link text with the blue of the background bars.

All in all, the mess in Figure 4-1 reminds me of my first apartment, which I "decorated" with a few Victorian-era antiques, a modern overstuffed recliner, one of those wicker peacock chairs that were all the rage in the 1980s, neon green, pseudo-bamboo window blinds, and, of course, the obligatory bookshelves made out of bricks and particle board.

By contrast, the revamped page in Figure 4-2 compares to a living room put together by a professional interior decorator. The following design changes pull this look together:

■ The page now uses just two fonts, both of which share the same plain, angular shapes.

■ The frame used for the agent's picture has the same shape and design as the four section graphics. If you look closely at the Martin Realty banner, you'll also see these shapes repeated in the background design. I simply copied the large and small polygons that form the photo frame, created multiple copies of each, and then varied the shapes by changing their color, rotating them, and resizing them.

■ All colors now coordinate throughout the site. (The home photo doesn't quite fit in the same color palette as the rest of the site, but that's unavoidable in situations like this, where your featured image may change regularly.)

- I replaced the amoeba-shaped buttons in the lower-left corner of the original page with a simple block of text. There's already lots going on visually here, and adding another graphic element in this position would be distracting.

- The new layout takes advantage of the entire window, whereas the original has a big block of unused space in the upper-right corner. With the new layout, there's room to include the company's phone number and the About Us, Staff Bios, and E-Mail links at the top of the page as well as at the bottom. So this redesign enhanced not just form, but also function.

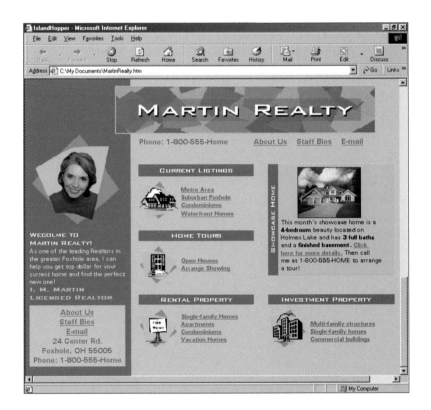

Figure 4-2
Common design threads run throughout this page to create a more cohesive, professional look.

---

see also | Chapter 8 explains how I created some of the custom graphics used on this page. For information on how I created the page background, check out Chapter 5.

Using Themes to Create a Unified Look

If you're not sure about your ability to put together a good design scheme or you just need some inspiration, FrontPage 2000 includes an assortment of design templates, called *themes,* on which you can base your site. To explore them, create a new, empty Web and then click Theme on the Format menu. The resulting Themes dialog box, shown in Figure 4-3, enables you to browse the available themes and also to customize the backgrounds, buttons, and other elements in a selected theme.

Figure 4-3
FrontPage offers a collection of themes that automatically format your page background, navigation buttons, and text using a particular artistic style and layout.

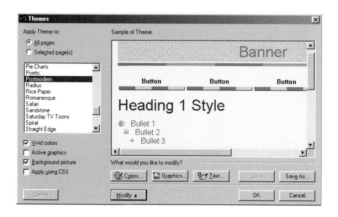

tip

You may recognize some of the themes; they're also featured in Microsoft Word 2000 and other Office 2000 programs. Microsoft PhotoDraw 2000 also offers templates and effects to help you build graphics that coordinate with the themes. If you use different Office programs to create the various elements of your Web site, you can work with one theme throughout to ensure that when you bring all those components together, everything's on the same design track.

Themes offer a good launching point for your design concept, and I'll give you an overview of how to use them in upcoming sections of this chapter. But first I want to mention a few caveats:

■ The number of themes installed with FrontPage by default is pretty limited, which means that you may not find a good fit for your content. And because everybody who uses Office 2000 has access to the same themes, you may discover that your site looks just like scads of others.

You can install additional themes found on the FrontPage program CD by scrolling to the top of the list in the box on the left side of the Themes dialog box and choosing Install Additional Themes. (You must have the program CD in your computer's CD-ROM drive.) You can broaden your selection even further by downloading additional themes from the Microsoft Office Update Web site. In FrontPage, click the Help menu and then click Office On The Web to access the Web site. If you see a world graphic, click your region. Click the Search Office Update link in the top bar, enter the word *Themes* into the search box, and then click Search Now to see a list of pages related to themes. Review this list to check the availability of additional themes. But again, remember that zillions of other people have access to the same themes. If you decide to use themes, as least take a look at sites offering content similar to yours to make sure that you don't wind up looking like a copycat.

■ You can customize many elements of a theme. For example, you can change the basic color palette, select a different font family, and replace the theme graphics with your own pictures. But when you start swapping graphics, substituting fonts, and shifting colors, you risk losing the design continuity the theme provides—which defeats the whole purpose of using a theme in the first place.

■ Some theme elements are formatted using Cascading Style Sheets (CSS), a Web technology that allows for more design control than you can get with plain old HTML. Unfortunately, some browsers choke on CSS. So I recommend that you clear the Apply Using CSS check box at the bottom of the Themes dialog box. FrontPage then alters the theme so that only features that can be formatted using basic HTML are included.

■ For the same reason, you may want to clear the Active Graphics check box. This option tells FrontPage that it's okay to use interactive graphics, such as *rollover buttons* (buttons that move when clicked or passed over with the mouse cursor). As with CSS, some browsers don't support the programming code used to create these effects.

see also | *For more on rollover buttons, check out Chapter 10.*

Applying a FrontPage Theme

When you apply a theme to an existing Web, FrontPage removes your current formatting and replaces it with the colors, fonts, backgrounds, buttons, and so on found in the theme. Although you can remove a theme from a page, doing so applies the default background formatting for a page (background color, hyperlink colors, and so on); it doesn't return you to your original formatting. So if your page uses other background settings, make a backup copy of your site before applying a theme.

---

see also | *For more about background formatting, see Chapter 5.*

With that legal disclaimer out of the way, here's how to apply a theme in FrontPage 2000:

1 On the Format menu, click Theme to display the Themes dialog box, which was shown in Figure 4-3 in the preceding section.

2 Choose the All Pages option to apply the theme throughout your site; choose Selected Page(s) to use the theme only on selected pages. (To select pages, close the Themes dialog box, click the View menu, click Folders, and then press and hold the Shift key while you click on the filenames of the pages you want to format. Then reopen the Themes dialog box.)

3 Click a theme in the list box to display a preview that shows you the colors, graphics, and layout of the theme. Drag the scroll box on the right side of the dialog box to scroll the preview display so that you can view all the theme elements that will be applied.

   If the theme contains a background picture, you can clear the Background Picture check box to hide the picture and display a solid-color background instead. Click the Vivid Colors check box to toggle between bolder and less-intense versions of the theme's color palette.

4 When you find a theme you like, click OK. If you're happy with certain aspects of the theme but want to modify others, hold off on that OK button and read the next three sections to find out how to customize the theme.

To remove a theme, choose No Themes from the list box in the Themes dialog box. If you applied the theme to selected pages only, you also can click Undo in the Edit menu or press Ctrl+Z to undo the formatting. The Undo command isn't available if you applied the theme to the entire Web. Again, though, remember that removing a theme returns the page to the default settings for the page background, link colors, and other page properties.

tip

If you customize a theme, be sure to save it so that you can use it again. Before leaving the Themes dialog box, click the Save As button, give the theme a name, and click OK. Be careful to click Save As and not the plain old Save button; if you click Save, you overwrite the existing theme with your modified one. (This warning applies only when you're modifying one of your own themes; FrontPage doesn't let you overwrite the official program themes.)

Adjusting Theme Colors

As I mentioned in the preceding set of steps, you can change from intense colors to less-saturated colors, and vice versa, by clicking the Vivid Colors check box in the Themes dialog box. But if you want to make further color adjustments, click the Modify button to reveal the Colors, Graphics, and Text buttons (shown near the bottom of the dialog box in Figure 4-3, found in the section "Using Themes to Create a Unified Look"). Click the Colors button to open the Modify Theme dialog box with the color options displayed, as shown in Figure 4-4. Here you can select a different color palette, create custom palettes, and apply colors individually to various design elements.

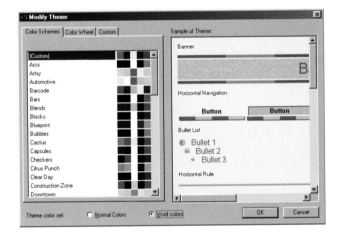

Figure 4-4
Click the Colors button in the Themes dialog box to display the Modify Theme dialog box, which has options for choosing a different color palette or changing the colors of a specific element.

Work your way through the dialog box in the following order:

1   On the Color Schemes tab, choose a color palette from the list on the left. The theme preview changes to show you how the various theme elements will look using the selected palette. Use the Normal Colors and Vivid Colors options at the bottom of the dialog box to toggle between the standard hues and their bolder counterparts.

2   To tweak the colors in the selected palette, click the Color Wheel tab, shown in Figure 4-5. Drag the hue marker, labeled in the figure, to shift all colors in the palette. As you drag, the color swatches and the theme preview reflect the adjusted colors.

   Drag the hue marker toward the center of the circle to create more saturated colors; drag outward to make colors less intense. Drag the

Brightness slider to the right to create lighter colors; drag it to the left to create darker shades.

Hue marker

Figure 4-5
When you drag the hue marker around the color wheel, you shift each color in the scheme.

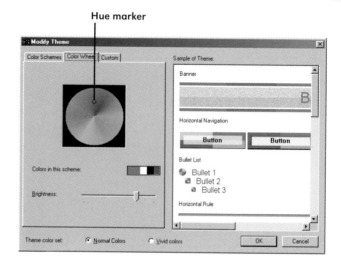

3   If you have trouble getting the color palette you want using the color wheel, click the Custom tab. On this tab, you can select a specific color for each element in the theme. Choose the element you want to change, and then select a color from the Color drop-down list.

4   When you finish tweaking colors, click OK to exit the Modify Theme dialog box and return to the Themes dialog box. Don't forget to click Save As to save your modified theme before you close the Themes dialog box, as discussed in the tip at the end of the preceding section.

see also   *Chapter 3 includes a more complete discussion of using color on the Web, including information on how to choose Web-safe colors.*

Changing Theme Graphics

You can't change the colors or style of a theme's pictures or graphics-based elements (buttons, for example), but you can replace them with your own graphics. Here's how:

1   Click the Graphics button at the bottom of the Themes dialog box. (If you don't see the button, click Modify to display it.) The Modify Theme dialog box reappears, but this time the options relate solely to graphics, as shown in Figure 4-6.

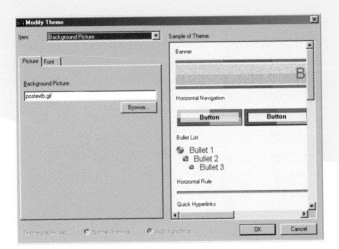

Figure 4-6
You can replace a theme graphic by selecting it from the Item drop-down list and entering the filename of the substitute graphic.

2 Select the item that you want to change from the Item drop-down list at the top of the dialog box.

3 Type the name of the replacement graphic you want to substitute. Be sure to enter the file's full pathname (for example, C:\My Documents\My Pictures\bluebutton.gif). Or if you're not sure about the pathname, click the Browse button, locate the file in the Select Picture dialog box, and click OK. The new graphic replaces the selected item in the theme preview.

Note that some theme components are made up of multiple graphics; if so, FrontPage gives you separate boxes for entering the name of each substitute graphic.

4 If the graphic includes type, you can alter the font, type style, and alignment. To get to these controls, click the Font tab.

5 After you finish making your graphics alterations, click OK to return to the Themes dialog box. As always, click the Save As button to save the customized theme if you want to be able to use it again in the future.

caution

Some theme graphics incorporate transparent canvas areas. When you view these graphics on a Web page, you see the page background through the transparent areas. As covered at the end of Chapter 9, setting the color of the picture canvas to match the page background ensures a smooth transition between the opaque and transparent areas of the picture. If you change the color of a theme background, you can ruin that seamless transition and wind up with a visible halo of canvas-colored pixels around the edges of the graphic. You can fix the problem either by restoring the theme's original background or opening the graphic in your image editing program and changing the color of those edge pixels to blend with the new theme background.

caution

Substituting Fonts

The final theme element within your control is the font used for the body type and various headings in the theme. Click the Text button in the Themes dialog box to access the font options. (Remember, if you don't see the Text button, click the Modify button to reveal it.) Choose the text element you want to tweak from the Item drop-down list, and then select the font you want to use from the Font list. The theme preview updates to show you how the new font looks. If you like what you see, click OK to close the Modify Theme dialog box and return to the Themes dialog box. And if you want to be able to use your customized theme again in future projects, save it by clicking Save As before you leave the Themes dialog box.

Plotting Out Your Page

After you've decided on a general design scheme, make a rough sketch of the layout of each page. Plot the position of each element that will appear on your home page as well as on other pages of the site. Then, when you're satisfied that the layout and design you have in mind will work well with the content you want to put on your site, get more specific. Figure out the exact pixel dimensions of each element—that is, how many pixels tall and how many pixels wide.

see also | *If you're not familiar with measuring in terms of pixels, Chapter 3 gives you the lowdown.*

Why bother getting this detailed? Because you'll save yourself lots of time and irritation. If you leap in and start creating your backgrounds, buttons, and other graphics without a plan, you'll undoubtedly have to do some resizing later. Your buttons may be a few pixels too wide to fit across the page, or your background may be a few pixels too narrow to fill the screen. On top of that, positioning elements in FrontPage isn't all that easy, especially if you turn off the program's CSS features to ensure broader browser compatibility. So play around with your layout on paper, not in FrontPage. You can also do your planning work in PhotoDraw, as I did in Figure 4-7. Click the New Picture button (labeled in Figure 4-7) to create a new, blank image. On the File menu, click Picture Setup to open the Picture Setup dialog box and then set the picture dimensions to match the size of the Web page you plan to create. Draw simple-shape placeholders for each of the major page elements, and then play with their sizes, colors, and positioning until you find a design that works. You can also use your actual text and graphics, but PhotoDraw might not process your layout changes as quickly as it will when working with simple shapes.

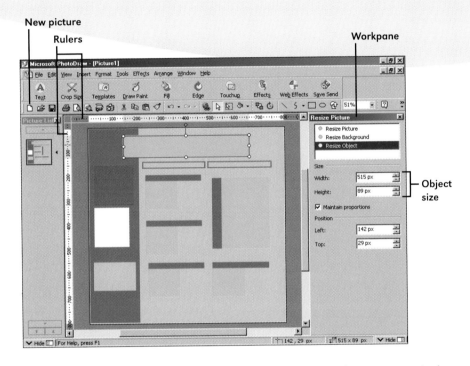

New picture

Rulers

Workpane

Figure 4-7
You can create rough layouts in PhotoDraw using placeholders for your various page elements.

When you've settled on a layout, turn on the PhotoDraw window rulers, if they're not already visible, by clicking the View menu and then clicking Rulers. Jot down the approximate size of each page element. Or select an object, click the Crop Size button on the visual menu, and then click Resize to display the Resize Picture workpane shown in Figure 4-7. Click Resize Object at the top of the workpane to display the object's exact dimensions in the Width and Height boxes.

Dealing with Layout Realities

At the risk of tempering any creative enthusiasm that the preceding few pages may have roused, I feel obliged to take a brief detour off the artistic highway and onto the technical back roads for a look at some harsh realities of digital design.

caution

Although PhotoDraw can export a picture as a Web page, you're better off creating the individual page elements separately and assembling them in FrontPage. This gives you the flexibility of reusing individual page elements throughout your Web and in other projects.

As I've mentioned many times already, not all browsers support all the design features that FrontPage and other sophisticated Web-building programs make available to you. This issue becomes especially critical in the area of page layout. The next two sections discuss two layout features, frames and CSS positioning, that pose serious browser-compatibility problems. You should use these features only if you're designing a site for a company intranet or another scenario in which you know that your audience will be using browsers that support them. Otherwise, skip to the section "Working with Tables" to discover the Web designer's secret weapon for page layout.

Frames

Some Web sites divide the available screen space into two or more separate windows. Because nothing in computerland can go by a simple, easy-to-understand name, these windows are known as *frames*. Each frame holds a separate Web page. As with any window, vertical and horizontal scroll bars enable the user to scroll the page display. Figure 4-8 shows an example of a frame-based page. The page includes three frames: a horizontal frame at the top of the page and two frames below. You don't see a scroll bar for the top frame because the contents of the page fit entirely within that frame.

Figure 4-8

Frames enable you to display multiple pages on-screen at the same time. But frames typically require more scrolling than a regular page, and some browsers don't support them.

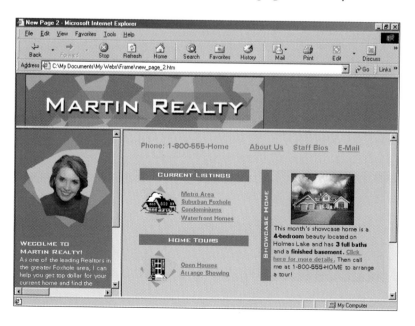

Frames were all the rage when they first became available. The thinking was that frames enabled people to keep multiple pages on-screen instead of having to click back and forth between them. But for several reasons, most Web designers now shy away from frames, and I suggest that you do the same.

First, users seem to prefer clicking links to scrolling pages to access content—and frame-oriented pages can require more scrolling than nonframe pages. Second, frames increase download time. Third, and most important, older browsers don't support frames, so most Web designers that use frames also create a frames-free version of their site and give people the option of which version to download. I'm assuming that you prefer to avoid strategies that double your workload, so I'm not going to explain how to create frames in this book.

Absolute Positioning and Other CSS-Based Formatting

The Position command on the Format menu and the Positioning toolbar in FrontPage 2000 give you precise control over the placement of text and graphics. You can specify positioning by entering page coordinates or by simply dragging an element into place, and you can change the way that text wraps around graphics. By using the Paragraph command, also on the Format menu, you can specify paragraph spacing, line spacing, indents, and other text spacing attributes typically available in word processing programs.

Unfortunately, these features come to you courtesy of CSS. I believe I've droned on sufficiently about CSS, but in case you dozed off, let me reiterate: if you use the formatting options that CSS provides, your pages may load incorrectly or not at all in some browsers. But don't fret—by using tables, discussed in the next section, plus a few other tricks discussed throughout this chapter, you can get nearly the same level of layout control without worrying about browser compatibility.

Working with Tables

Because tables can be created using basic HTML tags understood by the majority of Web browsers, many designers rely on them to lay out their Web pages. Figure 4-9 shows you the table that serves as the design framework for the revised real-estate site. The only element not placed in the table is the banner logo at the top of the page.

Figure 4-9
Tables enable you to achieve precise layout positioning without worrying about browser compatibility problems.

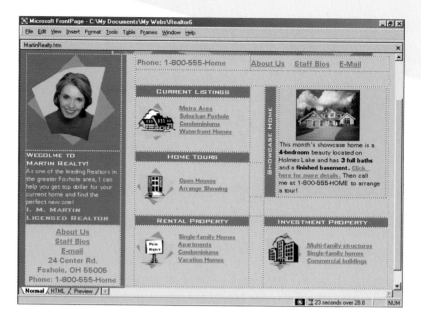

Tables make achieving complex page layouts easy—okay, not cakewalk-easy, but certainly much easier than trying to arrange stuff without them. After placing various page elements into table cells, you tweak spacing and positioning by adjusting the size of the cells and specifying the vertical and horizontal alignment of the cell contents with respect to the cell borders. You can even use a different background color for each cell, as I did in Figure 4-9.

Although I don't have room in this book to explain all the whys and wherefores of creating tables in FrontPage, I want to give you a basic primer so that you can start taking advantage of this useful feature. For more in-depth exploration of tables, check out the FrontPage online help system.

Ways to Create a Table

In FrontPage, you can create a table as follows:

■ On the Table menu, point to Insert and then click Table. The Insert Table dialog box, shown in Figure 4-10, appears. Specify the number of rows and columns in the table, table alignment, border size, and cell spacing and padding. (More about these attributes in a moment.) You can always change these table characteristics later, so don't worry too much about them now. Click OK to create the table.

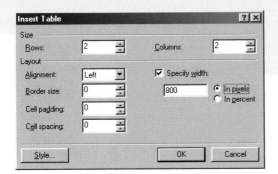

Figure 4-10
To let FrontPage create the table for you, click the Table menu, point to Insert, and then click Table and specify the table design in this dialog box.

■ On the View menu, point to Toolbars and then click Tables to display the Tables toolbar, shown in Figure 4-11. Click the Draw Table button, and then drag diagonally on the page to create the outside border for your table. Inside the table, drag horizontally and vertically to create the rows and columns of your table. If you make a mistake, click the Eraser button on the toolbar and drag over a line to wipe it away. To stop using the Draw Table or Eraser tool, click its toolbar button again or press the Esc key.

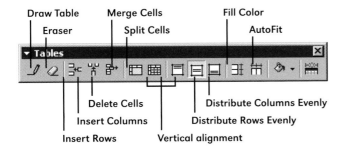

Figure 4-11
The buttons on the Tables toolbar give you quick access to major table formatting commands.

caution

Clicking the Style button at the bottom of the Insert Table dialog box accesses additional table formatting options. But these options rely on CSS—which, as I've repeated ad nauseam throughout this chapter, may cause your table to be displayed incorrectly in older browsers. Because the purpose of using tables is to avoid the browser headaches that more advanced layout features may cause, keep your clicker finger off this button.

- You can also create a table by clicking the Tables button on the Standard toolbar. (The button looks just like a table, conveniently enough.) When you click the button, a tiny grid display appears. Each square in the grid represents a table cell. Move your mouse cursor over the cells to specify the number of columns and rows you want in your table. (Watch the layout definition at the bottom of the display.) You can create as many as five columns and four rows using this method.

However you create a table, you add content to a cell by just clicking inside it and then using the same techniques you usually do to add elements to your page.

Table Formatting Options

To adjust table formatting, click inside your table, click the Table menu, point to Properties, and then click Table. You can also right-click the table and choose Table Properties from the shortcut menu. Either way, you see the Table Properties dialog box, shown in Figure 4-12, which is the central station for formatting your tables. You'll find some of the same options in the Insert Table dialog box, shown in Figure 4-10 (in the preceding section).

tip

You can move to the next cell in a table by pressing the Tab key. Press Shift+Tab to move back one cell.

Figure 4-12
The Table Properties dialog box allows you to adjust table formatting. FrontPage disables options according to the choices you make on the Compatibility tab of the Page Options dialog box.

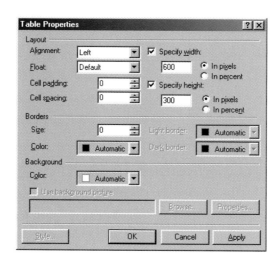

As in other FrontPage dialog boxes, the available options depend on the settings you choose on the Compatibility tab of the Page Options dialog box. (To display the dialog box, click the Tools menu and then click Page

Options.) Any features in FrontPage that aren't supported by the browsers or the server you specify on the Compatibility tab are disabled. The following list explains the options supported by most browsers:

■ **Alignment**   This option specifies the alignment of the table within the Web page. For example, if you choose Left alignment, FrontPage aligns the table to the left boundary of the page.

■ **Float**   This option specifies the alignment of a table that has a set width. If you choose Left from the Float drop-down list, the table is aligned to the left of the page and you can position text or other elements to the right of the table. If you choose Right, you can position elements to the left of the table. The Default setting aligns the table to the left and prevents you from putting any elements on the right.

■ **Cell Padding**   This option specifies the distance between the edges of the cells and the content within, measured in pixels. For example, enter 1 to create a 1-pixel margin around the interior of the cell. Unfortunately, you can't set cell padding for individual cells; all cells within a table will have the same padding. So I usually leave cell padding set to 0 and create margin space in a cell where needed by using one of the options described in the upcoming section "Adjusting Table Spacing and Layout."

■ **Cell Spacing**   This option specifies the space between each cell. When you set this value to 0, each cell butts right up against its neighbors. Again, I usually leave this one set to 0 and add spaces within the individual cells or insert an empty cell to create distance between one cell and another.

■ **Borders**   These options enable you to add a border around each cell (and thereby around the entire table itself). Use the Size option to set the border thickness, measured in pixels. Choose the border color from the Color drop-down list.

■ **Background Color**   This option specifies the background color for all cells in the table. If you select Automatic in the Color drop-down list, the cells are clear—that is, you see the page background behind them. (I'll explain how to select a page background in Chapter 5.) You can override the table background setting in any cell by choosing a different cell background color, as explained in the next section.

■ **Specify Width and Specify Height**   These check boxes and the corresponding options below them relate to table size. If you select the In Pixels option, the browser will display the table using the exact dimensions you enter in the Width and Height boxes. If you select the In Percent option, though, the browser adjusts the table size as necessary to fill up the specified percentage of the available window space. I recommend ignoring the In Percent option in most cases; as explained in Chapter 3, if the browser has to make the table larger or smaller to accommodate the browser window, text may reflow and affect your layout.

What happens if you clear the Specify Width and Specify Height check boxes? The browser first looks to see whether you've specified dimensions of the individual cells. If you haven't, the browser simply expands each cell as necessary to display the contents within. That sounds like an okay option, but it can actually cause your table to fall apart. Without any instructions for sizing a cell that holds text, the browser simply makes the cell as wide as necessary to keep the longest paragraph on one line (assuming that there are no line breaks in the paragraph).

That said, when you're creating a new table, clear the Specify Width and Specify Height check boxes temporarily. Otherwise, adjusting the size of individual cells can be a pain. Say that you set the table width to 600 pixels and you create three columns, each 200 pixels wide. If you reduce the width of column 1, FrontPage automatically increases the width of the other two columns to maintain your 600-pixel table width. But maybe you don't *want* the other two columns to be wider than 200 pixels— you just want the first column to be narrower than 200 pixels. With the Specify Width check box cleared, you can adjust the width of one column as needed without affecting the others. After you finalize your table design, go back and select the Specify Width and Specify Height check boxes so that FrontPage passes along the final table dimensions to the browser. Note that dragging a cell border with your mouse to resize it, as discussed later in this chapter, automatically selects the check boxes.

To see how your formatting choices affect the table without closing the Table Properties dialog box, click Apply. Like what you see? Click OK to close the dialog box. But if you think better of your changes, you must reenter the original settings and then click OK. Clicking Cancel after you click Apply doesn't restore your original formatting. Another way to remove the changes you make to the table is to click OK to close the dialog box and then click Undo on the Edit menu.

Cell Formatting Options

Whereas the Table Properties dialog box enables you to format the overall table, the Cell Properties dialog box enables you to format individual cells or groups of cells in a table. To display the Cell Properties dialog box, click inside the cell you want to change, click the Table menu, point to Properties, and then click Cell. Or right-click the cell and choose Cell Properties from the shortcut menu. Either way, the Cell Properties dialog box, shown in Figure 4-13, appears. Some of the options found here also appear on the Tables toolbar, shown earlier in Figure 4-11.

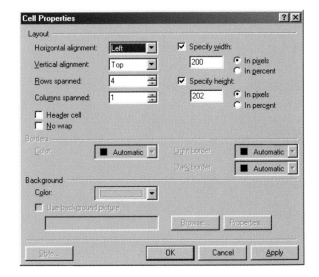

Figure 4-13
You can change the size, alignment, background color, and other options for selected cells here.

tip

You can apply the same formatting to a group of cells by selecting them before opening the Cell Properties dialog box. To select a range of cells, click inside the first cell and Shift+click in the last one. You can also click inside one cell, press and hold the Shift key, and use the arrow keys to select the surrounding cells.

Again, the available cell formatting options reflect your choices on the Compatibility tab of the Page Options dialog box. Here are the options supported by most browsers:

- **Horizontal Alignment**   This option specifies the position of the cell contents with respect to the left and right edges of the cell. Choose Left or Default to shove everything against the left edge; choose Right to align the contents with the right side of the cell. Choose Center to center the cell contents. Ignore the Justify option;

not many browsers support it—and even if they did, it produces ugly results.

■ **Vertical Alignment**   This option specifies how the cell content is positioned within the top and bottom edges of the cell. I can tell that you're clever enough to figure out what results you get if you select Top, Middle, or Bottom or click their counterparts on the Tables toolbar. (The Default option is the same as selecting Middle.) The Baseline option may be new to you, though.

Baseline is a type-related measurement that refers to the invisible line on which text rests. If you drew a line under the bottom of the word *bottom,* that line would be the position of the baseline. The tails of some letters, such as *y, g, j,* and *q,* dip beneath the baseline. When you apply this option to cells in the same row, the baseline for text in each cell should have the same position. This alignment applies only to the first line of text in each cell, and subsequent lines may have different baseline positions.

■ **Rows Spanned and Columns Spanned**   These values specify the height and width of a cell based on a particular number of table rows or columns. Suppose your table has four rows and two columns, for a total of eight cells. If you set the Rows Spanned value to 2 for the first cell, FrontPage resizes the first cell so that it's two rows tall. However, the cells that occupied row 2 get shoved to the right to make room for the taller cell; FrontPage doesn't simply merge two cells to create one double-decker cell. You still have eight cells, but now column 1 has three cells, column 2 has four cells, and the displaced cell hangs off the right edge of the table, all by its lonesome.

At times, a table with this kind of irregular layout may be just what you need. For example, maybe you want a piece of text or graphic to hang out over the edge of the rest of the table. But if you want a regular, rectangular table, the only option for making your cell twice as tall without changing the height of other cells in the same row is to merge it with the cell above or below. See the next section for details.

■ **Header Cell**   When selected, this option results in centered, boldface text—formatting that's standard for cells that contain column or row labels in data-oriented tables. Some browsers may apply the formatting somewhat differently from what you see in FrontPage, so I suggest that you pretend this option isn't there and use the text controls explored in Chapter 6 to apply whatever header formatting you want to use.

■ **No Wrap**   When this check box is cleared, text automatically wraps to the next line when it bumps up against the side of the cell. If you select the check box, the cell automatically expands as necessary to fit all text within a single paragraph on one line (unless you've added manual line breaks, a topic also mentioned in Chapter 6). Remember that surrounding cells will also be adjusted in tandem.

■ **Specify Height and Specify Width**   These options work just like their counterparts in the Table Properties dialog box except that they control the selected cells. The In Percent option, however, reflects the cell height measured as a percentage of the overall table size, not of the browser window. If you clear these check boxes, the cell size will be adjusted as needed to fit the cell contents. If you previously specified specific table dimensions as well as specific height and width values for the surrounding cells, however, FrontPage will respect those settings when sizing the current cell. That may limit the adjustment that FrontPage can make to the selected cell.

■ **Background Color**   This option specifies the background color for the selected cells. You can fill any cell with a solid color. Select the color you want from the Color drop-down list. Or click the Fill Color button on the Tables toolbar to change the background color of selected cells without monkeying around with the Cell Properties dialog box. If you choose Automatic, FrontPage defers to the background color setting in the Table Properties dialog box.

tip

If you move your cursor over a cell border, a double-headed arrow will be displayed. You can drag the border to adjust the size of the cell. If the border refuses to budge, either you're trying to make the cell smaller than its contents or you set specific table dimensions (in the Table Properties dialog box) and FrontPage is enforcing whatever cell size is needed to retain those dimensions. A cell also resists resizing if you set specific dimensions for another cell in the same row or column or if the contents of one of those other cells won't fit into a narrower or shorter cell. Also, remember that when you drag a cell border, FrontPage assumes that you want to make the cell a specific size and so selects the Specify Width or Specify Height check box for the cell.

tip

After you make your choices in the Cell Properties dialog box, click Apply to see how they affect your table without closing the dialog box. Or click OK to apply the changes and close the dialog box. As with the Table Properties dialog box, clicking Cancel after you click Apply doesn't restore your original formatting. To remove the changes you made, you can either manually reset the options in the Cell Properties dialog box or click Undo on the Edit menu after you close the dialog box.

Adjusting Table Spacing and Layout

You can adjust table spacing and change the number of cells, rows, and columns in your table at any time. The following list explains all these table maneuvers as well as how to select cells, which you must do before making some of these changes.

- **Select cells and cell contents** To select a single cell and its contents, press the Alt key while you click inside the cell. Or if you like doing things the hard way, click inside the cell, click the Table menu, point to Select, and then click Cell. But really, memorize that Alt+click tip—you'll be selecting cells a lot. (If you merely want to change the cell properties, you only need to click in the cell to select it.)

The Secret of Skinny Cells Some Web layout programs resist efforts to create an empty cell that's 1 pixel wide or tall. The program may insist on adding a nonbreaking space character to the cell, which results in a larger cell than you want. Even if you dig into the HTML code and delete the space character—it's written * *—the program reinserts the code as soon as you turn your back.

Here's the fix: You need to create a blank image that's 1 pixel wide by 1 pixel tall. Save the image in GIF format; name the file 1Pixel.gif or something similar that you can remember easily the next time you need the image. Then insert the image into the cell that you're having difficulty sizing. Now the program should respect your wishes and set the cell size to 1 pixel as you asked.

Unfortunately, you can't create a single-pixel image in PhotoDraw; the minimum image size is 10 pixels by 10 pixels in that program. So have a friend who uses Adobe Photoshop or some other program create the image for you.

To select a range of adjacent cells, click the first one and then Shift+click the last cell in the range. Or click in the first cell and then hold down the Shift key while you press the arrow keys to select the surrounding cells.

You also can click the Table menu, point to Select, and then click Column or Row to select all cells in the current column or row.

- **Add cells**   To add a single cell, click inside an existing cell, click the Table menu, point to Insert, and then click Cell. The new cell appears to the left of the cell you clicked.

- **Delete cells**   Select the cells you want to dump, click the Table menu, and then click Delete Cells. Alternatively, you can click the Delete Cells button on the Tables toolbar.

- **Merge cells**   Select the cells you want to join, click the Table menu, and then click Merge Cells. Alternatively, you can click the Merge Cells button on the Tables toolbar. You can merge only a rectangular selection of cells.

- **Split cells**   Select the cell, click the Table menu, and then click Split Cells. Alternatively, you can click the Split Cells button on the Tables toolbar. Either way, FrontPage displays the Split Cells dialog box, where you can specify how you want to subdivide the cell. Click OK to split the cell and close the dialog box. You can also divide cells by using the Draw Table tool on the Tables toolbar.

- **Add a row**   Click in the row that's immediately above or below where you want the new row to go. Then click the Table menu, point to Insert, and click Rows Or Columns to display the Insert Rows Or Columns dialog box. Click the Rows option, specify the number of rows you want to add, and then click Above Selection or Below Selection, depending on whether you want the new row above or below the current row. Click OK to insert the row or rows.

note

Pressing the Delete key on your keyboard doesn't delete selected cells; instead, it deletes the cell contents.

You can also click the Insert Rows button on the Tables toolbar to add a new row above the selected row. If you select multiple rows before clicking the button, FrontPage inserts an equal number of new rows.

- **Add a column**   You use the same process for adding a column as you do for adding a row, but this time, click in a cell that's immediately to the left or right of where you want to insert the column. In the Insert Rows Or Columns dialog box, click Columns, specify the number of columns you want to add, and choose the Left Of Selection or Right Of Selection button to specify where the new column should go. Click OK to create the new columns.

  Clicking the Insert Columns button on the Tables toolbar adds a new column to the left of the selected column. You can add multiple columns by selecting multiple columns before clicking the button; FrontPage adds as many columns as were selected before you clicked.

- **Divide an area evenly among cells**   To evenly divide the vertical space created by two or more cells, select the cells, click the Table menu, and then click Distribute Rows Evenly. To divide the horizontal area among multiple cells, click the Table menu and then click Distribute Columns Evenly. Alternatively, you can click the corresponding buttons on the Tables toolbar.

- **Match the table size to its contents**   If you want FrontPage to automatically resize the table to fit the table contents, click inside the table, click the Table menu, and then click AutoFit. Alternatively, you can click the AutoFit button on the Tables toolbar.

- **Adjust line spacing within a cell**   If you press the Enter key within a cell, FrontPage starts a new paragraph, which creates a double line space. If you want a single line space, press Shift+Enter instead. In this case, you're not creating a new paragraph, just creating a manual line break within the paragraph, as in Microsoft Word. (Some people refer to this type of break as a *hard break.*)

- **Insert space between two tables**   Put your cursor in the last cell of the top table, and press Ctrl+Enter. You can then press Enter (for a double line space) or Shift+Enter (for a single line space) to shove the two tables farther apart.

■ **Insert horizontal space between a cell's borders and its contents**
For text, you can place your cursor at the beginning or end of a line and then press the Spacebar to insert blank spaces (assuming that the cell is wider than the text). For a picture inserted into a table cell, you can use this same tactic or right-click the picture, click Picture Properties from the shortcut menu, and click the Appearance tab. Then adjust the Vertical Space and Horizontal Space values. Note that this space will also affect the distance between the picture and any text in the cell.

Making any of these changes can sometimes have unexpected consequences. If your table goes haywire after you add, delete, merge, or split cells, just click Undo on the Edit menu or use the Undo keyboard shortcut, Ctrl+Z. Then analyze your table to figure out why the change would throw the other cells into a frenzy. Usually, the problem relates to the fact that the size of cells in one row or column is dependent on the size of surrounding cells in the table. Change one cell, and the others have to adjust accordingly.

Toolbar Tweaking If the Tables toolbar—or any toolbar, for that matter—doesn't include some of the formatting commands that you use frequently, add your own buttons. On my Tables toolbar, I've added buttons for selecting the current row and column as well as for opening the Cell Properties and Table Properties dialog boxes. You can get detailed online help on this subject by clicking Microsoft FrontPage Help on the Help menu, clicking the Answer Wizard tab, typing *How do I customize a toolbar?* into the text box, and clicking the Search button. The help topic "View or customize toolbars" describes how to add and remove commands from toolbars.

But here's the short story: Click the Tools menu, and then click Customize to display the Customize dialog box. Click the Commands tab and then select the name of the menu on which the command resides from the Categories list. Then find the command name in the adjacent Commands list. Drag the command from the Commands list onto the toolbar where you want to put its button.

Don't like the design of the button that FrontPage uses? With the Customize dialog box open, click the command name on the toolbar and then click the Modify Selection button to display a menu. Point to Change Button Image to select a button design that's more to your liking.

You can further customize your toolbar by moving or removing buttons on the toolbar. If the Customize dialog box is closed, you can move a button to another position on the toolbar by pressing Alt as you drag the button. You can remove a button by pressing Alt as you drag the button off the toolbar.

Using Templates

You may have noticed that FrontPage offers several Web site templates, which you can select by clicking the File menu, pointing to New, and then clicking Web. When you create a Web site based on a template, FrontPage creates a set of pages and includes placeholder text and graphics on each page that you then replace with your own content. Page templates are also available, which you can access by clicking the File menu, pointing to New, and then clicking Page.

Personally, I don't find that using templates saves me a lot of time because it often takes me longer to replace and rearrange the template content than to start from scratch and build my own pages. But what I do find helpful is the option to create my own custom templates. This feature is especially great in corporate situations where several people contribute content to a site; having everyone work from the same templates helps ensure consistency.

If you want to create a site template, you have to use the FrontPage 2000 Software Developer's Kit (SDK), which is beyond the scope of this book. (For information about where to obtain this kit, search the Microsoft Web site for Knowledge Base article Q252975.) But creating a template for a single page is easy. Start with a new, empty page, and add the basic elements that you want the template to contain. You can create placeholder text and graphics along with instructions for replacing the placeholders with actual content, as is done in the FrontPage templates. If you apply a theme, that design information will also be saved as part of the template.

When you've got your template page ready to go, click the File menu, click Save As, and select FrontPage Template from the Save As Type drop-down list. Enter a filename, and click Save to display the Save As Template dialog box, shown in Figure 4-14.

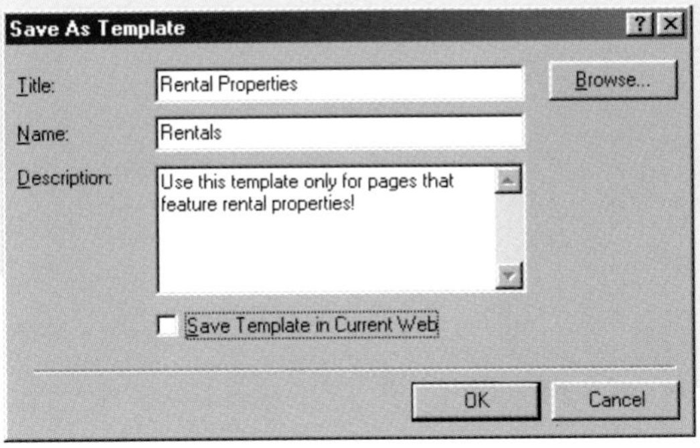

Figure 4-14
By saving your completed page as a template, you can easily use the same design again.

In the Title box, enter whatever title you want to use to identify the template, plus a short description. If you select the Save Template In Current Web check box, FrontPage stores the template file in the same folder as the current Web, assuming one is open. If you want to be able to access the template along with the FrontPage templates when you create a new page, however, *don't* select this check box.

To substitute the new template for one you previously saved, click the Browse button and select the template you want to overwrite. Finally, click OK to save the template. If the page has any additional files, such as graphics, you'll see the Save Embedded Files dialog box, which has options for saving these files. After reviewing these options, click OK. Assuming that you cleared the Save Template In Current Web check box in the Save As Template dialog box, the template and its description now appear along with the FrontPage templates in the New dialog box.

beautiful

BACKGROUNDS

All you need to know about . . .

- Setting background and link color defaults

- Filling the background with a solid color

- Creating tiled backgrounds

- Making sidebars

- Filling your background with a texture

- Designing repeating background patterns

- Creating color-block backgrounds

- Uncovering the secret of nonrectangular backgrounds

Just as you can make a meal look more enticing by serving it on fine china instead of on a paper plate, you can make your Web site more appealing by redesigning the background. Flip through the "before" and "after" page examples in Chapters 1 and 4, and you'll see just how dramatically this one change can improve your site.

In this chapter, you'll find recipes for creating some of the backgrounds featured in those examples, plus a few new designs tossed in for good measure. Of course, since we're talking about computer art here, you'll encounter a handful of technical side dishes as well. Although not as tasty as the artistic parts of the chapter, these technical bits hold the key to making sure that your site is displayed as planned, so take the time to digest them well.

Having just forced you to swallow more food metaphors than is probably healthy, I'll stop now so that you can push away from this introductory table and sink your teeth into the goodies provided in the rest of this chapter. (Sorry! That's the last one, I promise.)

Digging into Backgrounds

Before you start designing your background, you need to understand a bit about how Web page backgrounds work:

- **You can use a solid color or an image for a page background.** You tell Microsoft FrontPage 2000 your choice in the Page Properties dialog box, explained in the section "Setting FrontPage Background Defaults" on page 97.

- **Browsers repeat background images as necessary to fill the page.** Figure 5-1 shows how a page appears when a 200-by-200-pixel image is used for the background. I added the white overlay in the upper-left corner to show the size of the original image more clearly.

note

You can use many of the techniques presented in this chapter to create your site banners, navigation bars, and buttons, as well as backgrounds. In fact, for a cohesive look, you should tie the design of these elements to your background style. But since I wanted to present you with as many creative ideas as possible, I won't waste space showing you how to create a whole coordinated set of elements in this book. Instead, I'll use different design concepts for the examples in this chapter than I will in other chapters. You can then adapt the steps in any chapter to whatever element you're trying to create.

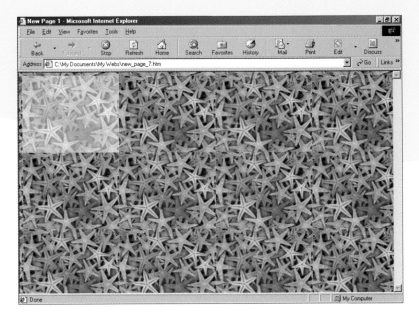

Figure 5-1
If you use an image for the page background, the user's browser repeats the image as many times as needed to fill the page.

■ **Pages with solid-color backgrounds load faster than pages with image-based backgrounds.** Why? Because you give your page a solid-color background by simply specifying the color in the HTML instructions that get sent to the browser, an addition that doesn't affect download time one whit. But with an image-based background, you're tacking on an extra image file to your page. The browser has to download the image file and then spend a little additional time tiling the image across the page.

■ **Use image tiles to create faster-loading image-based backgrounds.** Because browsers repeat background images to fill a page, you can create a great background *and* keep the download time small by using an image *tile*. A tile is a small image that creates a seamless design when repeated across the page by the browser. For example, to create the background shown in Figure 5-2, I used the tile shown in Figure 5-3. Tiled backgrounds reduce page-loading time because the browser has to download only one small graphic instead of a page-size image.

tip

When you use an image as your background, go ahead and specify a background color as well. The solid color appears while the background image loads, and it also serves as a substitute background if users turn off image loading in their browsers. If you don't specify a background color, the page appears using whatever color the user selected as the browser default. (See the section "Setting FrontPage Background Defaults" for more information about default settings.)

Figure 5-2
Although this background appears to be one big image, it's actually a small graphic tiled to fill the page.

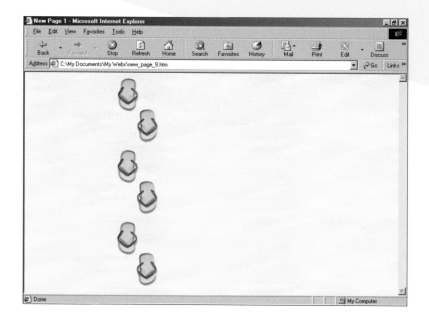

Figure 5-3
This image tile, which has a file size of just under 10 KB, generates the background shown in Figure 5-2.

■ **Site visitors can override your background formatting.** Most browsers provide an option that allows users to override your color choices and display pages using their own preferred colors for the background, text, and links. In most browsers, the default override colors are white for the page background, black for text, bright blue for unvisited links, and purple for visited links. Mind you, many people don't even know that they have this kind of control, especially those who are new to the Web. And you couldn't design around every possible set of override colors, even if you wanted to. But you should at least check to see that your pages look okay using the default override color scheme.

After loading your page in Microsoft Internet Explorer 5.5, you can apply the browser default colors by clicking the Tools menu, clicking Internet Options to display the Internet Options dialog box, and then clicking the Accessibility button at the bottom of the General tab. In the Accessibility dialog box, select the Ignore Colors Specified On Web Pages check box, as shown in Figure 5-4. Click OK to return to the Internet Options dialog box, and then click the Colors button to display the Colors dialog box, also shown in the figure. Selecting the Use Windows Colors check box sets the page background and text color as indicated by the Windows color scheme you specified for your system. Clearing the box enables you to choose your own custom background and text colors. The colors shown in Figure 5-4 represent the default color scheme.

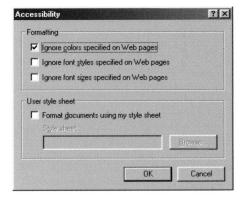

Figure 5-4
Most browsers, including Internet Explorer 5.5, enable the user to override the colors that you chose for your background, text, and text links.

Setting FrontPage Background Defaults

If you apply a theme to your Web site in FrontPage, as explained in Chapter 4, the theme specifies the background image or color. The theme also sets the default colors used for links, text, and other page elements. (I'm talking here about the defaults used while you're building your pages, not the user's browser defaults.) If you don't use a theme, you set the defaults on the Background tab of the Page Properties dialog box, shown in Figure 5-5. You can display the Page Properties dialog box by clicking the File menu and then clicking Properties; or by clicking the Format menu and then clicking Background. You can also display this dialog box by right-clicking anywhere on your Web page and then clicking Page Properties in the shortcut menu.

Figure 5-5
On the Background tab of the Page Properties dialog box choose the default link colors and page background you want FrontPage to use.

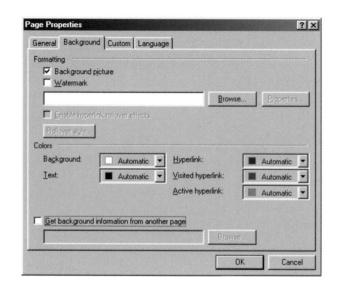

note

The steps for getting to the Page Properties dialog box assume that you're working on your Web in Page view (as do all other instructions in this book unless I specify otherwise). Also, the options in the dialog box depend on the Compatibility settings in the Page Options dialog box. (Click the Tools menu, and then click Page Options.) The options shown in Figure 5-5 appear when you tell FrontPage that you want your page to be compatible with both Internet Explorer and Netscape Navigator versions 3.0 and later, as is the case with most other examples and dialog boxes shown in this book.

From top to bottom, the Page Properties options shown in Figure 5-5 work like so:

■ **Background Picture** To use an image as your page background, select this check box and then enter the name of the picture file you want to use in the text box. Or click the Browse button to display the Select Background Picture dialog box, shown in Figure 5-6. If the picture is part of one of your existing FrontPage Web folders, you can access it through this dialog box. To grab an image from some other location, click the button labeled Search Computer to display the regular file-opening dialog box, where you can rifle through all the folders on your computer or local network. Alternatively, you can click the button labeled Search Web to locate a background on the Internet, select a file from the URL drop-down list, or click the Clip Art button to open the Microsoft Clip Gallery and select a clip-art graphic.

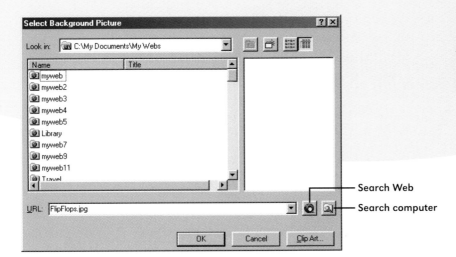

Figure 5-6
If you want to use an image as your page background, click the Browse button in the Page Properties dialog box and select the image from this dialog box.

- **Watermark**   Select this check box to prevent the picture from scrolling with the Web page. In other words, the background stays put when the user scrolls to display the rest of the page. I'm not a big fan of this option because you have to design your page so that the image works well behind any content that may scroll over it. Also, watermark backgrounds confound some browsers.

- **Properties**   This button opens a dialog box that contains options for changing the file format of the background image, adding alternative text (captions that are displayed if the user chooses to download the page without images), and setting up the picture to link to another page. Although these options are vital for regular page graphics, as explained in Chapter 10, I can't imagine why you'd want to apply them to a background image. If you do, you must click OK to close the Page Properties dialog box after selecting your image and then reopen the dialog box. Only then does the Properties button become available.

- **Enable Hyperlink Rollover Effects**   Select this check box to tell FrontPage that you plan to add animation effects to linked text and graphics. But be aware that some browsers don't support these effects. Chapter 10 gives you a brief introduction to this subject.

■ **Colors**   Use these five drop-down lists to set the default colors for the page background, text, and text links. As I mentioned earlier, you can specify both a background image and a background color. The background color appears while the page is loading or serves as the background if the user turns off image loading in the browser. It's not a critical feature, but since it doesn't add to page download time and looks nice, why not take advantage?

see also | *See Chapter 3 for a primer on Web color, a subject that's a little more complex than most people realize.*

■ **Get Background Information from Another Page**   If you want to use the same background settings you designed for another page on the same Web, select this check box. Then enter the filename, or click Browse and select the file.

Laying Down Background Tiles

You can use any old image as your page background, assuming that you've saved it in either the GIF or JPEG file format, as discussed in Chapter 9. But in practical terms, only very small pictures make suitable backgrounds. Remember, the more pixels in your image, the bigger the image file size, and the longer your site visitors must wait for your pages to load. A picture large enough to fill the screen of a monitor set to a typical screen resolution—800 pixels wide by 600 pixels tall—simply takes too long to download.

Microsoft PhotoDraw 2000 Version 2 includes Web templates that create stylish page backgrounds, like the one shown in Figure 5-7. But because these templates produce page-size background images with very large file sizes, they're better suited as backgrounds for Microsoft PowerPoint presentations or Microsoft Word documents. The background in Figure 5-7 has a file size of 200 KB and takes about 1½ minutes to download over a 28.8-Kbps modem, for example. Later in this chapter, you'll find information about using other PhotoDraw tools to create more efficient background images using tiles.

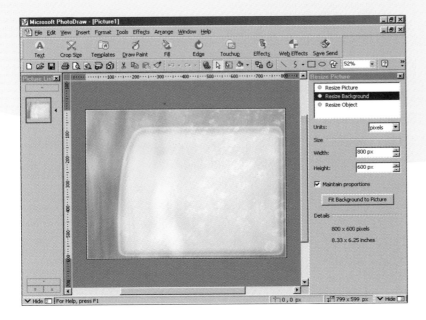

Figure 5-7
The backgrounds generated by the PhotoDraw Web Graphics templates look great, but because they generate very large files, they're better suited for use in PowerPoint or Word than on a Web page.

The Clip Gallery, available from inside FrontPage and PhotoDraw, offers a collection of background images as well. These images are sensibly small and designed to tile across the page, as discussed earlier. If you want to investigate the clip-art backgrounds, turn to Chapter 8 to find out how the Clip Gallery works. But I urge you to try your hand at creating your own custom backgrounds too. Once you know a few tricks, which I'll pass on in the next few sections, designing a background is really very easy and gives you much more flexibility than using a prefab background tile.

note

The instructions in this chapter show you how to create tiled backgrounds using PhotoDraw Version 2. But if you use some other graphics program, you can easily adapt the concepts to your own software.

see also | *Chapter 8 introduces you to the PhotoDraw program interface and explains how to create new pictures and work with the drawing tools.*

Solid-Color Sidebars

One of the most popular styles of page backgrounds features a color bar running down the left side of the page. (See Figure 4-2 in Chapter 4 as an example.) This *sidebar,* as it's known, creates a great frame for a site's major links or other important information that you want to set off from the rest of the page. It also adds visual interest to pages that use a white background. Best of all, the file size of the tile needed to create a sidebar background is very small, keeping download time minimal.

Making the tile for this background design involves a really complex skill: you have to be able to draw a rectangle. If you're up to the challenge, work your way through these steps:

1 Create a new image by clicking the New Picture button on the Standard toolbar, which is labeled in the upcoming Figure 5-9.

2 The next step is to set the picture size. For this project, you need an image that's 100 pixels tall and at least 1300 pixels wide. You want to make sure that your tile stretches beyond the right edge of the user's monitor. The highest screen resolution width most people use is 1280 horizontal pixels, so a 1300-pixel-wide tile should be more than adequate. (To create the examples in this chapter, I used slightly narrower tiles so that they could be printed in this book at a decent size and still fit on the page.)

To specify the picture dimensions, click the File menu and then click Picture Setup to display the Picture Setup dialog box, shown in Figure 5-8. On the Active Picture tab, select Pixels in the Units drop-down list, enter the dimensions into the Width and Height boxes, and make sure the Landscape Orientation option is selected, as shown in Figure 5-8. Click OK to close the dialog box.

Figure 5-8
Select the Pixels option from the Units menu, set the picture dimensions to 100 pixels tall by 1300 pixels wide, and choose the Landscape Orientation option.

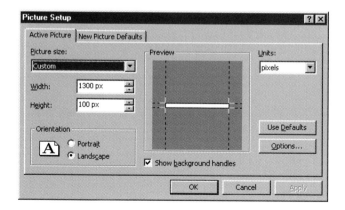

3 If you don't see the rulers along the top and left side of the PhotoDraw work area, click the View menu, and then click Rulers to display them.

4 Click the Rectangle button on the Standard toolbar, labeled in Figure 5-9, to activate the rectangular drawing tool. The workpane, also shown in the figure, displays the Edge options, which control the color, size, and style of the border PhotoDraw applies to the rectangle. Click the Straight Line option in the list, as in the figure, and set the Width value to 1 point.

New picture

Selection handle   Selection outline   Fill Color   Rectangle   Workpane

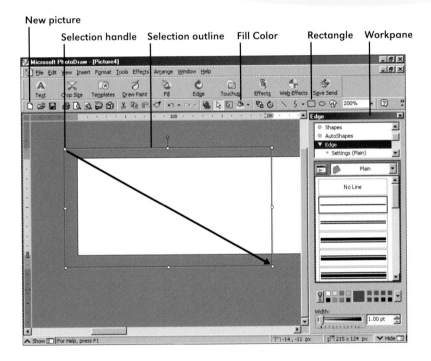

Figure 5-9
Draw a rectangle that's as wide as the sidebar you want to have on your Web page.

---

see also | *Chapter 3 shows you how to use the color picker at the bottom of the workpane to select colors.*

---

caution

Be sure to create your rectangle so that it hangs off the left, top, and bottom edges of the picture canvas, as shown in Figure 5-9. Your actual image tile will still be 100 pixels tall by 1300 pixels wide (assuming that's the size you specified in step 2) because anything off the canvas gets dumped when you save the picture for use on the Web. But because of some odd notion in PhotoDraw's brain, if you make the tile exactly the same height as the canvas, you sometimes wind up with a thin, white border at the point where two tiles meet.

5   To create the sidebar, drag from the left edge of the picture to the 200-pixel mark on the horizontal ruler. This will give you a sidebar that has a width of 200 pixels. If you want a wider or narrower sidebar, adjust the size accordingly.

After you release the mouse button, PhotoDraw displays a *selection outline* around the rectangle. You see round *selection handles* around the perimeter of the selection outline, as shown in Figure 5-9. (The top, green, handle is for rotating the rectangle, which you don't want to do for this design.)

6   Select the sidebar color by clicking the arrow on the Fill Color button, labeled in Figure 5-9. You can also select a fill color by clicking the Fill option in the list at the top of the workpane and then selecting the color from the workpane's color picker.

7   If you want to make further adjustments to the width of the rectangle, drag a side handle. (If you somehow deselected the rectangle, click it to redisplay the handles.) Or for more precise sizing, click the Crop Size visual menu, labeled in Figure 5-10. (The visual menu looks like a toolbar, but it's really a menu bar in disguise.) Click Resize on the menu to display the Resize Picture workpane, and then click Resize Object in the list at the top of the workpane. The Width and Height boxes show the current dimensions of the sidebar. If you want to adjust the sidebar width but not the height, clear the Maintain Proportions check box. Then enter a new Width value and press Enter.

8   On the File menu, click Save to save your picture in the PhotoDraw format, which has the file extension .mix. You want to retain a copy of the tile in this format so that you can edit it easily later if needed.

9   Now save a copy of the tile for your Web page. Chapter 9 explains this process fully; the remaining steps here show you how to save the file in the GIF format, which retains transparent areas. Click the File menu, and then click Save For Use In, which unfurls the Save For Use In Wizard. On the first screen of the wizard, select On The Web and then click Next. (You may think that choosing the As A Background In Microsoft PowerPoint, FrontPage, Or Word option is the right choice here, but if you go that route, your empty canvas areas don't remain transparent.)

Visual menu

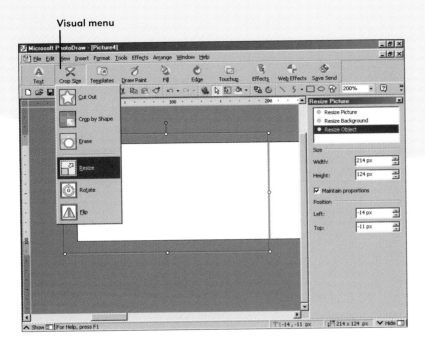

Figure 5-10
For precise sizing of your sidebar, rely on the size controls that appear in the workpane when you choose Resize from the Crop Size visual menu.

10 On the second screen, Select As A Picture and click Next.

11 Select Let the Web Page Background Show Through, and click Next.

12 Select My Web Page's Background Is A Tiled Image, and then click Next. (Again, this choice seems odd because you're *creating* a tiled image to use as your background, but trust me—this is the option you want.)

13 Click Save. PhotoDraw displays the Save As dialog box and selects the GIF format for the file. Give the picture a name, select the folder where you want to save the file, and click Save.

14 Switch to FrontPage, click the Format menu, and then click Background to open the Background tab of the Page Properties dialog box. Select the Background Picture check box, click the Browse button, select the image tile you just created as your background image, and then click OK. To close the Page Properties dialog box, click OK. As we Americans like to say when we want to make people think we know how to speak French, *voilà*. Your new tiled background appears.

note

What about the empty portion of the picture canvas? As long as you save the image in the GIF file format, using the options discussed in these steps, the empty areas remain transparent. When you load the tile image as your background image in FrontPage, whatever background page color you specify in the Page Properties dialog box will show through the transparent areas. You could fill the empty part of the picture with the page's background color to achieve the same effect, but going the transparent route gives you more long-term flexibility. Should you decide to change the Web page background color, you don't have to redo the tile image—just choose a different background color in FrontPage.

You follow these same basic steps to create all the sidebar variations explained in the next section, as well as most other kinds of background tiles. So you may want to tag this page with a sticky note, paper clip, or whatever device you use to help you keep track of vital life information.

Gradient Sidebars

For a variation on the solid-color sidebar background, fill the sidebar with a gradient. The sidebar shown on the left in Figure 5-11 shows a gradient that fades from dark to light orange.

Figure 5-11
Use the workpane options to adjust the gradient effect.

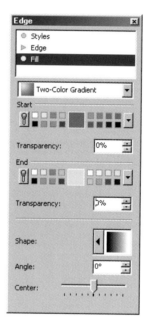

To fill your sidebar with a gradient, follow the same steps outlined in the preceding section, but instead of choosing a solid fill in step 6, apply a gradient fill, as follows:

1 Click Fill in the list at the top of the workpane, and then select Two-Color Gradient from the drop-down list, as shown on the right in Figure 5-11. (If you don't see all the workpane options shown in the figure, drag up on the workpane's title bar to undock the workpane. Then drag a corner of the workpane to adjust the size as you do any window.)

2 Click the Shape arrow to display thumbnails representing the available gradient designs. Choose the first thumbnail in the menu, which creates a left-to-right gradient.

3 Set the Angle value to 0 degrees. If you change the value, PhotoDraw rotates the gradient pattern.

4 Choose the initial gradient color by selecting it from the Start color picker. This color appears on the left side of the sidebar. The color you choose from the End color picker appears on the right side of the sidebar.

5 Set the transparency of each color. If you want the sidebar to be fully opaque throughout, leave both Transparency boxes set to 0. To make either color slightly transparent, raise its transparency value. At 100 percent, the color disappears altogether. Note that wherever the gradient isn't fully opaque, whatever solid background color you choose in the FrontPage Page Properties dialog box will show through the sidebar.

6 Drag the Center slider to move the gradient *midpoint*—the position at which the two colors meet.

7 From here, follow the instructions I gave in the preceding section, "Solid-Color Sidebars," to adjust and save your tile.

Shadowed Sidebars

To give your sidebar some depth, add a shadow at the right boundary of the sidebar. For this effect, you first need to draw a straight line alongside the filled part of your sidebar rectangle. Here's the drill:

1 Click the Line button on the Standard toolbar to activate the line tool and display the Edge options in the workpane, as shown in Figure 5-12. Set the line color to match the color of your rectangle by clicking the

tip

If you want to create gradients that include more than two colors, choose Designer Gradient instead of Two-Color Gradient from the workpane drop-down list. PhotoDraw then displays a menu of available multihued gradients in the workpane. For Designer Gradients, you can change the shape and angle of the gradient, but you can't adjust the individual colors. (You can use the Color Effects filters described in Chapter 9 to tweak all the colors as a group, though.) The Transparency value in this case adjusts the opacity of the entire gradient rather than a single color.

caution

Although gradient sidebars (and other graphics featuring gradients) look cool on a monitor that's set to display 16-bit color (about 65,536 colors) or higher, they most likely will appear speckled if viewed at only 8-bit color (256 colors). For more about why this is so, see Chapter 3. I don't worry too much about this issue when creating sidebars because even if people do view the page at only 256 colors—which is becoming more and more uncommon anyway—the speckles simply create a bit of a pattern in the gradient sidebar, which doesn't look too awful in my opinion. Still, when you're creating a gradient, you may want to set your own monitor to 8-bit color so that you can see the worst-case scenario. The problem will be more pronounced with some colors than others.

Eyedropper button and then clicking inside the rectangle. (I chose a contrasting color for the line in the figure so that you could distinguish the line from the rectangle.)

Figure 5-12
Hold the Shift key and drag with the Line tool to draw a straight line at the edge of the filled rectangle.

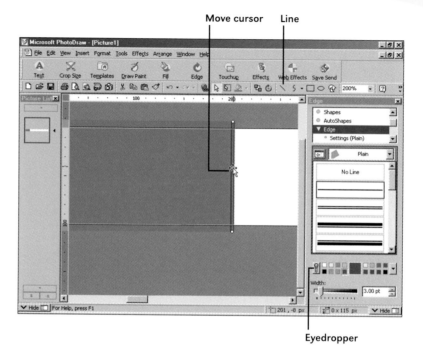

2 Create the line by pressing and holding the Shift key as you drag from the top of your rectangle to the bottom. When you hold the Shift key when dragging instead of simply dragging, PhotoDraw constrains the line to 15-degree angles, which only lets you draw at a 15-degree angle, 30-degree angle, 45-degree angle, and so on.

3 When you release the mouse button, the line becomes selected, as shown in Figure 5-12. Press the arrow keys on your keyboard to nudge the line so that it's smack up against the right edge of the filled area of the rectangle. If the line doesn't respond, place your cursor over the line until you see the move cursor (the four-headed arrow cursor), shown in the figure, and click. Then try pressing the arrow keys again.

4 The width of the line plays a role in determining the width of the shadow. So if you want a fat shadow, set the Width value in the workpane to

about 3 points. For a skinny shadow, set the value to 1.00. You can always change the value later, so don't sweat this decision too much.

5   Click the Effects visual menu, and choose Shadow from the menu. The Shadow options appear in the workpane, as shown on the right side of Figure 5-13.

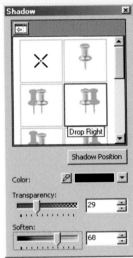

Figure 5-13
Adding a shadow is easy: just click a shadow-style thumbnail in the Shadow workpane.

6   Click the Drop Right shadow icon, as shown in the figure. (It's the second icon in the second row.)

7   To change the shadow color, click the Color arrow to display the standard color picker. You can also click the eyedropper and then click a color in your picture.

8   Drag the Transparency slider to make the shadow more or less opaque.

9   Drag the Soften slider to the right to create a fuzzier shadow; drag to the left to give the shadow more distinct edges.

10 If you want to adjust the position of the shadow with respect to the line, click the Shadow Position button. PhotoDraw then selects the shadow, and you can use the arrow keys or drag the shadow around to position it. Click the Finish button, which appears while the shadow is selected, to glue the shadow in place. Keep in mind that for this graphic, you're

tip

You may wonder why I didn't just give my sidebar a shadow by selecting the rectangle that forms the sidebar and then applying the shadow effect. The reason is that you get more flexibility in sizing the shadow if you apply it to a separate line—you increase or decrease the line width to adjust the shadow size. However, you can't get quite as soft a shadow with the line method. Try both techniques and see which one gives you the effect you want.

adjusting only the horizontal placement of the shadow. The vertical portion of the shadow will extend off the canvas, as does the rectangle that forms the sidebar portion of your background tile (assuming you followed my advice in the section "Solid-Color Sidebars" earlier in this chapter).

11 Save your tile in the PhotoDraw format so you can adjust the shadow in the future as necessary, and then resave the tile for the Web. ("Solid-Color Sidebars" also contains instructions for this step.)

Ragged-Edged Sidebars

By applying one of PhotoDraw's Edge effects, you can give your sidebar an irregular border like the one shown on the left side of Figure 5-14. The Designer Edges are really meant to use as frames around entire images, but they work swell for this purpose too, with a little tweaking on your part, as I'll explain momentarily. Here are the steps:

1 First, draw a straight line along the edge of the sidebar, following the same steps given in the preceding section. You need a fairly thick line— try 20 points to start with and adjust later as needed. (In this case, you really do need the separate line; applying the effect to the rectangle is possible but doesn't produce very satisfactory results.) Set the line color as usual.

2 Put the PhotoDraw Content CD (the Number 2 CD) in your computer's CD-ROM drive. You can access a few edge treatments without the CD, but for the greatest assortment of styles, PhotoDraw needs to pull files off the CD.

3 Click the Edge visual menu, and select Designer Edges from the menu. The workpane now shows a list of edge designs, as shown in the right half of Figure 5-14. The designs are separated into three gallery types: Artistic, Paper, and Traditional. Select a type from the Gallery Type drop-down list (labeled in the figure) to see its offerings.

Expand Gallery

Gallery Type

Figure 5-14
Although they're meant to create photo frames, you can use the PhotoDraw Designer Edges effects to create a stylized border for your sidebar.

tip

To see more edge styles at a time, click the Expand Gallery button, labeled in Figure 5-14. Click the button again to collapse the gallery to its original size.

4 Click an edge thumbnail to see how the effect looks on your sidebar, but don't panic at what you see initially. Chances are, the frame that PhotoDraw applied is too small for the line. If so, the program hides whatever areas of the rectangle don't fit within the frame. To remedy the situation, click the Stretch To Fit button in the workpane. You can also tug at the selection handles on either end of the line to stretch line and edge effect together.

5 PhotoDraw applies the edge effect to both sides of your line. If you don't want the left edge of the line to be visible, move the line behind the rectangle. To do this, click the Arrange menu, point to Order, and then click Send To Back. Now the line rests just underneath the rectangle. Press the right or left arrow key to nudge the line and expose more or less of the line's right edge.

6 Save the graphic in the PhotoDraw format and then in the GIF format for the Web, as described earlier, in the section "Solid-Color Sidebars."

tip

Remember that the graphic you're creating will be tiled on the Web page. If you choose an effect with a distinct edge pattern, you may wind up with noticeable tile edges like the ones in Figure 5-1. So choose an effect with random, abstract edges rather than a highly stylized effect. If you do want to create a patterned edge, see "Repeated Background Patterns" later in this chapter to find out how to design the tile so that it meets seamlessly with its neighbors.

If you don't find a Designer Edge that floats your boat, PhotoDraw has lots of other options for you. Select the line, and then select Artistic Brushes, Photo Brushes, or Theme Brushes from the Edge visual menu. The workpane then displays thumbnails of the prefab edges available for the menu option you chose, as shown in Figure 5-15. After displaying one group of thumbnails, you can access another by selecting a different group from the Gallery Type drop-down list.

Figure 5-15
For more ways to trim your sidebar, dig out the Artistic Brushes, Photo Brushes, or Theme Brushes edge option.

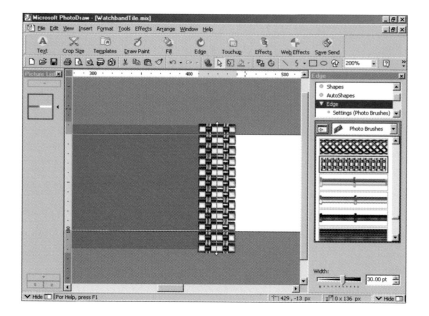

The Artistic Brushes effects mimic the strokes you can create with traditional art tools, resulting in irregular edges similar to those shown in Figure 5-14. Photo Brushes effects decorate the line with tiny repeating images; Theme Brushes effects format your line using designs that coordinate with the themes in the FrontPage Themes dialog box. Figure 5-16 shows examples of sidebar borders created using one of the

Photo Brushes effects and one of the Theme Brushes effects. Again, if you want to use an edge that features a strong pattern, like these, see the section "Repeated Background Patterns" to find out how to make it work correctly.

Figure 5-16
The left sidebar edge effect was created using a Photo Brushes edge, and the right was created using a Theme Brushes edge.

Horizontal Stripes

As you've worked your way through all the variations on the vertical sidebar background, you may have figured out that you can use the same basic technique to produce a background with stripes that run horizontally across the page, as shown in Figure 5-17. The difference between the background tile shown in Figure 5-17 and the one used to create the vertically oriented sidebars is that the tile in Figure 5-17 is tall and skinny instead of short and wide. You can see the tile under construction in Figure 5-18. I first created a dark green rectangle and then added a black line, a gray rectangle, and a white line. (The separate components in the tile appear in the scratch area to the left of the tile in the figure.)

Figure 5-17
You can use a tall, thin tile to fill your background with horizontal bands of color like this.

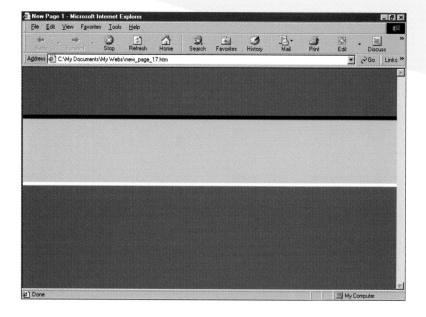

Figure 5-18
Here you see the four components that make up the image tile used to create the background shown in Figure 5-17.

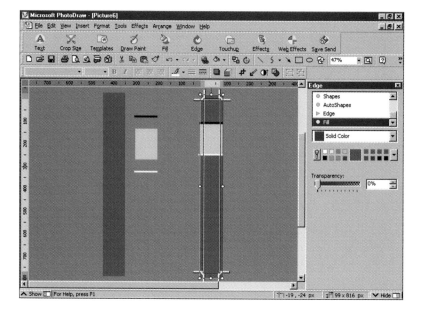

As you can see from the example in Figure 5-17, a vertical tile offers a great way to segment your page into horizontal sections. You do sacrifice some layout flexibility, though, when you use a background to subdivide your page. If you want to change the size of a section of the page, you have to re-create the background tile. If you want flexibility *and* horizontal color bands, you can use a table and then fill a row of cells with a solid color to create the color bands. Chapter 4 explains how to work with tables.

Textured Backgrounds

For a simple, elegant way to add some visual interest to your page, add a textured background. If you want a simple textured background, you can do the job with a small square tile.

PhotoDraw provides an official command, Format Background, that automates the process of creating textured Web backgrounds. Although this feature certainly makes creating a background simple, it also limits you in some ways. So I'll show you both the easy, automated option and the also easy, but more flexible, manual way.

Whichever method you use, the trick to this effect is using a very subtle texture. If the texture is too pronounced, a noticeable pattern will appear when the image is tiled.

Using PhotoDraw's Format Background command

1 Put the PhotoDraw content CD (that's the number 2 CD) into your CD-ROM drive so that the program can access all the available texture images.

2 Create a new blank image, following the same instructions laid out in step 2 of the section "Solid-Color Sidebars" earlier in this chapter. But this time, you can use a square tile instead of one that will run the whole width of the browser window. A tile size of 100 pixels tall by 100 pixels wide usually works well, but there's no hard-and-fast rule on this.

caution

Why not go really small with your tile—say, 10 by 10 pixels? After all, each pixel adds to the image file size, right? While that's true, the browser also needs a certain amount of time to duplicate and place each of your background tiles. So although an itsy-bitsy tile may take less time to download, the finished background may actually take longer to display than if you use a larger tile. Also, some Macintosh browsers have problems with tiles smaller than 64 pixels wide. Finally, remember that the more original random texture information you give the browser to work with, the less likely you are to wind up with a visible pattern in the tiled background. You can use a smaller tile if the texture features a very tiny grain pattern—think sand on a beach—than if the texture has a larger grain, like in a slab of marble, for example.

3   Click the Web Effects visual menu, and choose Format Background. The workpane changes to show the Format Background options. Choose Texture from the top drop-down list to display thumbnails of the available texture fills in the list, as shown in Figure 5-19. The textures are organized into categories, but if you choose All from the Gallery Type drop-down list, as in the figure, you can peruse all textures in the same list.

Figure 5-19
Click one of the thumbnails in the workpane to apply the texture to your image tile.

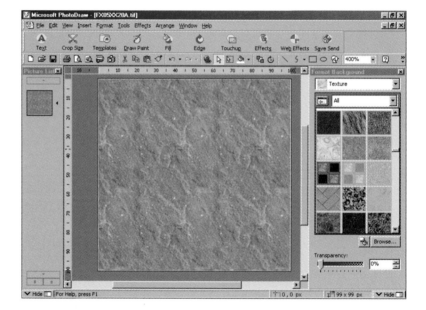

4   Click the texture that you want to use. You can drag the Transparency slider to make the texture more or less opaque.

5   To see how the tiled background will look, click the File menu and then click Preview In Browser. PhotoDraw taps Internet Explorer on the shoulder, and Internet Explorer responds by displaying the proposed background. If you like what you see, close the browser and move on to step 6. If not, return to PhotoDraw, click another texture thumbnail, and choose Preview In Browser again.

6   If you want, you can click Save on the File menu to save a copy of the picture in the PhotoDraw native format so that you can easily swap out the texture with another one later. Of course, creating a whole new background tile is about the same amount of work as saving and opening an existing one, so do what makes you happy.

7 Save the tile for use on the Web by following the file-saving instructions provided at the end of Chapter 9. In this case, your tile doesn't contain any transparent areas, so you can choose either the GIF or JPEG format; pick the one that delivers the best trade-off between file size and image quality.

Okay, that's the official background creation method. What's my problem with it? First, many of the textures in the list aren't really textures per se, but patterns that don't tile seamlessly in the browser. Second, you can't modify the textures in any way except to adjust the overall transparency. If you instead use the top-secret method described in the following steps to create your background tiles, you gain a lot more design flexibility. The only drawback is that you can't use the Preview In Browser command to preview the tiled background; you have to use a slightly more involved process to pull the image up in FrontPage to see whether you did a good job. I think the trade-off is well worth it. Try this method for yourself and see whether you agree.

Creating custom textures in PhotoDraw

1 Create a new picture that is 100 pixels wide by 100 pixels tall. (See the section "Solid-Color Sidebars" earlier in this chapter if you need help.)

2 Click the Rectangle button on the Standard toolbar, and drag to create a rectangle that's slightly bigger than your image canvas. (See the aforementioned "Solid-Color Sidebars" for the scoop on why you need an oversized rectangle.) Don't worry about the size or exact shape of the rectangle—just make sure that it hangs off the edge of the canvas all the way around.

3 Fill the rectangle with the color that you want to use as the primary shade for the background. You can choose the color by clicking the arrow on the Fill Color button. (It's labeled in Figure 5-20.) Hint: Lighter, more pastel shades make better backgrounds than dark, bold shades.

4 Click the Effects visual menu, and then click Designer Effects. The workpane displays thumbnails representing PhotoDraw's collection of

special effects. Scroll down the list until you find the Texturizer effect, shown in Figure 5-20. Click the thumbnail to apply the effect to your rectangle.

Figure 5-20
Use the Texturizer effect to create custom texture fills.

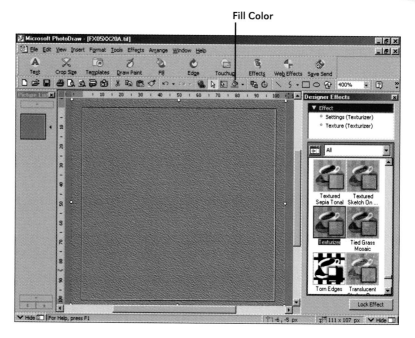

5 To explore all the texture variations you can create, click Texture (Texturizer) at the top of the workpane. PhotoDraw reveals the texture controls shown in Figure 5-21. Click the Texture arrow to display a flyout menu showing thumbnails of all the texture patterns. Now, *these* are what I call *textures*.

You can use the Light Position option on this workpane to change the direction at which the "light" falls on the texture, which will change the pattern of highlights and shadows in the texture. The Scale option changes the size of the shapes used to create the texture, and the Relief option makes the hills and valleys in the texture more or less pronounced.

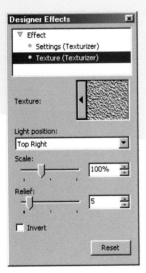

You can make the texture less pronounced by lowering its transparency. To adjust the transparency, click Settings (Texturizer) at the top of the workpane. Then drag the Transparency slider, which lives all by its lonesome in the workpane.

6   On the File menu, click Save to save the picture in the PhotoDraw format (.mix) so that you can continue to adjust the texture later if needed. Then save your image tile as explained at the end of Chapter 9. Again, because this tile doesn't contain any transparent areas, you can choose either GIF or JPEG as the file format. Chapter 9 will help you make the right call.

tip

For best results, use a low Relief value, remembering that your texture becomes more visible when it's tiled across an entire page. Lowering the Scale value gives you smaller and more random texture grains, which can also help prevent visible patterns when the image is tiled.

tip

To preview your image tile without saving it, click the File menu, point to Send To, and then click Microsoft FrontPage. In the Send To Microsoft FrontPage dialog box, click As Background On Active Page. Then click the Options button to display the Export Options dialog box. Click the Save Picture As One Image option, and select either JPEG or GIF in the Save Images As Type drop-down list, depending on the format you want to use. Click OK twice to close the dialog boxes. PhotoDraw launches FrontPage if it's not already open and displays your image as the background.

Repeated Background Patterns

Several times in this chapter, I alluded to problems that can occur when a background tile features a distinct object or pattern, such as the tiles shown in Figure 5-16. You have to be sure that you create the tile so that the pattern aligns perfectly when the image is tiled in the browser—it's the same concept as lining up two pieces of wallpaper to avoid a noticeable break in the pattern.

Figure 5-22 shows close-up views of the tiles that I used to create the sidebars shown in Figure 5-16. (I copied the two tiles into the same picture here in order to show both in the same PhotoDraw window.) In each case, I positioned the edge pattern so that if you were to join the top and bottom of the canvas—which is just what happens when the image is tiled in the browser—the pattern would match up perfectly.

Figure 5-22
Make sure that the portion of the pattern at the top of the canvas matches up perfectly with the portion at the bottom of the tile.

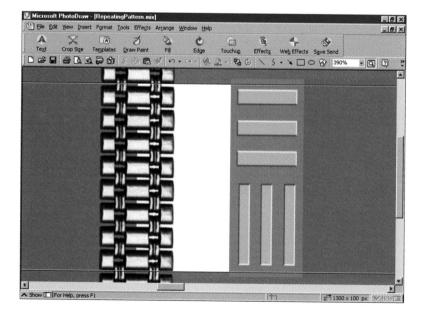

note

Remember to match the top and bottom of the PhotoDraw picture canvas, not the rectangle or line that you drew to create the tile (which should hang off the edge of the canvas, for reasons explained in the first example in this chapter). Anything beyond the canvas gets clipped away when you save the file, so it's the canvas edges that matter when you're matching patterns.

Getting patterns to line up perfectly can be a headache, especially with complex patterns. For best results—and the least amount of stress on you—choose patterns that have distinct, repeating shapes, like those in Figure 5-22. Patterns that include space between each shape also make things easier.

For two more examples of patterned tiles, flip back to Figure 5-2 at the beginning of this chapter and Figure 1-6 in Chapter 1. Figure 5-3 shows you the positioning of the flip-flop pattern that I used to create the Figure 5-2 background. I applied a background texture to the whole tile and created the flip-flops by drawing a single line and then applying the flip-flop design available in the Photo Brushes collection of edge effects. For Figure 1-6, I used a similar approach but made the left edge of the tile transparent, filled the right portion with a green-and-white texture, and used a clip-art shape from the PhotoDraw Content CD to separate the two.

Faux Backgrounds

You now know how to create backgrounds that feature sidebars, horizontal bands of color, and textures. But how do you create a background that segments your page into multiple blocks of color, as in Figure 5-23? You could create a page-size image with this design and use the image as your background, but that means a huge image file and serious download waits. Tiles won't work either because they fill the screen with a single pattern of color, not large areas of color like the ones in this example. The answer, as with most Web design challenges, lies in the creative use of tables. In Figure 5-23, I set the page background color to yellow, created a table, and then filled the cells in the upper-right corner with blue and filled the cells in the lower-left corner with green. It's a quick, easy answer, and what's more, you can easily change the pattern as needed by reformatting the cells.

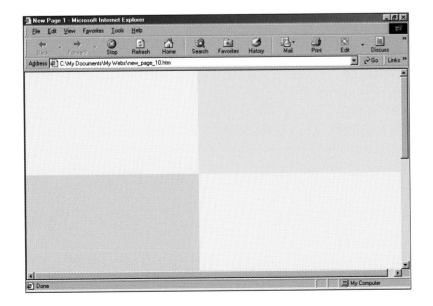

Figure 5-23
You can create color-block backgrounds like this by using tables.

For another example of using tables to create part of your background, see the Coho Winery site shown in Figure 1-7 in Chapter 1. I used a textured tile to create the rose-shaded areas of the background and created a table to hold the page contents. Then I set the background color for the table cells in the middle of the page to pale yellow. I left the other cells set to the Automatic background option, which lets whatever page background you chose appear behind the cell.

Figure 4-2 in Chapter 4 also relies on a table for background design. For the page background, I used a horizontal image tile with a blue sidebar. In the Page Properties dialog box in FrontPage, I set the overall page background color to tan. I filled the cells at the bottom of the sidebar with tan as well, and I filled the cells that hold the Showcase Home information with light green. I filled other cells with dark blue to create the divider lines and section-head backgrounds. (Figure 4-9 shows the actual table layout.)

Many designers take advantage of tables in this fashion, which helps explain the predominance of rectangular shapes on the Web—rectangular sidebars, rectangular banner heads, rectangular buttons, and rectangular text layouts. This trend doesn't stem from a lack of creativity on the part of the Web design community, but from the gridlike nature of tables. You know that saying, "When all you have is a hammer, everything looks like a nail"? Well, when all you have is a table cell, everything looks like a rectangle.

"But wait," you say, "some Web page backgrounds have color blocks with *curved* edges. How do they make those?" Ah, I feel just like a renegade magician giving away the secret to pulling a rabbit out of a hat—a trick, incidentally, that is apparently easier than getting rabbits out of my garden. But back to the secret of backgrounds that have nonlinear edges, such as the one shown in Figure 5-24: they're simply curved border graphics created in a drawing program and imported into FrontPage, usually into a table cell. Figure 5-25 shows you a behind-the-scenes look at the structural makeup of the design in Figure 5-24.

You can use the techniques outlined in Chapter 8 to produce curved shapes like the ones used in the background in Figure 5-24. Before you get all fired up about making curve shapes and inserting them all over your Web site, though, stop to remember that graphics take time to download, while you can specify a solid background color for a page or a table cell and not affect download time at all. That's why rectangles, boring as you may find them, usually are the better choice.

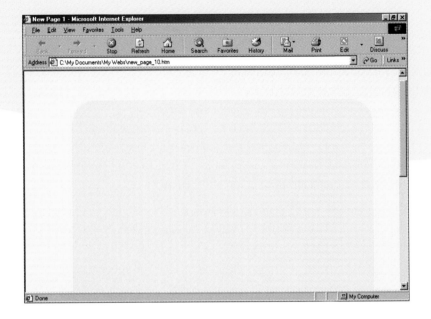

Figure 5-24
*How do you create backgrounds
that feature nonrectangular
shapes?*

Corner graphic   Corner graphic

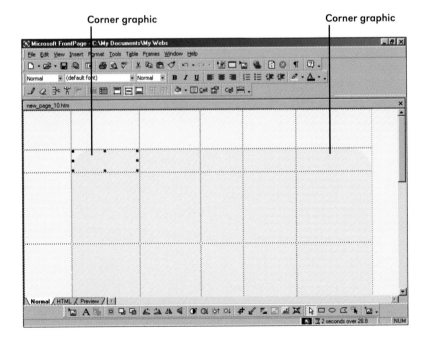

Figure 5-25
*The secret: A simple shape graphic
placed in a table cell creates the
curved edge of the blue region.*

Is Your Background Color Blind?

When you're designing a page background, select a design that ensures text legibility. That means avoiding busy textures or patterns and using reverse type (light type on a dark background) only for short headlines and other large type elements. These basic guidelines go a long way toward making your site easily readable. But you need to go a step further in your design thinking if you want your site to be accessible to people who have color perception problems—a condition commonly known as color blindness. Color-blind people have problems distinguishing red from green and may also have difficulty telling blue from yellow. So if you put red text on a green background, for example, or add a yellow button to a blue navigation bar, your site may be confusing to color-blind visitors.

Here are a few ways that you can make your site welcoming to color-blind visitors:

- Don't ask visitors to follow color-based instructions, such as "Click the red button" or "Follow the green arrows." Instead, use different shapes, patterns, or text labels to indicate navigation elements. Also, stick with the conventional underline formatting for hyperlinks.

- Aim for a high degree of contrast between text and background. Black text on a white background delivers the greatest contrast. For obvious reasons, don't rely on color alone to provide contrast—medium-blue text on a medium-red background, for example. Instead, create contrast through a mix of light, dark, and medium shades.

You can use PhotoDraw to evaluate your pages from a contrast viewpoint. First, take a "screen shot" of your page by pressing the Print Screen key, which puts a picture of whatever is on-screen into the Clipboard. Open a new picture in PhotoDraw, and press Ctrl+V (the keyboard shortcut for the Paste command on the Edit menu) to display the screen shot in PhotoDraw. Then click the Effects visual menu, click Color Effects, and choose Grayscale from the Touchup Effect drop-down list in the workpane. Finally, click the Grayscale button in the workpane to convert your picture to grayscale as shown on the next page.

(continued)

Is Your Background Color Blind? (continued)

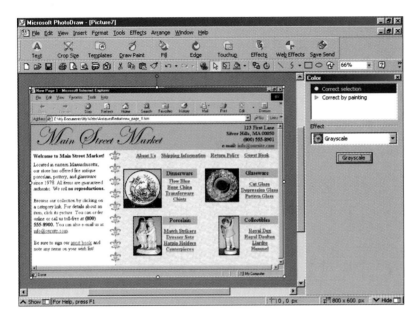

■ Keep in mind that a person with color-perception problems may also see slightly less contrast between light and dark objects or between highly saturated and less-intense colors than people with normal vision. In other words, when your site looks okay to you, boosting color, saturation, and contrast a little more improves things for the color-blind visitor.

■ If you know someone who has trouble distinguishing color, ask for an evaluation of your pages. Although the grayscale test will give you a good idea of whether your site needs more contrast, input from someone who deals with color problems on a daily basis will be even more valuable.

PART

two

THE FINE
print

In a former life, I worked as an editor for a consumer magazine.
With each new issue, the editorial and art departments locked horns because of our different priorities. The artists wanted hip, graphics-heavy pages featuring big pictures, teeny type, and "cool" design concepts such as twisting columns of pale yellow text placed atop a picture of a turquoise sea. We editors, on the other hand, wanted articles that people could actually *read*.

In the end, we always came to a compromise that resulted in both readability and design flair. The chapters in this second part of the book will help you achieve a similar balance between style and sensibility on your Web pages. First I'll walk you through the process of adding and formatting your regular body text in Microsoft FrontPage—a task that's surprisingly more complex than formatting text for print documents. Then I'll show you how to create some cool text effects that you can use for banner heads and other large type elements.

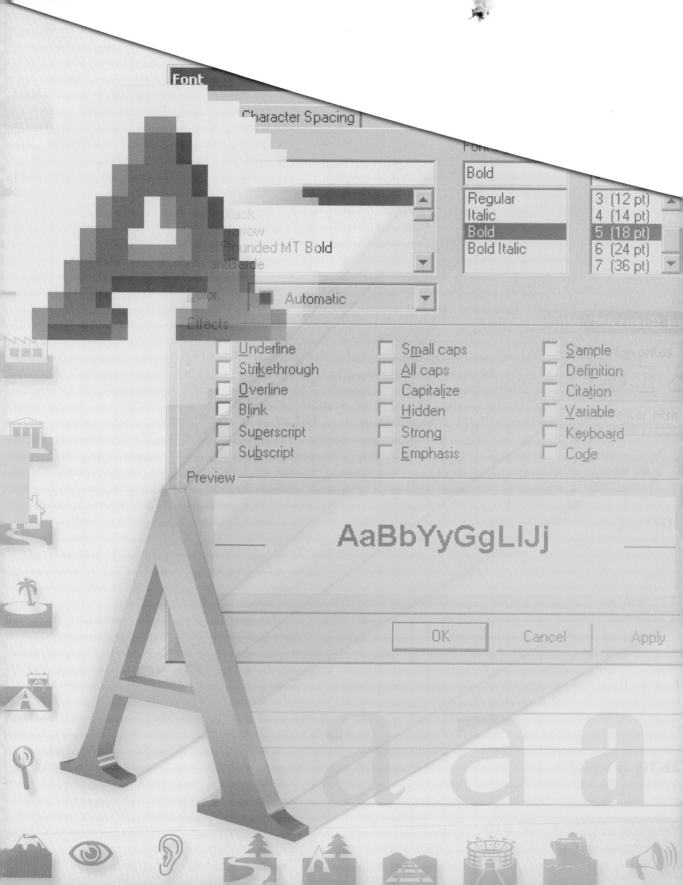

6

everyday

TEXT

All you need to know about...

- Adding text to your Web pages
- Changing text color, font, alignment, and size
- Formatting text using HTML paragraph styles
- Choosing the best Web fonts
- Creating smooth characters with anti-aliasing
- Understanding the Web's approach to type size
- Adjusting text spacing
- Inserting special symbols

In the first word processing programs, text formatting controls were pretty limited. You could choose from two or three fonts, change the type size, adjust spacing between paragraphs, and create bold, italic, and underlined text. Today, every modern word processing program—as well as Microsoft FrontPage 2000 and nearly every other program that includes text capabilities—provides a huge range of formatting options. You can choose from a virtually unlimited number of fonts, apply text special effects, and control the spacing not just of paragraphs, but also of lines, words, and even individual characters.

Before you run to the keyboard to explore this glorious realm of typographic possibility, however, you should know that the Web has a few cruel technical jokes in store for would-be type artisans. I don't want to give away the punch lines just yet, but suffice it to say that how your text appears on other people's monitors ultimately is in their control, not yours.

Don't get me wrong—I'm not saying that you should just throw up your hands and go about your hunting and pecking without any regard to type design. But you do need to understand the technical side of things and then be a little creative—literally and figuratively—with text formatting. This chapter tells you what you need to know to be successful in the challenging world of Web typography.

Creating Text in FrontPage

You can add text to a Web page in FrontPage in three ways: type it directly into an open page, copy and paste it from an existing text document, or create a text graphic using Microsoft PhotoDraw 2000 or some other graphics program. Chapter 7 explores the graphic side of text; the next few sections explain the first two type options.

Typing and Editing Text

You create text in FrontPage using the same techniques you use in Microsoft Word and most every other word processing program on the planet. Here's a quick how-to:

- Click to display a blinking vertical line—known far and wide as the *insertion marker*—which indicates where the next letter you type will appear. Then type away.

- Press the Enter key to end the current paragraph, insert a double line space, and start a new paragraph. Press Shift+Enter to create a line break, which starts a new line within the same paragraph and inserts just a single line space.

■ Before you can make certain formatting or editing changes, you must select the text you want to alter. Just drag over the text you want to select. The selected text appears highlighted.

■ You can also double-click a word to select the entire word. For longer blocks of text, try this: click before the first letter you want to select, and Shift+click after the last letter.

■ Want to deselect text? Just click on it.

■ Press Delete to wipe out selected text. When no text is selected, Delete erases the character to the right of the insertion marker and Backspace deletes the character to the left.

■ To reposition the insertion marker within text, just click where you want the insertion marker to go.

Bringing in Text from Another Source

In addition to entering new text in FrontPage, you can import text from other Web pages or documents, as follows:

■ **Insert an entire document**   On the Insert menu, click File, and select the document's filename from the Select File dialog box. (You may need to select the document's file format from the Files Of Type drop-down list before you can access the file.) FrontPage dumps the document's contents onto the current Web page. Some of the page's original formatting may not survive the transition; you can use the techniques outlined in the rest of this chapter to reformat the page if necessary.

   FrontPage accepts Word files as well as files saved in standard text formats, such as .txt and .rtf. You can also insert documents that you create in other Microsoft Office programs.

■ **Paste text from an open document**   In the document that contains the text you want to use, select the text, click the Edit menu, and then click Copy. The Copy command makes a copy of the text and dumps the copy into the Clipboard, a temporary storage tank for data. Switch to FrontPage, click the Edit menu, and then click Paste to copy the text in the Clipboard onto your page. Again, you may need to tweak the text formatting in FrontPage.

lingo

A *font,* sometimes also called a *typeface,* is a complete set of letters, numbers, and other typographic characters that share a common design.

note

If you select text before you apply formatting, your changes affect only the selected text. If no text is selected, your changes affect any new text you type from the current position of the insertion marker forward.

Formatting Text

Now we get to the complicated stuff. Formatting text for the Web requires some different strategies than those you use when creating print documents. The following list gives you the basic instructions for choosing fonts, setting type size, applying type styles, and adjusting text spacing in FrontPage. Later in this chapter, we'll examine the specific issues that make each of these tasks a bit more complex than they appear on the surface.

■ **Apply an HTML paragraph style** HTML *paragraph styles* enable you to apply a particular set of formatting attributes—font, type size, alignment, and type style (bold, italic, and so on)—with one click. In essence, these paragraph styles work just like the ones in Word and other word processing programs, although the level of formatting you can achieve with HTML styles is much more limited. To apply a paragraph style in FrontPage, click anywhere in the paragraph you want to format and then select the style from the Style drop-down list, which appears on the Formatting toolbar, as shown in Figure 6-1. (If you don't see the Formatting toolbar, click the View menu, point to Toolbars, and then click Formatting to display it.) The upcoming section "Using HTML Paragraph Styles" provides more details about the formatting that's applied with each of the styles.

Figure 6-1
You can apply text formatting using the controls on the toolbars.

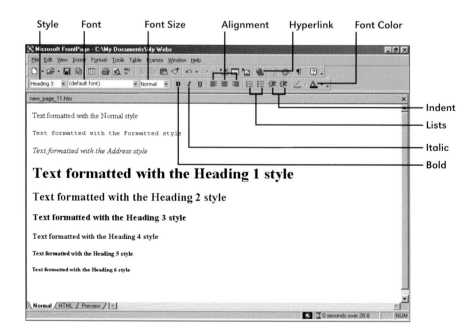

- **Change the font**   The Font drop-down list, labeled in Figure 6-1, lets you specify the font for selected text. If you select Default Font, FrontPage uses the default font associated with the current paragraph style.

  You can specify a default proportional font and a default fixed-width font for each Web page. Click the Tools menu, and then click Page Options to open the Page Options dialog box. Click the Default Font tab, and select the fonts from the drop-down lists.

  See "Choosing Web-Friendly Fonts" later in this chapter to find out which fonts work best for Web text and why the user's browser might not honor your font choices.

- **Change the type size**   Choose a size from the Font Size drop-down list, also labeled in Figure 6-1. If you select Normal, FrontPage uses whatever size is associated with the current paragraph style. To use some other size, select it from the list. But again, the browser might not render the type at the size you see on your screen. The section "Sizing Type: It's All Relative" explains this bit of business.

- **Make text bold or italic**   The Formatting toolbar includes Bold and Italic buttons, just like Word and other Office programs. Clicking the buttons toggles the formatting on and off. Some paragraph styles automatically boldface text, in which case the Bold button has no effect, however. Likewise, the Italic button has no effect when the Address paragraph style is used because that style already calls for italic.

lingo

Characters in *proportional* fonts consume varying amounts of horizontal space—the letter *m* is wider and thus takes up more space than the letter *i,* for example. All characters in a *fixed-width* font, also known as a *monospace* font, are allotted the same amount of space regardless of their individual widths. All the styles in the FrontPage Styles drop-down list except Formatted use a proportional font; the Formatted style uses a fixed-width font.

caution

As for that U (for Underline) button to the right of the Italic button, ignore it. The conventional way to indicate a text link is with an underline, so you don't want to underline nonlinked text. And when you assign a link to text, FrontPage adds the underline for you automatically. Come to think of it, the Underline button has absolutely no reason to stay on your Formatting toolbar. So press and hold the Alt key as you drag the button off the bar. Now you have room to add a button for a more worthwhile command.

see also | *For more about customizing toolbars, see Chapter 4.*

■ **Change the paragraph alignment**   Click one of the three alignment buttons, labeled in Figure 6-1, to specify how you want the individual lines in a paragraph to align with respect to the left and right edges of the paragraph. You can center the type or align it to the left or right.

tip

When you're creating a bulleted or numbered list, pressing Enter creates a new line, complete with a new bullet or the next sequential number. To get rid of the bullet or number and go back to the regular formatting applied by the Normal style, press the Backspace key.

■ **Create a bulleted or numbered list**   Several of the HTML paragraph styles apply list formatting. If you want to create a bulleted or numbered list but don't like the font or type size attributed with the list styles, apply some other style and then use the two list buttons labeled in Figure 6-1. The left button formats the paragraph as a numbered list; the right button formats the paragraph as a bulleted list. You can toggle the list formatting on and off by clicking the toolbar buttons. And you can change the default bullet shape and numbering style that FrontPage uses by clicking the Format menu and then clicking Bullets And Numbering.

see also   *For information on how to use a graphic as a bullet, see Chapter 7.*

■ **Move the paragraph right or left**   Click the indent buttons, also labeled in the figure, to shove the paragraph to the left or right. Each click moves the text another notch. See the section "Spacing Things Out" at the end of this chapter for other ways to adjust the position of text on the page.

tip

Many font designers include a separate bold or italic version of each of their fonts. A few of these variations appear in the Font drop-down list as separate fonts. For print projects, you should use the designer's bold or italicized fonts because each character is crafted individually and thus looks better than if you simply apply the generic bold or italic formatting to the regular version of the font. But for your Web pages, going with the bold or italic formatting makes more sense. If the user doesn't have the bold version of the font installed, the browser will revert to the default font, which means the text won't be bold. Ditto for italics. When you apply the bold or italic formatting in FrontPage, on the other hand, you're inserting a standard HTML tag (formatting instruction) that tells the browser to boldface or italicize the type no matter what font is used.

■ **Change the text color**   Click the arrow on the Font Color button to display the standard FrontPage color picker, and select a text color. The Automatic option uses whatever default text color you specify on the Background tab of the Page Properties dialog box. (To open the dialog box, click the Format menu and then click Background.)

see also   See Chapter 3 for help with picking colors in FrontPage.

The Highlight Color button on the Formatting toolbar applies a translucent stroke of color over the selected text, much like a real-life highlighter pen. This feature is unavailable when you disable formatting features that require Cascading Style Sheets (CSS). (You perform that task on the Compatibility tab of the Page Options dialog box, as explored in Chapter 1.)

The Font dialog box, which you can display by clicking the Format menu and then clicking Font, offers a slew of Effects check boxes that provide yet more formatting options. As you check and uncheck the Effects boxes, the preview shows you what each effect does. Go ahead and play around in the dialog box, but then click Cancel and forget that these check boxes exist. You can't rely on some of the effects to work properly in all browsers, and the remaining effects are downright lame.

Formatting Text as a Link

To format a word or phrase as a link, select the text and then click the Hyperlink button, labeled in Figure 6-1. FrontPage displays the Create Hyperlink dialog box, in which you can specify where you want to take visitors when they click the text.

Linked text appears in the colors you set on the Background tab of the Page Properties dialog box, introduced in Chapter 5. Click the Format menu, and then click Background to open the dialog box. Choose the color for unvisited links from the Hyperlink drop-down list; select the color for a clicked link from the Visited Links drop-down list. The Active Hyperlink option sets the color that appears when the mouse cursor touches the link.

lingo

The word *hyperlink* refers to any Web element that displays another page (or part of a page) when clicked. Most people now just use the more casual term *link,* but FrontPage sticks with the official terminology. I think *hyperlink* sounds like it's straight from a sci-fi movie— "Scotty, hyperlink us to the planet surface now!"—so I generally use *link.*

Using HTML Paragraph Styles

The FrontPage Style drop-down list, labeled in Figure 6-1, lists the HTML paragraph styles that can be recognized by any browser. If you click the Format menu and then click Style, you can access a slew of additional styles available via CSS. Because not all browsers support CSS completely yet, I don't cover those styles in this book. If you're creating pages for a corporate intranet and know exactly which browsers your audience uses, I encourage you to investigate CSS styles, though, because they can save you a lot of formatting time and also expand your formatting options.

The styles in the Style drop-down list fall into three categories: body text styles, headline styles, and list styles. In Figure 6-1, you can see the formatting that's applied by the three body text styles—Normal, Formatted, and Address—along with the six headline styles.

The remaining six styles are designed for creating lists—bulleted lists, numbered lists, and so on. Three of the list styles—Bulleted, Menu, and Directory—create ordinary bulleted lists, and Numbered List does what its name implies. Defined Term and Definition work together to create a list that alternates between one normal line and one indented line. Because you can achieve the same results by simply using the indent and list buttons on the Formatting toolbar, you may not find too much use for the list styles, but they're at your disposal if you need them.

You can override most aspects of a style's formatting by making selections from the Formatting toolbar, as explained in the preceding sections. But depending on how users set up their browsers, the page might still be displayed using the style's default font and type size. The next few sections give you the background you need to understand this annoying fact.

Choosing Web-Friendly Fonts

An incredible number of fonts exist, and type designers create new fonts every day. The next two sections explain how to ferret out the fonts that work best for Web text.

Stick with "Safe" Fonts

Over time, you've probably amassed a pretty big collection of fonts. Some were installed with your computer's operating system, and others were added with programs such as FrontPage, Word, or Internet Explorer. If you display the Font drop-down list in FrontPage, as shown in Figure 6-2, you can see what each font installed on your computer looks like.

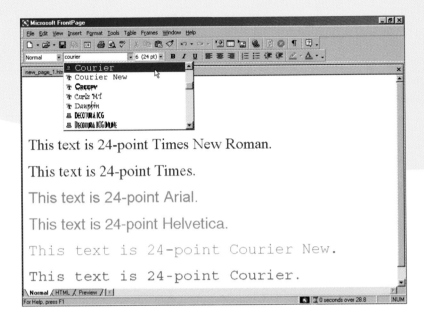

Figure 6-2
When designing Web pages, avoid the fancy fonts in the Font drop-down list and stick with the standard fonts.

Even though the Font drop-down list may offer a bounty of fonts, only a handful are suitable for the bulk of your site's text. Why? Because if people who visit your site don't have the fonts you used installed on their computers, their Web browsers substitute default fonts. What's more, even if people *do* have your fonts, they might be able to configure their browsers to overrule your font choices and automatically substitute the default fonts.

Most browsers allow the user to specify a proportional default font and a fixed-width default font, just as you can when setting your page defaults in FrontPage. The browser substitutes the user's default proportional font for any page text that you formatted using proportional type and substitutes the user's default fixed-width font for any type you formatted using fixed-width type.

On a computer running Microsoft Windows, the most common initial user defaults—the settings in force when the user first installs the browser—are Times New Roman for the proportional font and Courier New for the fixed-width font. On a Macintosh computer, the initial defaults are Times and Courier, which are close cousins of Times New Roman and Courier New. Figure 6-2 shows these fonts, along with another popular pair of proportional fonts, Arial (Windows) and Helvetica (Macintosh).

In some cases, the font turf battle between the Web designer and the browser is of no great consequence. Your text might not look as good

lingo

Fonts that feature very narrow characters are called *condensed* fonts. Fonts with especially wide characters are known as *expanded* fonts.

as it would if it were displayed as you specified, but as long as your fonts and the user's default fonts aren't too different, it's no harm, no foul. However, if you choose a font that has unusually wide or narrow characters, or extraordinarily tall or short characters, and the browser substitutes a font that uses more standard character shapes, the flow of your text may change significantly. For example, take a look at Figures 6-3 and 6-4. For the page shown in Figure 6-3, I first created a table in FrontPage, as explained in Chapter 4. Then I added into the various table cells all the text except the type in the school banner. I used two highly stylized fonts for the Book Fair headline and the Calendar headline. I chose a very narrow typeface for the remaining text.

Figure 6-3
A problem waiting to happen, this page uses an unusually narrow font for the body text and two highly stylized fonts for the section headlines.

Figure 6-4 shows the same page as it appears when I set the browser to substitute Times New Roman for proportional fonts and Courier New for fixed-width fonts. In this page, all the original fonts are proportional fonts, so everything appears in Times New Roman. Because Times New Roman characters are fatter than those of the original condensed font I used for the body text, some parts of the page are no longer displayed correctly. The book fair section of the page still looks okay, although the lines wrap differently around the picture and the headline no longer spans the width of the article. But the table cells that hold the calendar and contact information aren't big enough to accommodate the extra girth of the substitute font. As a result, the name of the school district now takes up two lines, and the bottom two calendar dates break unnaturally between the month and the day.

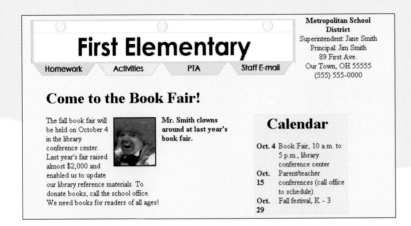

Figure 6-4
Here you see the page from Figure 6-3 as it appears when the browser substitutes Times New Roman for the original fonts.

> **see also** | *In this example, I specified a precise width for the cells in the table but left the Specify Height option unchecked throughout. So the table grows in height when the text reflows to the next line. For more information about table sizes and controlling cell height and width, flip back to Chapter 4.*

Obviously, you can't do anything to prevent people from choosing to override your fonts, and you have no way to know what fonts they'll substitute. But frankly, with the exception of visually impaired people, who often substitute fonts they find easier to read, most people don't even know they have the *option* to use fonts other than what the page designer ordered. Most of the time, if the browser does any font substituting, it's because the font isn't installed on the user's computer. So the best way to make sure text appears as you formatted it is to stick with standard fonts found on almost every computer. That way, you don't give the browser a reason to stick its nose in your typography business.

What constitutes a "standard" font? Well, computers running Windows usually have at least three installed fonts: Arial, Times New Roman, and Courier New. Macintosh systems typically have three similar fonts: Helvetica, Times, and Courier, respectively. Again, Figure 6-2 shows you all these fonts.

Figure 6-5 offers a look at six other fonts that are widely available. The first three fonts, Comic Sans MS, Impact, and Verdana were included with Internet Explorer 3.0. The other three fonts, Andale Mono (formerly known as Monotype), Georgia, and Trebuchet MS, were included with

Internet Explorer 4.0. All these fonts also are included with various versions of Windows and Office. (Do note, however, that just because a program includes a font doesn't always mean that the user will install it.)

Figure 6-5
These fonts are also used widely but are not 100 percent safe.

Comic Sans MS looks like this on-screen.

Impact looks like this on-screen.

Verdana looks like this on-screen.

Andale Mono looks like this on-screen.

Georgia looks like this on-screen.

Trebuchet MS looks like this on-screen.

tip

If you're missing any of the fonts shown in Figure 6-5, which are part of what Microsoft calls its Web Core Fonts, you can download them free of charge from the typography section of the Microsoft Web site, *www.microsoft.com/ typography*

As you can see, all the standard fonts are pretty darned plain. But for body text, plain is good. Readability is key, and these fonts have become popular over time because they are very readable. Save the special text treatments for banners, headlines, and other big text elements. You can create those elements as graphics, as explained in the next chapter, so that you don't have to worry about whether or not people have the same fonts as you.

To see how your page looks using different default fonts in Internet Explorer 5, click the Tools menu and then click Internet Options to display the Internet Options dialog box. Click the Fonts button at the bottom of the dialog box to open the Fonts dialog box, shown in Figure 6-6. Choose a proportional font from the Web Page Font list and a fixed-width font from the Plain Text Font list. Click OK to return to the Internet Options dialog box, and then click the Accessibility button to display the bottom dialog box in Figure 6-6. Select the Ignore Font Styles Specified On Web Pages check box, and then click OK twice to put all the dialog boxes away. Internet Explorer reloads your page using the default fonts you just chose.

Figure 6-6
*Like most browsers, Internet
Explorer enables the user to
select two default fonts and to
automatically substitute those
fonts for the ones specified by the
Web designer.*

I should point out that the Accessibility dialog box also enables users
to completely reformat your pages using their own custom style sheets.
My feeling is that people who are technically savvy enough to create their own style sheets know how this option can mess up a page and
also know how to restore the original formatting if necessary. So don't
worry about designing for this crowd; there's just no way to create a page
that works with every possible formatting scheme.

tip

When you're formatting text in FrontPage, you can specify more than one font for selected text. If the first specified font isn't
available on the user's system, the browser looks for the next font listed. Specifying additional fonts decreases the odds that the
browser will have to substitute the default fonts. But you need to add the extra font names manually into the HTML code. Select
the text, and then click the HTML tab at the bottom of the FrontPage window. The text appears highlighted in the HTML window.
You should see a <FONT FACE> tag followed by an equal sign and then the name of the font, which is surrounded by quotation
marks. Click just to the left of the closing quotation mark, type a comma, and then add the name of the second font. Your finished
tag should look something like this: *<font face="Arial, Helvetica">*

Go Sans Serif for Better Legibility

Fonts can be divided into two main categories: *serif* and *sans serif*. A serif is a little extra stroke tacked onto the ends of certain letters or numbers. Sans serif fonts go without this adornment—*sans* means *without* in French, if that helps you keep the two straight. Figure 6-7 shows close-ups of characters set in Times New Roman, a serif font, and Arial, a sans serif font. (Fonts such as Webdings, which contain only pictorial characters, don't belong in either the serif or sans serif camp. But these fonts aren't terribly practical, so I don't cover them in this book.)

Figure 6-7

Serif fonts such as Times New Roman (top) are easier to read in print than sans serif fonts such as Arial (bottom). But most people prefer sans serif fonts for on-screen reading.

Serif
Sans serif

If you come to Web design from a print-publishing background, you may be surprised to learn that although serif fonts are easier to read on paper, most people find on-screen type more legible when a sans serif font is used. Go figure!

Actually, there's a good reason for the switch. When creating a typeface, font designers specify the amount of space around each character. Most fonts were designed for the printed page, so the spacing is appropriate

What About Font Embedding? A relatively new type option, called *font embedding,* enables Web designers to provide site visitors with a copy of the fonts used on a page. The fonts are encrypted in a way that makes them available for use in a browser but not in other programs. This setup protects the people who design fonts for a living; if people who view the font want to use it in their own documents, they have to buy it.

As you can imagine, font embedding is a concern among font designers because if a hacker broke the encryption code, the designers' ability to be compensated for their work would be jeopardized. At present, several companies are trying to develop a font-embedding option that will offer a high level of protection against hackers. (You can read about the solution proposed by Microsoft at *www.microsoft.com/typography/.*)

On the Web designer's side of the fence, embedding can be problematic because it's implemented through CSS, which means that not all browsers support it. So my recommendation is—yup, you guessed it—format your text using one of the universally available fonts and forget about embedding for now.

for high-resolution printing, where the edges of characters are crisp and well defined. But on-screen text is displayed at a much lower resolution, which results in type that's a little blurry around the edges. The blurring makes the characters appear a little closer together than they do in print. Throw in the extra strokes that adorn serif characters, and the spacing gets even tighter, making the individual characters harder to distinguish.

Microsoft, among others, offers a few fonts designed especially for on-screen use. Figure 6-8 compares two of these fonts, Verdana and Georgia, with their traditional print counterparts, Arial and Helvetica in the sans serif camp and Times and Times New Roman in the serif contingent. (The figure is a screen shot that shows how the characters appear on-screen; the printed versions of these fonts would of course look slightly different.) Notice that the characters in the screen-oriented fonts are a little wider, blockier, and farther apart than their print-oriented cousins.

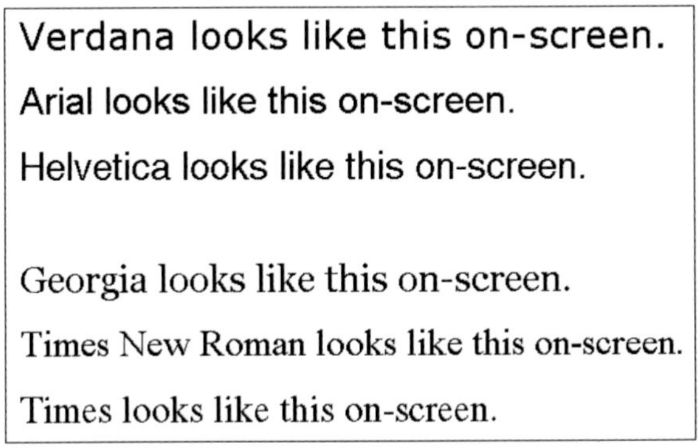

Verdana looks like this on-screen.

Arial looks like this on-screen.

Helvetica looks like this on-screen.

Georgia looks like this on-screen.

Times New Roman looks like this on-screen.

Times looks like this on-screen.

Figure 6-8
Verdana and Georgia, two fonts designed expressly for screen display, feature slightly larger, rounder letters and roomier character spacing than the default Windows fonts, Arial and Times New Roman, and the default Macintosh fonts, Helvetica and Times.

Don't Anti-Alias Small Type

Because everything on-screen is made up of square pixels, the edges of curved or diagonal lines look jagged, or, as we pixelheads say, *aliased.* (See Chapter 3 for more information about pixels.) Some programs offer text *anti-aliasing,* an effect that smoothes out the jagged edges in type— which, of course, is full of curves and diagonal lines. Figure 6-9 shows you a close-up of some text with and without anti-aliasing.

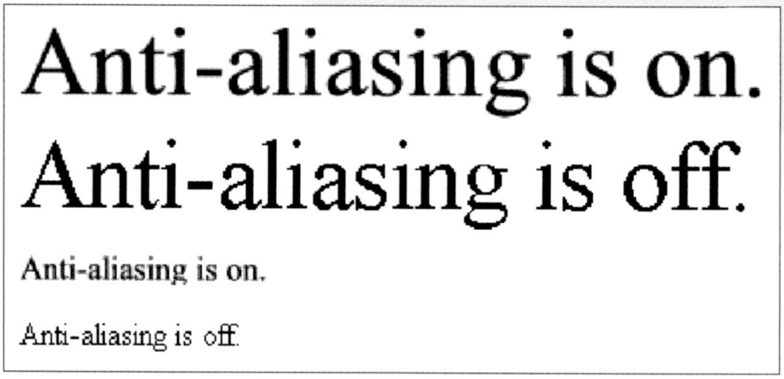

Figure 6-9
*When you create a text graphic,
turn on anti-aliasing for type
over 12 points but leave it off
for smaller type.*

Anti-aliasing is on.
Anti-aliasing is off.

Anti-aliasing is on.

Anti-aliasing is off.

As you can see, anti-aliasing improves the look of large on-screen type but makes small type harder to read. The general rule is to anti-alias type over 12 points in size but to leave anything smaller alone. (The upcoming section "Sizing Type: It's All Relative" explains points and other type-sizing details.)

You can't apply anti-aliasing to text that you type in FrontPage. So if you want your large headline type to be anti-aliased, you need to create it as a graphic in a drawing or image editing program that offers an anti-aliasing filter. In PhotoDraw, the feature is called Smoothing; Chapter 7 explains how to apply the effect to your text.

Limit Yourself to Two or Three Fonts

You can always spot a page designed by a type novice because it looks as though the corner store had a clearance sale on fonts. Every headline appears in a different, wacky font. Body text, too, uses obscure, offbeat fonts—the more, the merrier!

I've already mentioned the technical problems that can arise if you give in to the temptation to indulge in unusual fonts when formatting text in FrontPage. But even when you create text elements as graphics—in which case, you're free to pick whatever font you desire—you need to use some restraint. Otherwise, your page starts to look disjointed, and the fonts draw attention to themselves and away from your message.

For a professional, polished look, limit yourself to three—that's right, *three*—fonts. That gives you one font for your company logo or other corporate-identity elements, which might require a specialty font, plus two everyday fonts for other text. The traditional type formula for printing calls for a serif font for body text and a sans serif font for headlines, but as I discussed earlier, those roles get reversed for screen text.

If your pages are very text-heavy, you can add visual interest through the use of color and different type styles—bold, italic, and a combination of bold and italic.

Sizing Type: It's All Relative

When you create a print document, each text character winds up the exact size you specified when you formatted the type. On the Web, things aren't so reliable. I know, you're sick of that refrain by now, but I'd be remiss if I didn't sing it one more time. As is the case with fonts, when you set the size of your text in FrontPage, all you're really doing is telling the browser what sizes *you* think work best. The browser might not respect your wishes. (Note here that I'm talking only about text that you enter and format in your Web design program, not type created as a graphic.)

As I already discussed, most browsers allow the user to set two default fonts, one proportional and one fixed-width font. In addition, users typically can specify a default size for proportional and fixed-width text. The text sizes that you specify in FrontPage merely tell the browser how large to make each piece of text *relative to the user's default text size*.

This system was put in place so that the size relationship between headlines and body text would remain constant no matter what default text size a user selected. For example, suppose you created 12-point body text and made your headlines just slightly larger—say, 14 points. If a user set the default text size to 14 points and the browser didn't enlarge the size of your headline text by the same percentage, your body text and headlines would all wind up the same size.

caution

Don't italicize small text; it's difficult to read on-screen. And as I warned earlier, never underline text in a Web page, as you might do to add emphasis to printed words. By convention, text links are underlined, so you'll confuse people if you underline words that aren't links.

lingo

The values you see in parentheses next to the seven sizes in the Font Size menu state the text size in *points,* a traditional unit of type measurement. In print, one point translates to roughly 1/72 of an inch. But unless the user sets the browser's default type size to 12 points—the size associated with Size 3—this point measurement isn't accurate. Remember, everything's sized relative to the user's default type size. In addition, the size at which 12-point type appears on-screen varies depending on the screen resolution of the monitor. (See Chapter 3 for more about how screen resolution affects the size of objects on your Web pages.) The computer platform on which your page is viewed also comes into play—type on a Macintosh computer usually appears about one or two points smaller than it does on a computer running Windows, for reasons I won't even try to explain because it makes my head hurt just thinking about it. The bottom line is: use the specified point sizes as a guide, but don't take them too seriously.

caution

When you're formatting your type in FrontPage, choosing Normal from the Font Size drop-down list results in the type size specified by the current paragraph style. You can make the text larger or smaller by selecting another size from the list. You get a choice of seven sizes, which appear in the list as 1 through 7. Size 3 represents the user's default font size. (This is the size applied when you use the Normal paragraph style.) The other sizes result in text that's incrementally smaller or larger than the user's default.

Now that you've digested the basics of sizing text on the Web, allow me to throw in one more wrinkle: Most browsers offer a setting that ignores your custom size formatting altogether! If you work your way back to Figure 6-6, you can see the Internet Explorer 5.5 option related to this feature. When the Ignore Font Sizes Specified On Web Pages option is selected, the browser always renders the text at the size dictated by the paragraph style that you applied, no matter what other sizes you may have selected from the Font Size drop-down list.

As we say in the computer business…"Aaaaarrrrrrrggh!!!"

Given all these variables, what's the best approach to take when sizing type? Well, you'll find lots of recommendations out there, and frankly, nothing is a surefire answer because you can never know what default viewing options everyone in your audience will choose. Here's how I handle the dilemma, though. I rely on just a handful of paragraph styles: Normal for all body type; Heading 2 or Heading 3 for headlines (Heading 1 is usually just too big); and sometimes Bulleted List and Numbered List for list text. I then specify both the font and the size for each bit of text. In a best-case scenario, the page appears exactly as I formatted it. In a worst-case scenario, the page appears in the user's default font, using the size associated with the paragraph style. That way, the basic structure of the text content will always be kept intact, no matter what. Of course, you should always preview your pages and make sure they won't totally fall apart if that worst-case scenario occurs.

Spacing Things Out

HTML doesn't offer very sophisticated text-spacing options. The earlier section "Formatting Text" explains how to indent text, adjust the paragraph alignment, add a single space between lines (press Shift+Enter), and end a paragraph, which automatically creates a double space between the last line of the current paragraph and the first line of the next paragraph.

FrontPage offers many other advanced spacing options, including ways to fine-tune the space between characters, between the lines in a paragraph, and between paragraphs. But all these formatting options require CSS. Feel free to take advantage of these features if you know that everyone who visits your site will be using browsers that support CSS.

If you're worried about CSS support—which is a reasonable concern—try these tricks for gaining some additional control over your text spacing without using CSS:

lingo

Publishing gurus refer to the process of adjusting of the amount of space between characters as *kerning*. The amount of space between lines is known as *leading*, pronounced "ledd-ing."

- Insert nonbreaking spaces. A nonbreaking space is a special space character whose main purpose is to prevent the browser from breaking a line of text between two words or characters that should stay on the same line—for example, between someone's first initial and last name. But you can also use nonbreaking spaces to add space between the left and right boundaries of a table cell and the text within. For example, if using a normal indent doesn't give you enough space between the left edge of a cell and the text, click before the first letter and press the Spacebar to shove the text to the right. You can insert a nonbreaking space by clicking the Insert menu and then clicking Symbol to open the Symbol dialog box (discussed in the next section). The first symbol in the dialog box is a nonbreaking space character. You also get a nonbreaking space when you press the Spacebar two or more times in succession. On the first tap of the Spacebar, you get a regular old space character; after that, FrontPage inserts one nonbreaking space code ( ) for each tap.

   Don't use nonbreaking spaces to indent lines of text unless you're working with a fixed-width font, however. Here's why: Suppose you're creating a site for your gardening club and want to add a list showing each member's name and phone number. You type the name *Bill*, press the Spacebar 10 times, type Bill's number, and press Enter to start the next line. You type the second name, *Mona*, and press the Spacebar 10 times. You'd expect that your cursor would be directly underneath the first character in Bill's phone number because each name has the same number of letters. But each character in a proportional font doesn't consume the same amount of horizontal space. *Bill* takes up less space than *Mona,* for example. So ten spaces after *Mona* puts you beyond the first character in Bill's phone number. If the difference happens to be equal to a single nonbreaking space, you're in luck; if not, you're stuck because you can't subtract a fraction of a space.

■ As an alternative to using nonbreaking spaces to adjust text in a table, you can use empty columns or rows to add space where it's needed. Using the gardening club example, you could put the member names in one column, add the phone numbers in another column, and insert an empty column in between to separate the two.

see also *See Chapter 4 for the full story on tables, including additional ways to position text within a table cell.*

■ Finally, here's a trick I mentioned in Chapter 4 but that bears repeating here: you can insert an empty single-pixel GIF image to serve as a "spacer" in your text. See the sidebar "The Secret of Skinny Cells" in Chapter 4 to find out how to create a spacer graphic. After inserting the graphic, select it, click the Format menu, click Picture Properties, and use the options on the Appearance tab of the Picture Properties dialog box to adjust the width, height, and alignment of the spacer graphic until you achieve the space you want.

see also *Chapter 10 explains more about adjusting picture properties in FrontPage. Note that although resizing a regular graphic in FrontPage can reduce image quality, you can adjust the dimensions of a spacer graphic as needed to create the page space you need. After all, you can't damage the quality of an invisible graphic.*

Inserting Special Symbols

Your computer keyboard, like a typewriter, includes keys for creating typographic symbols such as dollar signs, ampersands, and so on. But what if you need some other character—say, a trademark or a copyright symbol? You can add it in FrontPage as follows: Click the Insert menu, and then click Symbol to display the Symbol dialog box, which contains standard typographic symbols plus letters that use special punctuation found in some non-English words (accent marks, umlauts, and so on). Select the symbol, and click Insert to close the dialog box and insert the character.

By the way, some specialty fonts, such as Webdings and Zapf Dingbats, provide nothing but symbols, some of which are really just tiny pictures. You can insert these symbols by copying them from the Windows Character Map or using their ASCII codes (keystroke combinations assigned to each character), but I don't advise it. If the browser substitutes a default font, the symbols won't appear properly on the Web page. To include symbols other than those found in the FrontPage symbol dialog box, create the symbol as a graphic, as explored in Chapter 7.

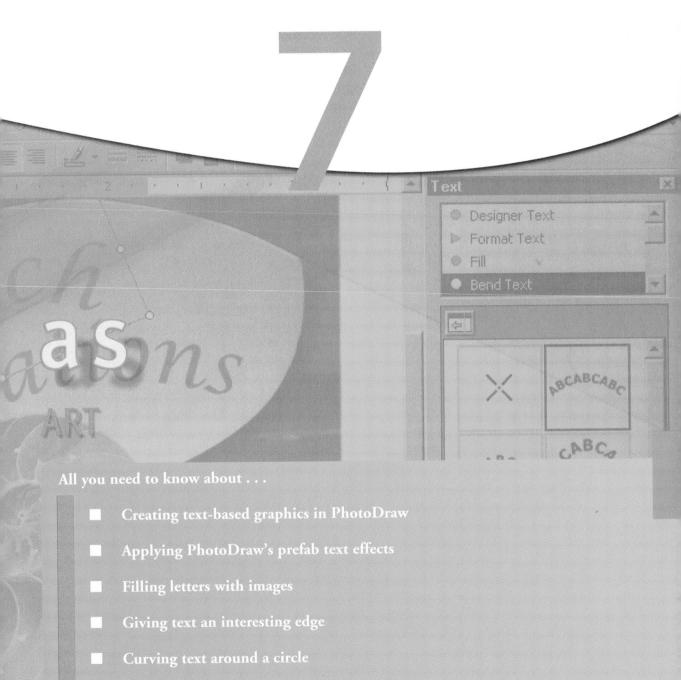

All you need to know about . . .

- Creating text-based graphics in PhotoDraw

- Applying PhotoDraw's prefab text effects

- Filling letters with images

- Giving text an interesting edge

- Curving text around a circle

- Using pictures as letters

- Creating fancy bullets

note

Examples in this chapter feature Microsoft PhotoDraw 2000 Version 2, but if you don't have that program, you can easily adapt the concepts to any drawing or painting program.

Most people don't think of text as art. But as this chapter proves, a few special formatting techniques can give ordinary letters as much impact as any photo or illustration. You'll find out how to perform such text tricks as filling characters with images, adding edge effects, and more.

These effects are ideal for banner heads, company logos, and other large type elements on your Web site. Use them in moderation, though; a page covered with too many text effects is as ugly as a roadway littered with billboards. In other words, just because you *can* doesn't always mean you *should.*

Creating Text in PhotoDraw

You can create just about any sort of artistic text you can imagine in PhotoDraw. But whatever effect you have in mind, the first step is to add your basic text to a new picture. Here's how:

1   Click the File menu, and then click New to display the New dialog box. Select any page size and click OK to create a new, empty picture canvas.

2   Click the File menu, and then click Picture Setup to set the canvas size to match the dimensions of the text you plan to create. Remember to set the unit of measurement to pixels and size your graphic according to the guidelines provided in Chapter 3.

3   On the Text visual menu, shown in Figure 7-1, click Insert Text. PhotoDraw displays the Text workpane and automatically creates and selects some sample text. You see the selection outline and handles around the text, as illustrated in the figure.

note

PhotoDraw puts all your text on a single line. If you want the text to wrap to a new line, press Enter to insert a manual line break.

4   Type your text. Because the sample text was selected, PhotoDraw replaces it with your text. The text appears both in the picture area and in the text-entry box in the workpane. (If you accidentally deselected the sample text before typing, reselect it by dragging over it in the text-entry box.)

5   Select a font, type size, and style from the drop-down lists at the bottom of the Text workpane, which you can see along the right side of the program window in Figure 7-1. PhotoDraw applies your settings to all the text you just typed, selected or not. (You can also choose these formatting settings before you begin typing, but if you do, PhotoDraw deselects the sample text, and you'll need to reselect it to replace it with your own words.)

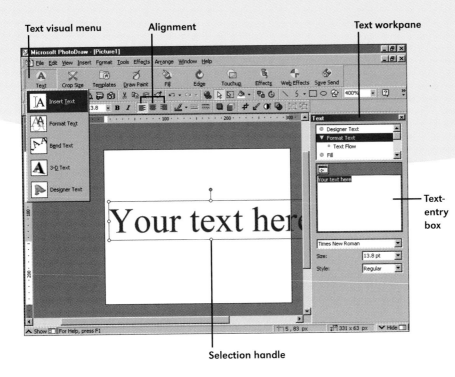

Text visual menu   Alignment   Text workpane

Figure 7-1
To insert text, click the Text visual menu, click Insert Text, and then type away.

Text-entry box

Selection handle

6 Set the text alignment by clicking one of the alignment buttons on the Formatting toolbar. I labeled the buttons in Figure 7-1. You can center text or align it to the left or right. PhotoDraw aligns the text with respect to the edges of the selection outline.

After you create your text, you can change the formatting and apply special effects at any time. You can also delete or add characters if necessary. Just click the text in the picture area to select it, and then use the editing and formatting techniques outlined in the rest of this chapter.

caution

To retain full text editing capabilities, save your picture in the native PhotoDraw format (.mix) before closing it. Chapter 9 explains how to save pictures in PhotoDraw.

note

PhotoDraw considers all the text you just entered in the text-entry box as a single *text object*. Any formatting or effects you apply affect all characters in the text object. So if you want to create two different styles of text, create each as a separate text object. To start a new text object while the Text workpane is open, you must click the Text visual menu and click Insert Text again.

Adding or Deleting Characters

To add characters to a text object that you just created, click in the text-entry box to position the insertion marker, and then type the new characters. (If the Text workpane is no longer open or you want to edit another text object, click the text in the picture area. Then click Format Text on the Text visual menu.)

Press Delete to wipe out the character to the right of the insertion marker; press Backspace to erase the character to the left of the marker. You can also drag over entire words or phrases to select them and then press Delete. Or, to replace the selected characters with new text, just start typing.

To delete an entire text object, click it in the picture area and press Delete.

Changing the Font, Size, or Type Style

To change the font or the type style of a selected text object, just use the Text workpane options or their counterparts on the Formatting toolbar. Remember, all characters in a text object get the same treatment, even if you select only a few of them in the text-entry box before you make your changes.

To change the type size, you can use the Size drop-down list in the Text workpane or the Font Size drop-down list on the Formatting toolbar. Or, for on-the-fly sizing, drag one of the selection handles that appear around the perimeter of the selection outline. (You can see the handles in Figures 7-1.) Drag a corner handle to enlarge or reduce the text while keeping its original proportions; drag a top or bottom handle to change the text height only; drag a side handle to change the width only.

Moving and Rotating Text

To move a text object, click the selection outline to display a four-headed arrow cursor and then drag the text. Instead of dragging, you can also press the arrow keys on your keyboard to nudge the text in the direction of the arrow. To position text more precisely, click the Arrange menu and then click Arrange to display the Arrange workpane. Type the page coordinates for the text in the Left and Top option boxes. PhotoDraw calculates the position relative to the edge of the picture, using pixels as the unit of measurement.

see also For more about positioning text with respect to other picture objects, see Chapter 8. In addition to relocating the text, you can change its stacking order—that is, move it on top of or underneath another object.

You can rotate text by clicking Text Flow in the Text workpane list to display the options shown in Figure 7-2. Click Vertical to rotate the text 90 degrees clockwise. Click Horizontal to rotate the text 90 degrees counterclockwise.

For more rotation options, click the Custom Rotate button (labeled in Figure 7-2) to display the Rotate workpane, which contains icons representing four different angles of rotation (0 degrees, 90 degrees, 180 degrees, and 270 degrees). Click an icon and watch your text spin accordingly. To rotate the text to some other angle, enter the value (in degrees) in the Custom box below the icons. Alternatively, you can rotate the text object by dragging the green rotate handle that hangs off the top of the selection outline, as shown in Figure 7-2.

note

Contrary to the names of the Orientation options, Horizontal and Vertical don't always result in horizontal or vertical text. For example, if you select a vertical text object and then click the Vertical option, PhotoDraw spins your text 90 degrees clockwise, which gives you horizontal text.

Rotate handle   Custom Rotate

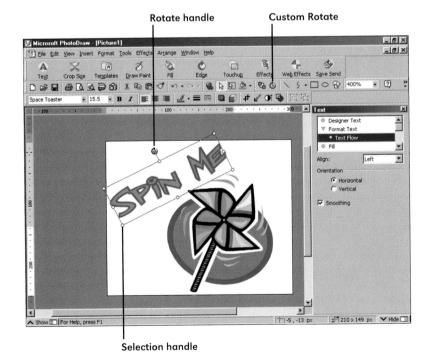

Selection handle

Figure 7-2
To rotate a text object to a custom angle, drag the green rotate handle.

Anti-Aliasing Text

Chapter 6 introduced you to the concept of text anti-aliasing, an effect that manipulates pixels around the edges of each character to make the text appear less jagged on-screen. In PhotoDraw, the Smoothing option applies anti-aliasing. After selecting a text object, click Format Text at the top of the Text workpane and then click Text Flow to display the Smoothing check box, as shown in Figure 7-2. Clear the box if you don't want PhotoDraw to anti-alias the text. Remember that while anti-aliasing is a good option for large text, it can make small text (less than 12 points) more difficult to read.

Giving Text the Treatment

Typography geeks use the term *type treatment* to refer to special effects applied to text. Whatever term you use, PhotoDraw makes it surprisingly easy to create some darned cool text effects.

Chapter 5 provides instructions for using PhotoDraw's fill, edge, and shadow effects; Chapters 8 and 9 introduce you to some additional effects. You use the same techniques to apply these effects whether you're working with graphics or text, so I won't explain them in detail again here. Instead, the remaining examples in this chapter give you some ideas about how you can combine the various effects already covered, plus a few new tricks, to lend added interest to your text.

However, before I launch into those examples, I want to offer a few quick tips:

■ First, the technical stuff: Whenever a text object is selected and the Text workpane is displayed, you can click Fill or Edge in the list at the top of the workpane to access the same options found in the Fill and Edge workpanes. You can fill your text with a solid color, gradient (multiple bands of color), texture, or picture, and you can outline your text with a solid color or with one of the edge effects. See Chapter 5 for a closer look at these options.

■ PhotoDraw offers prefab type treatments that format your text using stylized fonts and a variety of effects. To check out these treatments, click Designer Text on the Text visual menu or in the Text workpane. Personally, I find the selection pretty limited, but you can use one of these effects as a starting point if you need inspiration. Click a thumbnail in the workpane to apply the effect to your text.

tip

The font and size restrictions that apply to text you type in FrontPage, explored in Chapter 6, don't come into play when you're creating text graphics in PhotoDraw. Your text lives by the graphic laws of the land, not the text laws. Still, don't overload your page with graphics that use too many different fonts or wild effects. No matter what type of text you create, the ultimate objective is an easy-to-read message. Also, your effects will work better on fat, blocky text than on skinny script text.

You can then change the color, outline, and so on by using the standard techniques for formatting text. Be sure to put the number 2 PhotoDraw program CD in your CD-ROM drive before you start so that you get access to all the available effects.

■ Keep in mind that any graphics—whether text graphics or plain pictures—increase the page download time. So if you're already pushing the limits of a reasonable download wait, don't make the situation worse by creating your text as graphics. Instead, stick with the standard HTML text that you can create in FrontPage.

■ After you finish your text object, save it first in the PhotoDraw native format (.mix) so that you can edit it easily later. Then save it as either a GIF or a JPEG image, depending on the text effect you created. Chapter 9 explains all aspects of saving files in PhotoDraw.

Filling (and Stroking) Text with Meaning

The text examples in Figures 7-1 and 7-2 use solid-color interiors and outlines, which are perfectly acceptable options for simple headlines and the like. But when you want to give your text some extra oomph, consider filling your characters with an image, as I did in the top example in Figure 7-3, or using a special outline, as in the bottom example.

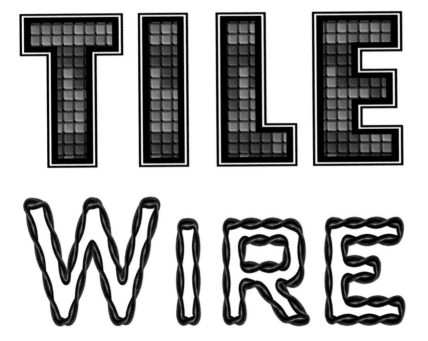

tip

Applying special effects in PhotoDraw or any program involves a lot of effort on the part of your computer, so the effect may take a few seconds to appear. To speed things up while you're experimenting, create a one-character or two-character text object and play around with different settings on that small object. Note the settings of the effects you apply as you go. When you generate an effect you like, create your real text object and reapply those same settings.

Figure 7-3
To reinforce the meaning of your words, fill or outline the characters using a design related to the subject.

lingo

The following steps explain how to create the type treatment shown at the top of Figure 7-3. I filled this text with one of the texture images provided on the number 2 PhotoDraw program CD.

1 Create your basic text, as outlined earlier in this chapter.

2 Put the number 2 PhotoDraw program CD in your CD-ROM drive. Click Fill in the list at the top of the Text workpane, and select Texture from the drop-down list. You see thumbnails of the available texture images in the workpane. Click the image that you want to use as your text interior. For this example, I used the Straight Edge 3 texture, as shown in Figure 7-4.

3 If necessary, adjust the Color, Transparency, and Scale values in the workpane to modify the fill. (Click the scroll arrows at the bottom of the workpane to display these options if they're hidden, as they are in Figure 7-4. Or undock the workpane by dragging it by its title bar.)

Figure 7-4
The tile pattern you see in the interior of these letters is simply an image from the PhotoDraw Texture collection.

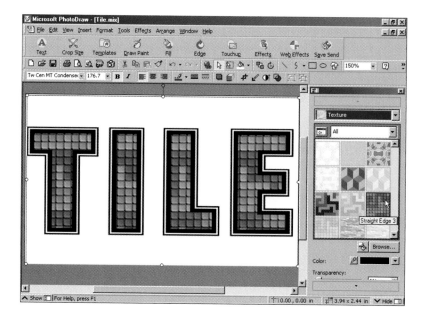

4 Click Edge in the list at the top of the Text workpane. Select Plain from the Gallery Type drop-down list, and then select the line style, color, and width you like.

Although you can fill your text with any image that catches your eye, choosing a design that's somehow related to the text, like the tile image in Figure 7-4, reinforces the meaning of the text. I took this same approach to create the wire example in Figure 7-3, but this time I relied on an edge effect rather than a patterned interior to make the visual point.

After creating your text as usual, you can create this effect by taking the following steps:

1 Click Fill in the list at the top of the Text workpane, choose Solid Color from the drop-down list, and then select the color of your page background from the color picker. For the example text, I selected white.

2 Click Edge at the top of the Text workpane, and then select Photo Brushes from the Gallery Type drop-down list. Select the Burl Twist brush, as shown in Figure 7-5. Adjust the Width value as you see fit. To change the transparency of the outline or the placement of the line with respect to the character's fill, click Settings (Photo Brushes) in the list at the top of the workpane. For this text effect, I selected On Top from the Placement drop-down list.

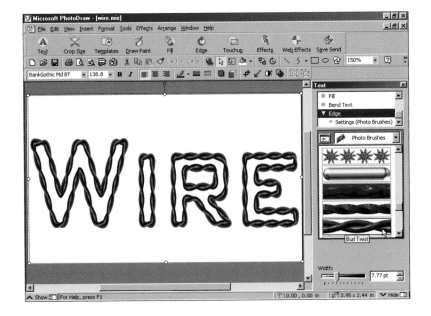

Figure 7-5
This text has a white solid fill and a Photo Brush edge effect.

Bending Your Words

Advanced graphics programs enable you to *fit text to a path,* which means that you can create text that flows along an angled or curving line, tilting up when the line tilts up, curving down where the line curves down, and so on. PhotoDraw doesn't offer full-fledged text-on-a-path formatting, but you can bend text so that it text follows a circle or curve, as I did in Figure 7-6. (This text is slightly rotated from horizontal as well as curved.)

Figure 7-6
I used PhotoDraw's Bend Text feature to make the text follow the same curve as the shell's edge.

To try out this feature, click your text object to select it and then click Bend Text in the list at the top of the Text workpane. Or, if the Text workpane isn't open, click Bend Text on the Text visual menu. Either way, you see the workpane options shown in Figure 7-6. Click the thumbnail that represents the style of curve you want, and then drag the Amount slider to adjust the degree of the curve.

To enhance the effect I created in Figure 7-6, I added a slight shadow in a contrasting color behind the text. Figure 7-7 shows the original and shadowed examples together. When text and background share similar color values—that is, they're both about the same brightness and intensity, as in this picture—the contrasting shadow makes text more legible. Enhanced contrast is especially critical to making your site accessible to people with color-perception problems, as discussed in Chapter 5.

Figure 7-7
Adding a white shadow behind the text increases legibility by creating more contrast between the text and the shell.

Using Pictures as Characters

Just as text can serve as art, pictures can stand in for certain letters and numbers, as shown in Figure 7-8. You can replace a character that has a simple shape—*o, i, l,* or *c,* for example—with a similarly shaped graphic that offers a pictorial representation of the meaning of a word.

Figure 7-8
A button graphic stands in for the letter o.

tip

Don't forget that you can press the arrow keys on your keyboard to nudge a selected text object or graphic in the direction of the arrow.

The trick is to create your text as two text objects, one containing the letters that will come before graphic and a second containing the rest of the letters. Then insert the graphic and drag the three components into place.

Creating Stylish Bullets

Want to decorate your bulleted lists with something a little spicier than the simple circles and squares that FrontPage's bulleted list formatting offers? PhotoDraw offers you countless ways to create graphic bullets. Figure 7-9 gives you a close-up look at a few bullets that I created using various PhotoDraw features. The following text—which, sadly, doesn't enjoy the glamour of designer bullets—explains how to create each of these bullets.

Figure 7-9
You can create these bullets using a Photo Stamps painting tool (left), a Designer Clip Art shape (middle), and 3D effects.

■ The glowing sphere on the left side of Figure 7-9 looks like it might take a while to create, right? And it would if you tried to paint it from scratch. But in fact, I created this bullet in seconds using PhotoDraw's photo stamps, which enable you to "paint" with tiny photographic objects. You click to paint a single copy of the object, like the bullet in the figure, or drag to lay down multiple copies of the object.

Again, put the number 2 PhotoDraw program CD into your CD-ROM drive to access all the photo stamps. Click the Draw Paint visual menu, and then click Photo Stamps. Thumbnails representing the available objects appear in the Paint workpane, as shown in Figure 7-10. Click a thumbnail, and then click on your picture canvas. If you're not happy with what you see, click Undo Last in the tiny Paint toolbar that appears when you choose the Photo Stamps command, and try again.

Photo Stamps cursor

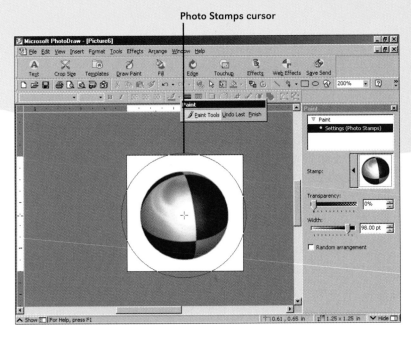

Figure 7-10
To create a single bullet, select an object from the Paint workpane and then click once in the picture area.

You can adjust the size of the object by dragging the Width slider. Your change affects your next click or drag; you can't adjust the size after the fact as you can with other PhotoDraw objects. Click Settings (Photo Stamps) at the top of the Paint workpane to display a Transparency option, which adjusts the opacity of the object, and a Random Arrangement check box. When the check box is selected, PhotoDraw alters the size and angle of each object you paint. If you clear this check box, PhotoDraw creates all the objects at the same size and orientation.

When you're happy with your bullets, click the Finish button on the Paint toolbar.

■ The middle bullet in Figure 7-9 is a clip-art graphic included in the PhotoDraw Designer Clip Art collection. To browse the available shapes, put the number 2 PhotoDraw program CD in your CD-ROM drive, click the Insert menu, and then click PhotoDraw Content. The Insert PhotoDraw Content dialog box appears. Locate the Designer Clip Art folder and double-click it to display folders containing different subject categories. Double-click a folder to see thumbnails of all the graphics in that folder; double-click the graphic you want to use. The graphic in Figure 7-9 lives in the Shapes folder.

tip

In most cases, the size of the Photo Stamps cursor is larger than the shape that you will create when you click. If you want the bullet to fill the canvas, raise the width value until the cursor falls partially off the canvas, as shown in Figure 7-10.

tip

Some of the Designer Clip Art graphics are simple black-and-white drawings that you can customize by applying your own fills, edges, and other effects.

■ To create the bullet on the right in Figure 7-9, I simply drew a triangle and then applied a 3D effect. To explore the 3D features, click the Effects menu and then click 3-D. After selecting a basic 3D design, click the various items in the list at the top of the 3D workpane to reveal options for adjusting the effect.

see also | *In Chapter 8, you'll find out how to draw simple shapes in PhotoDraw.*

PART

three

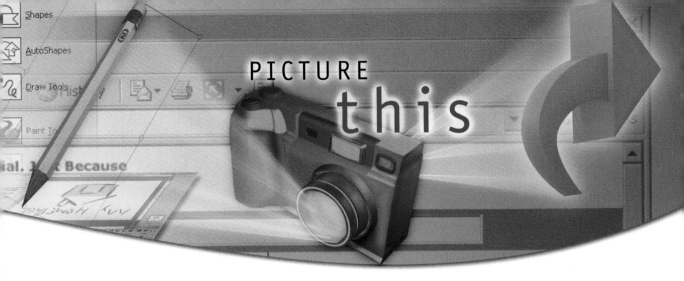

PICTURE
this

As you already know if you've explored the first two parts of this book, Microsoft PhotoDraw 2000 makes creating cool page backgrounds and text graphics incredibly simple. But those projects represent just the start of the design projects that you can do in PhotoDraw. In the next three chapters, I'll show you how to use the program's drawing, painting, and photo editing tools to create custom logos and illustrations, enhance and retouch digital photos, and create rollover buttons and animated images. You'll be surprised at just how quickly and easily you can turn out professional-looking graphics, even if you have absolutely no experience.

To wrap up the book, the last chapter walks you through the process of adding all the elements you've created in earlier chapters to your Web pages in Microsoft FrontPage. You'll find out how to insert and position pictures, turn them into clickable links, and handle a few final bits of graphics housekeeping that you need to check off your list before sharing your newly designed Web site with the world.

Shapes

AutoShapes

Draw Tools

Paint Tools

Photo Stamps

Text

press F1

8

simple
DRAWINGS

All you need to know about . . .

- Finding your way around in PhotoDraw
- Drawing and editing simple shapes
- Painting naturalistic images
- Applying special effects
- Stacking objects to create pictures
- Making quick work of designing cool buttons
- Using clip art

note

This chapter, like others, shows you how to create graphics using PhotoDraw 2000 Version 2. But you can easily adapt most of the concepts covered here to just about any graphics software. Some tool names and operations may work a little differently, but the basic approach is the same no matter what program you use. Also keep in mind that this book isn't intended to provide all the details of PhotoDraw but rather to give you the basics you need to get started. If you need more information about the program, click the Help menu and then click Contents And Index to access the PhotoDraw online help system.

note

If you don't see a toolbar that I reference or show in a figure, click the View menu, point to Toolbars, and then click the toolbar name. The Standard toolbar and the Formatting toolbar are labeled in Figure 8-1. If a button that I mention isn't visible, click the More Buttons button, labeled in Figure 8-1, to display buttons that won't fit in the available window space. PhotoDraw rearranges your buttons on the fly to keep visible the ones you use most frequently.

Perhaps you're blessed with a budget that allows you to hire a professional artist to create graphics for your Web site. If so, I urge you to take full advantage of that option. Custom art is well worth the price you'll pay a talented artist.

But what if your budget barely covers a box of colored pencils, let alone a professional artist? You can create your own graphics with the drawing and painting tools in Microsoft PhotoDraw. Not an art major? Don't worry. As you'll find out in this chapter, PhotoDraw offers plenty of design aids to help the artistically challenged.

Opening Pictures

Your first order of business is to open a picture. You have three options:

- **Create a new picture** To create a canvas at the default picture size, click the New Picture button on the Standard toolbar. (See Figure 8-1.) Or click the File menu, and then click New to display a dialog box where you can select a picture size. Either way, you can always change the canvas size later.

- **Open an existing picture** To display the Open dialog box and track down your file, click the File menu and then click Open. Or just click the Open button, labeled in the figure. If you want to see previews of your pictures before opening them, click the File menu and then click Visual Open. PhotoDraw hauls out the dialog box shown in the middle of Figure 8-1, which enables you to browse thumbnails of your picture files. Double-click a thumbnail to open the picture.

- **Import a picture from a scanner or a digital camera** Depending on your scanner, you might be able to scan directly into PhotoDraw. Click either the Scan Picture button, labeled in Figure 8-1, or the File menu and then Scan Picture. Similarly, you might be able to download pictures from your digital camera to your computer. After connecting your camera to the computer, click the File menu and then click Digital Camera. Alternatively, click the Digital Camera button, labeled in Figure 8-1. If you use a camera memory-card reader, however, bypass this option and open the files directly from the reader just as you would from a floppy disk or hard drive. To enable PhotoDraw to process your edits more quickly, save the image files to your hard drive after you open them.

Formatting toolbar

Standard toolbar

Visual menu

New picture   Scan Picture

Open   Digital Camera

More
Buttons

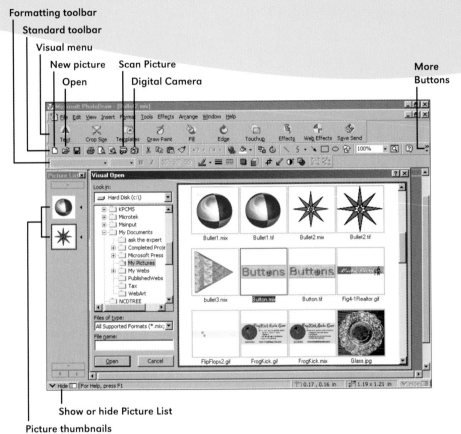

Show or hide Picture List

Picture thumbnails

Figure 8-1
To browse thumbnails of your existing pictures, use the Visual Open command on the File menu.

tip

See that Hide button beneath the Picture List in Figure 8-1? You can click it to close the Picture List to make more room for your picture. When you click the Hide button, it becomes the Show button; click it to reopen the Picture List. You can similarly hide and reveal the workpane, which appears on the right side of the program window when you select a tool, by clicking the Show/Hide button in the lower-right corner of the window.

When you first launch PhotoDraw, a dialog box appears offering you these same options plus a few others. Click the button representing the route you want to take, and click OK. If you don't want PhotoDraw to display the dialog box in the future, select the Don't Show This Dialog Box Again check box before you click OK.

For every open picture, regardless of how it got its start, you see a thumbnail in the Picture List, which runs down the left side of the program window. But only one picture is active and available for editing at a time. Clicking a picture's thumbnail makes that picture active and hides the picture that was formerly on stage.

Zooming In and Out

PhotoDraw gives you several ways to zoom in for a closer view or pull back to see more of the picture:

■ Choose a magnification percentage from the Zoom drop-down list, labeled in Figure 8-2, or double-click the value currently shown, type a new value, and press Enter. Choose Fit Background from the Zoom drop-down list to see the entire picture on-screen; choose Selection to zoom in on a selected object; and choose Fit All to see the picture plus everything in the *scratch area*, which is that gray area surrounding the picture. You can also access these last three options by clicking the View menu and then pointing to Zoom.

■ Click the View menu, and then click Pan And Zoom to display the Pan And Zoom window, shown in Figure 8-2. You also can open the window by clicking the Pan And Zoom button, labeled in the figure. To zoom in and out, respectively, drag the Zoom slider or click the icons above and below it. To view an area that isn't currently visible, drag the viewfinder box over the area you want to see. Click the Zoom To Background button in the lower-right corner of the window to zoom the display so that the entire picture fits on-screen.

■ Press the plus key on your keyboard's numeric keypad to zoom to the next magnification level in the list; press the minus key to zoom out one step.

However you zoom, you're not changing the size of the picture, just magnifying the on-screen display. The upcoming section "Basic Picture Editing" explains how to change the picture dimensions.

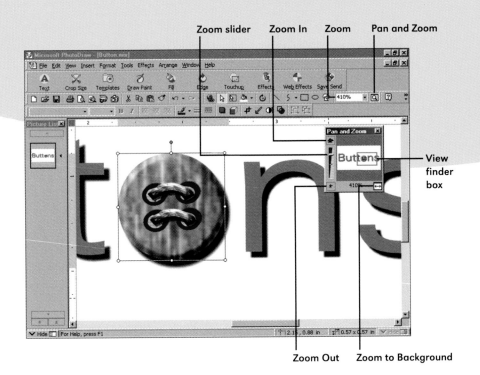

Figure 8-2
To change the view size, use the Pan And Zoom window or press the plus and minus keys on your numeric keypad.

Changing the Canvas Color or Design

Every picture rests on a virtual canvas officially known in PhotoDraw as the *picture area*. I'll stick with *canvas* because that's the professional term, and I know that want you to sound like a pro when you swap stories with your artist friends.

By default, the canvas appears white in PhotoDraw, as shown in Figure 8-3, but it's actually transparent and doesn't appear in printed pictures. For Web pictures, whether or not the canvas appears depends on the format in which you save the file. If you use the GIF format, you can leave the canvas transparent or make it visible. If you use the JPEG format, the canvas is always visible.

see also | *Chapter 9 explains all your saving options in detail.*

note

The gray area around the canvas is the scratch area. You can put text and picture elements in the scratch area to keep them nearby until you need them. If you save the picture in the PhotoDraw format (.mix), the scratch area contents are saved with the file. However, objects in the scratch area don't print, and they're dropped from pictures saved in other file formats.

tip

When you apply a Texture background from the Format Background workpane, PhotoDraw *tiles* (repeats) a small image as many times as needed to fill the canvas. With some fills, you may get visible "seams" where two tiles meet. If you want to eliminate the seams, you can create a faux background by drawing a rectangle that completely covers the canvas, as explained later in this chapter, and then use the Texturizer special effect, discussed in Chapter 5, to fill the rectangle with your own custom texture.

Background handle   Canvas   Scratch area   Format Background workpane

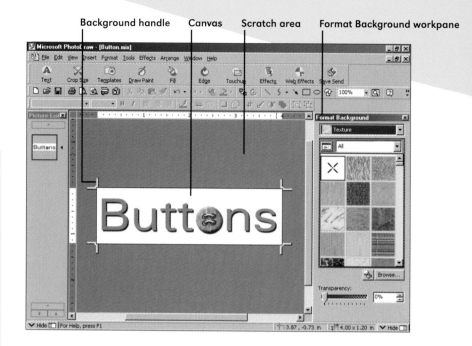

If you want something other than a plain white canvas, choose Format Background from the Web Effects visual menu. The Format Background workpane appears, as shown in Figure 8-3. You can fill the background with a solid color, a texture, or a picture. Choose your preference from the drop-down list, and select the fill. If you raise the Transparency slider past 0, the fill becomes translucent.

To return to the default white canvas, choose Solid Color from the drop-down list and then click the white color swatch or choose No Color from the color palette.

Sizing the Canvas

Anything that's off the canvas gets dumped when you save the picture in any format except the PhotoDraw format. So before you save your picture as a JPEG or GIF file for use on the Web, make sure that all objects fit within the canvas boundaries. If necessary, you can enlarge the canvas.

The easiest way to resize the canvas is to drag the background handles, labeled in Figure 8-3. To show or hide the handles, click the View menu and then click Background Handles. You can also adjust the canvas size by choosing Resize from the Crop Size visual menu and entering specific dimensions in the Resize Picture workpane. Be sure to click Resize Background in the list at the top of the workpane before you enter the width and height values.

Creating Simple Graphics

At the beginning of this chapter, I promised that even people with no drawing skills could easily create graphics in PhotoDraw. To prove my point, the upcoming section "Object Lessons: Forging Shapes into Pictures" provides a step-by-step breakdown of how I created the button graphic featured in Figures 8-2 and 8-3. Before leaping into specifics, though, I want to introduce you to PhotoDraw's major drawing, painting, and editing tools.

Drawing Primer

You access PhotoDraw's drawing tools via the toolbar buttons labeled in Figure 8-4, which appear near the right end of the Standard toolbar. Clicking the AutoShapes button displays a menu of icons representing the drawing tools; click the icon for the tool you want to use. The most common tools also have their own toolbar buttons so that you don't have to slog through the AutoShapes menu to get them.

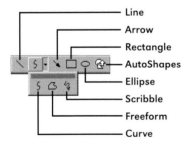

Line
Arrow
Rectangle
AutoShapes
Ellipse
Scribble
Freeform
Curve

Figure 8-4
The drawing tool buttons reside on the Standard toolbar, which you hide and display by clicking the View menu, pointing to Toolbars, and then clicking Standard.

To use any tool but the Scribble, Curve, and Freeform tools, just drag in your picture to create the shape. With the Scribble tool, you draw as you would using a pencil: as you drag the mouse, PhotoDraw lays down a line that follows your cursor.

The Curve and Freeform tools offer the flexibility of freehand drawing with the added convenience of some automatic input from PhotoDraw.

caution

Remember that if you're creating a tile to use as your Web page background, you want the canvas to be slightly *smaller* than the objects that make up the tile, for reasons discussed in Chapter 5. In no case, however, do you want a canvas that's significantly larger than your picture. Empty canvas around the edges of the picture adds to file size unnecessarily.

tip

But they're a little more complex to use than the other tools. Here's the scoop:

■ The Curve tool offers assistance with drawing freeform curving lines. Try it out: Click to set the start of the line, move the mouse to where you want to position the midpoint of the first curve, and click, as shown in the top example in Figure 8-5. Now move the mouse to adjust the curve, as shown in the second example, and double-click to end the line. Or just single-click to start a new segment and add more curves. The third example in the figure shows the finished line.

■ Use the Freeform tool to get help with drawing straight line segments. Click to set the start of the first segment, move the mouse, and click again to set the end of the segment. Keep clicking to create additional segments.

   If you drag instead of click, the Freeform tool works like the Scribble tool. When you release the mouse, PhotoDraw sets the endpoint of the segment. To finish off the shape or line, double-click. The bottom example in Figure 8-5 shows a line I created with this tool and indicates where I clicked and dragged.

Figure 8-5
The Curve tool helps you draw precise curved lines; the Freeform tool works like a combination of the Line tool and the Scribble tool.

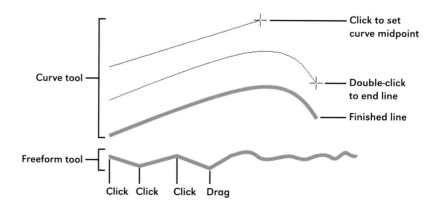

When you select a drawing tool, PhotoDraw displays the Edge workpane, where you can specify the size and style of the shape's *stroke,* or outline. If you create a closed shape—that is, not an open line—you can fill the interior with a solid color, a texture, a picture, or a gradient. To display the fill options, click Fill in the list at the top of the Edge workpane. Or choose an option from the Fill visual menu.

see also | *For a thorough explanation of the Fill and Edge workpane options, flip back to Chapter 5.*

Painting vs. Drawing

Choose Paint Tools from the Draw Paint visual menu to display the Paint workpane, shown in Figure 8-6. Select Paint Tools from the Gallery Type drop-down list to paint with a brush that creates strokes resembling those made by a traditional paintbrush, airbrush, highlighter pen, or pencil, depending on the brush style you choose from the list below the Gallery Type drop-down list.

Paint floating toolbar

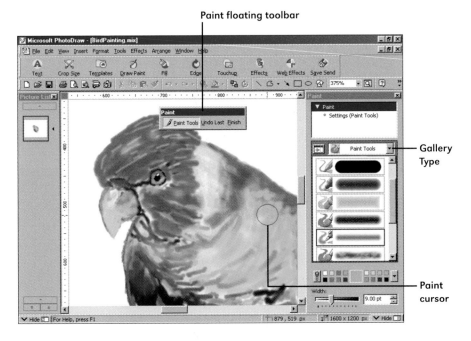

Figure 8-6
The painting tools enable you to work more as you would with traditional art tools, but you don't get the same editing flexibility afforded by the drawing tools.

To paint, you simply drag to lay down free-form strokes of color, just as with the Scribble tool. But unlike the Scribble tool, which creates a single independent object each time you drag, the paint tools enable you to drag multiple times and tell PhotoDraw to regard all the strokes as one object. For example, I painted all the strokes in the bird picture shown in Figure 8-6 during a single painting session, so the end result was a single object.

After you select Paint Tools, PhotoDraw displays a small toolbar, known as a *floating toolbar,* which appears in the figure. The toolbar offers three buttons: Paint Tools, Undo Last, and Finish. Paint all the strokes you want your object to contain, and then click Finish. Any time prior to clicking Finish, you can click Undo Last to erase the previous paint stroke. (Don't choose the normal Undo command on the Edit menu, or you undo all your paint strokes.) You can change the brush, color, width, or transparency of the next stroke you paint by using the options in the Paint workpane. The paint cursor, labeled in Figure 8-6, indicates the size of your brush.

To rub out just a portion of a stroke, select Erasers from the Gallery Type drop-down list in the Paint workpane, select an eraser style, and drag over the stroke. If you want to lessen the impact of the eraser, click Settings (Erasers) in the list at the top of the workpane and then raise the Transparency value past 0. Now when you drag over painted pixels, PhotoDraw simply lowers their opacity instead of making them fully transparent.

Although you'll probably find painting more intuitive than working with the drawing tools, painting does have some disadvantages. For example, you give up the flexibility of being able to adjust the characteristics of each stroke independently after you complete the shape because PhotoDraw merges all the strokes into a single object. Another drawback to painted objects is that they're pixel-based, while drawn shapes are vector objects. (Chapter 2 explains the difference.) You can enlarge a vector object as much as you want without any quality loss, but that's not the case with painted objects, as I explain in Chapter 3. For these reasons, I don't paint very often. You can achieve a look similar to the strokes created by the painting tools by using a drawing tool with one

Hey, Isn't That Cheating? I feel duty bound to confess a secret about the painting in Figure 8-6: I'm not really a talented enough painter to create something like that from scratch. So what's the trick? I opened a photograph that I shot at our local zoo and then simply painted on top of it, as if I were tracing a picture with colored pencils. After finishing the painting, I deleted the photo from the picture.

This trick offers a way to create a stylized version of a photographic subject without having to watch those how-to-paint-a-landscape-in-30-minutes shows on public television. Many of the PhotoDraw Designer Effects also give photos a hand-painted look. But I want to emphasize one point: Use only your *own* photos for this purpose. Copying from someone else's photograph without permission is as legally dangerous—not to mention as ethically reprehensible—as reproducing the original photo.

of the Artistic Brushes edges, and you wind up with far more editing flexibility down the line.

> **see also** You can "stamp" your page with tiny photographic images by selecting Photo Stamps in the Gallery Type drop-down list in the Paint workpane. To see this feature in action, visit the upcoming section "Quick Buttons and Bars" and also travel back to the last section in Chapter 7, which explains how to create custom bullets with a Photo Stamps brush.

Basic Picture Editing

After you draw or paint an object, you can alter its size, shape, location, and more using the following techniques. If you came to this chapter after exploring Chapter 7, which explains how to create text in PhotoDraw, you already know most of these tricks—they apply whether you're working with a text object or a graphic object. But I'll present them again here to save you the trouble of thumbing back to Chapter 7.

- **Select a single object** Before you can edit an object, you must select it. Simply clicking the object gets the job done. PhotoDraw surrounds the object with a rectangular selection outline, which is trimmed with white *selection handles* and a green *rotate handle*, labeled in Figure 8-7. Some shapes that you draw with the AutoShapes tools also sport one or more yellow *adjustment handles*. More about all the handles momentarily.

- **Select multiple objects** Click the first object and hold the Shift key while you click the others. Or press Ctrl+A to select all objects in the picture. You can also drag around the objects you want to select.

- **Resize a selected object or an entire picture** Drag a corner selection handle to resize a selected object proportionally; drag a side handle to adjust the width only; drag a top handle to adjust the height only. For precision sizing, display the Resize workpane by choosing Resize from the Crop Size visual menu. Click Resize Object at the top of the workpane, and enter the new dimensions. As long as the Maintain Proportions check box is selected, PhotoDraw automatically adjusts the height when you adjust the width, and vice versa.

Figure 8-7
You can move a selected object by dragging it or by pressing the arrow keys on your keyboard.

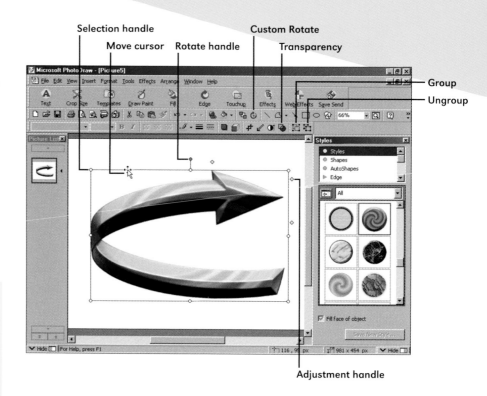

caution

Remember, you can enlarge shapes that you create with the drawing tools as much as you want without worrying about quality loss, as long as you continue to save the picture in the PhotoDraw format. (Other formats convert the shapes to pixels.) But painted objects, which are pixel-based just like photos, are not immune to damage. Although you may not notice any quality loss in PhotoDraw, it may be visible when you print the picture or display it on your Web page. Note also that applying some effects, such as the 3D effects, rasterizes vector shapes (pixelizes them). So be sure to set the shape's size before you apply those effects.

To resize the entire picture instead of a single object, click Resize Picture in the workpane instead of Resize Object before entering the new dimensions.

■ **Rotate a selected object** Drag the green rotate handle, labeled in Figure 8-7. Or click the Custom Rotate button, also labeled, to display the Rotate workpane, where you can enter a custom rotation angle or choose one of four preset angles.

■ **Reshape a drawn object** If yellow adjustment handles appear when you select an object, you can drag them to reshape the object. The changes you can make depend on the shape, so just drag a handle to see what's possible. If you're familiar with Bézier curve drawing tools, PhotoDraw enables you to edit curve points as you can in high-end drawing programs. Check the PhotoDraw help system for details on how to access the curve-editing functions.

■ **Move a selected object**   Position the cursor over the selection outline to display the four-headed arrow cursor, as shown in Figure 8-7, and then drag the object. (If you don't see the cursor, click the selection outline again. PhotoDraw sometimes gets distracted.) You can also press an arrow key on your keyboard to nudge the object slightly in the direction of the arrow. Press Shift plus an arrow key to nudge the object in larger increments.

■ **Change the outline (stroke) or interior (fill) of a drawn object** Choose an option from the Edge or Fill visual menu, respectively. For more about these options, see Chapter 5.

■ **Adjust the transparency of a selected object**   Drag the Transparency slider in the Fill or Edge workpane to make the interior or outline of a shape more or less transparent. But if you want to modify the entire shape, click the Transparency button, labeled in Figure 8-7, to display the Transparency workpane, and adjust the Transparency slider there instead.

■ **Align two or more selected objects**   Click the Arrange menu, and point to Align to display a submenu of alignment options. You can align objects vertically or horizontally. If the Relative To Background option is selected, PhotoDraw aligns the objects with respect to the canvas. Otherwise, the program aligns the objects with respect to the first object you selected.

■ **Grouping selected objects**   To temporarily combine selected objects into one, click the Arrange menu and then click Group. Or just click the Group button, labeled in Figure 8-7. Why group? Because you can then move, size, and duplicate the objects as a single entity rather than applying the same edit to each one individually. You also lock in the relative positioning of all the

tip

By default, PhotoDraw nudges the object one pixel with every press of an arrow key and 10 pixels when you throw in the Shift key. You can set up different nudge distances, however. On the Tools menu, click Options to display the Options dialog box. Click the General tab, and then change the Small Nudge and Large Nudge values (in pixels).

tip

PhotoDraw offers a collection of effects that apply a set of formatting attributes to drawn objects with one click. To explore the effects, choose Styles from the Web Effects visual menu and then select a design from the Styles workpane, shown in Figure 8-7. I used the design selected in the figure to give the arrow its fill, edge, and three-dimensional effect. Note that these styles are *not* related to the Cascading Style Sheets (CSS) styles I've been warning you about throughout earlier chapters, and they won't result in browser incompatibility problems. See the upcoming section "Quick Buttons and Bars" for more speed-formatting tricks.

objects in the group, so you can't accidentally alter their arrangement with an errant click or drag.

To break a grouped object back into its original components, click the Ungroup button, also labeled in the figure, or click the Arrange menu and then click Ungroup.

■ **Duplicate a selected object**   Press Ctrl+D, or choose Duplicate on the Edit menu. You also can press Ctrl as you drag an object. The duplicate emerges from the original and follows your mouse cursor as you drag.

■ **Copy a selected object to another picture**   Press Ctrl+C (the keyboard shortcut for the Copy command on the Edit menu), open the second picture, and press Ctrl+V (the shortcut for the Paste command). If both pictures are open, you can make the second picture the active picture and then simply drag the object's thumbnail from the Object List (explained in the next section) into the second picture.

■ **Move a selected object to another picture**   Press Ctrl+X (the shortcut key for the Cut command on the Edit menu), open the second picture, and press Ctrl+V to paste in the object. If you want to create a new picture to hold the object, just drag the object to the Picture List.

■ **Insert another picture**   To insert another picture into the active picture, click the Insert menu, click From File, and then select the file. Click Visual Insert on the Insert menu to browse thumbnails of your files. To add a clip-art graphic from the Microsoft Clip Gallery, click Clip Art on the Insert menu. The upcoming section "Using Clip Art" details the Clip Gallery.

■ **Delete a selected object**   Press Delete.

■ **Save a picture**   To save a picture for the first time, click the File menu and then click Save to open the Save As dialog box and go about the usual save routine, which is fully covered in Chapter 9. After you save a file for the first time, you can just press Ctrl+S to resave it.

Shuffling the Stacking Order

Every PhotoDraw object exists on its own layer, independent of all the other objects. If you drag one object atop another, the top object obscures the bottom one. This assumes that both objects are fully opaque, of course. If you set the Transparency value for the top object to greater than 0 percent, the bottom object becomes partially visible through the top object.

As an example, see Figure 8-8, which shows the logo banner that I created for the Martin Realty Web page discussed in Chapter 4. The text, on the top layer, is fully opaque and so covers everything immediately below it. But I set the Transparency value for the blue rectangle, which rests just below the text, to 40 percent, so you can still see the random shapes in the layers below. A faded bar like this helps to separate text from a busy background.

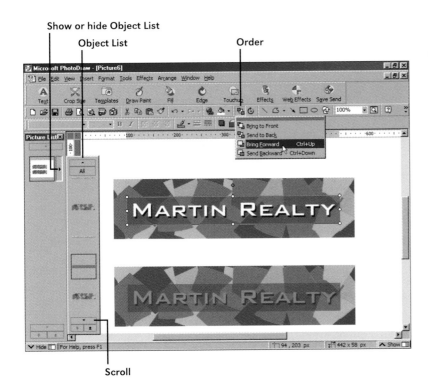

Figure 8-8
Click the arrow next to the thumbnail in the Picture List to display the Object List, which shows the stacking order of all objects in the picture.

To see the *stacking order* of all objects in your picture—that is, which one is at the top, the middle, and so on—click the arrow to the right of the picture's thumbnail in the Picture List. (See Figure 8-8.) PhotoDraw shows the Object List, which contains thumbnails of each object. A dark outline surrounds the selected object's thumbnail.

You can send an object forward or backward in the stack by dragging the object's thumbnail up or down in the Object List. Or click the Order button, labeled in the figure, and select one of the four options. (You can also access these commands by clicking the Arrange menu and then pointing to Order.) In the bottom example in Figure 8-8, I moved the blue rectangle to the top of the stack, so the characters now peek out through it.

If all the object thumbnails aren't visible in the Object List, click the arrows at the top and bottom of the list to scroll the display. Clicking All at the top of the list selects all the objects in the picture. To close the Object List, click the arrow next to the picture's thumbnail again.

Quick Buttons and Bars

Earlier, in the section "Basic Picture Editing," I introduced you to the Styles command, found on the Web Effects visual menu, which you can use to apply prefab designs to a selected object. The Styles effects are particularly well suited for creating buttons, bars, and other navigation graphics. But using Styles effects is only one of several fast routes to generating this type of graphic. Play around with these other techniques too:

■ Click Photo Stamps on the Draw Paint visual menu to display a collection of photographic objects that you can "stamp" onto the page, many of which are designed to be used as buttons. (Put the number 2 PhotoDraw program CD into your CD-ROM drive first so that you can access the entire collection.) After you choose an object, click Settings at the top of the Paint workpane and deselect the Randomize Arrangement check box so that the shape will appear at the orientation you see in the workpane thumbnail. Then click once on your canvas. If you don't like the result, click Undo Last in the floating Paint toolbar, adjust the workpane settings, and try again. Click Finish to close the deal. I used this technique to create the top-left button in Figure 8-9.

If the photo object you create is smaller than the picture canvas, PhotoDraw adds empty pixels around it to make it the same size as the canvas. Use the Crop tool, discussed in Chapter 9, to trim away the extra pixels from the object, and then trim away the excess canvas using the techniques explained earlier in this chapter, in the section "Sizing the Canvas."

tip

If you have trouble selecting an object in a stack by clicking in the picture, display the Object List and click the object's thumbnail instead.

Figure 8-9
I created all these buttons with just a few clicks using PhotoDraw's prefab effects tools.

- I created the top-right button in Figure 8-9 by simply drawing a line using one of the Theme Brushes edge effects. Select the Line tool, and then select Theme Brushes from the Gallery Type drop-down list in the Edge workpane. Select a brush style (simpler is better if your button will contain text), and then hold down the Shift key while dragging to draw a short horizontal line. Adjust the Width value in the workpane to make the line thicker or thinner; drag a selection handle at either end of the line to adjust the line length.

- To create a simple 3D button like the lower-left example in Figure 8-9, create a basic shape with a drawing tool and apply a solid-color fill and edge. On the Web Effects visual menu, click Emboss And Embed to display the Emboss And Embed workpane, which contains thumbnails representing different effects that create three-dimensional effects that work well for buttons. Click a thumbnail and then click Settings (Emboss or Embed) at the top of the workpane to adjust the effect. If you decide that you want to remove the effect, click Emboss And Embed at the top of the workpane and then click the first thumbnail (the one with the big *X*).

■ The final example in Figure 8-9 starts with a simple circle. Hold the Shift key and drag with the Ellipse drawing tool to create a circle. Fill the circle with a texture. Apply an edge if you like. Click Glow on the Web Effects visual menu to display the Glow workpane, which contains thumbnails representing effects that add a colored halo around your shape. The effect is similar to adding a shadow, but Glow enables you to create multicolored shadows and also gives you more control over the size of the shadow. Click a thumbnail in the Glow workpane to choose a basic design, and then use the other settings in the workpane to refine the effect.

■ Click Web Graphics on the Templates visual menu to launch a wizard that walks you through the steps of creating buttons, bars, and other Web elements based on PhotoDraw design templates. (Be sure to put the number 2 PhotoDraw program CD into your CD-ROM drive before you begin so that you can access all the templates.)

Object Lessons: Forging Shapes into Pictures

Reading about drawing, painting, and editing is all well and good, but you won't really get a good feel for how PhotoDraw works until you try it for yourself. To that end, the following sections provide click-by-click rundowns of how I created the clothing button that serves as the *o* in the Buttons text graphic shown at the top of Figure 8-10. The button consists of seven shapes stacked on top of one another. You can see these individual elements at the bottom of the figure.

Here's how to create the button components and meld them together into the finished button:

1 Draw the button base by holding Shift and dragging with the Ellipse drawing tool.

2 On the Web Effects visual menu, click Styles and select the effect shown in Figure 8-10. The effect applies a thick, black stroke around the shape, which I didn't want, so I next clicked Plain on the Edge visual menu and selected No Line in the workpane to remove the stroke.

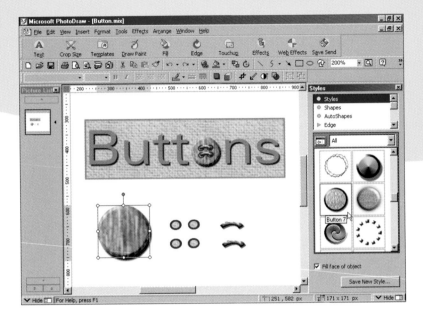

Figure 8-10
The button in the text graphic is actually seven separate shapes stacked on top of one another.

3 Hold Shift and drag again with the Ellipse tool to create the first buttonhole, using a plain, single-line, narrow edge. Click the Eyedropper tool in the Edge workpane, and then click the darkest part of the filled button base to use that color as the edge color. Fill the hole with the same fill that you plan to use as the background. This creates the illusion of a real buttonhole—where you'd see the fabric through the hole. I used the same texture fill you see in the background of the finished graphic at the top of Figure 8-10.

4 Press Ctrl+D to duplicate the hole. Then move it and the original hole into place to form the top pair of buttonholes.

5 Select both holes, click the Arrange menu, point to Align, and then click the Align Top option. (If the Relative To Background option at the bottom of the Align submenu is selected, click it to deselect that option before you align the shapes.) PhotoDraw lines up the two circles with each other, using the top of the shapes as the reference point.

6 Click the Arrange menu, and then click Group to glue the two holes together.

7 Press Ctrl+D to duplicate the pair of holes. Drag the duplicate pair into place below the first pair.

8 Hold Shift and click the top pair to select both pairs of holes. On the Arrange menu, point to Align, and then click Align Left to align the two pairs of holes by their left edges.

9 Finally, glue the two pairs of holes together by clicking the Arrange menu and then clicking Group. Reposition and resize the group of holes as needed to fit properly on top of the button base.

10 All that's left is to create the threads running between each pair of holes. Click the AutoShapes button on the Standard toolbar, and click the Arc shape from the Basic Shapes submenu. Drag to create a simple arc. The resulting shape includes regular selection handles, plus two yellow adjustment handles.

11 Resize, reshape, and rotate the line as needed to stretch the arc in a gentle curve between the centers of the two top holes. Drag a white selection handle to adjust the size; drag a yellow handle to adjust the degree of the curve. Drag the green rotate handle to spin the arc.

12 Click Photo Brushes on the Edge visual menu and select the Brown Rope effect, as shown in Figure 8-11. Used for small lines, this edge effect gives the look of twisted thread more than rope. Adjust the Width value in the Edge workpane until you're happy with the thickness of the thread. You'll adjust the color of the thread in the next step.

13 Click Color Effects on the Effects visual menu to display the Color workpane. Click Colorize in the Effect drop-down list. Click Correct Selection in the list at the top of the workpane, and then click the Eyedropper tool and click a light shade of purple in the button base. Drag the Amount slider in the workpane to intensify the thread color shift.

see also | *Chapter 9 explains color effects in more detail.*

14 To give the thread a three-dimensional look, click the Web Effects visual menu and then click Emboss And Embed. Select a thumbnail from the Emboss And Embed workpane. I chose Emboss 1, which is the top-right thumbnail in the workpane.

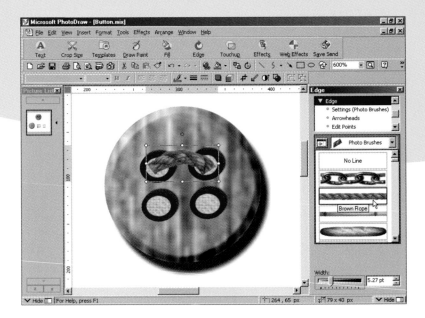

Figure 8-11
I used the Arc shape tool to draw a curved line and then applied the rope edge effect to create the thread.

15 To further define the thread, apply a slight shadow to it. On the Effects visual menu, click Shadow to display the Shadow workpane. Click the Drop, Down Right shadow thumbnail. Click the Shadow Position button, and press the arrow keys on your keyboard to nudge the shadow into place. I also dragged the selection handles around the shadow so that the shadow extends slightly beyond the ends of the thread, so that the thread appears to get darker as it goes into the hole.

16 After you're done fooling with the shadow position and size, click the Finish button on the Position toolbar. Adjust the Transparency and Soften sliders in the Shadow workpane as you see fit.

17 Press Ctrl+D to duplicate the thread, and then move the copy over the bottom pair of buttonholes.

18 If you want to resize, reshape, or move the entire button, group all the objects together. Press Ctrl+A to select everything, click the Arrange menu, and then click Group.

That's all there is to sewing up the button project—har har. Incredibly easy, eh? I won't tell your friends if you won't.

Using Clip Art

If you don't have the time or patience to create your own graphics, you can take advantage of the enormous selection of clip art found in the Microsoft Clip Gallery, which comes with Microsoft Office 2000, as well as some stand-alone Microsoft products, including PhotoDraw.

To browse the clip art, put the Clip Gallery CD into your CD-ROM drive, click the Insert menu, and then click Clip Art. PhotoDraw displays the Microsoft Clip Gallery window, shown in Figure 8-12. Click an icon in the list to display thumbnails of all the clips in that category, or type a word in the Search For Clips box and press Enter to see clips related to the word. For example, I typed "bird" to display the clips shown in Figure 8-13.

Click the Back and Forward buttons, labeled in Figure 8-13, to travel between the pages of thumbnails. Click the All Categories button to return to the category icons shown in Figure 8-12.

When you find a graphic you like, click it to display the mini-menu shown in Figure 8-13. Click the Insert Clip button to add the graphic to your picture; click the Preview Clip button to display a larger preview of the graphic. After you import a graphic into PhotoDraw, it behaves like any other graphic except that you can't ungroup the shapes that make up the picture.

PhotoDraw offers its own collection of clip-art drawings and photos, which you access from the number 2 PhotoDraw program CD. After putting the CD in your CD-ROM drive, click the Insert menu and then click PhotoDraw Content to open the PhotoDraw Clipart folder on the CD and browse thumbnails of the available clips. When you find a clip that you like, double-click it to insert it in your picture.

tip

You can insert clip art directly into FrontPage, but I recommend that you prepare the graphic in PhotoDraw and then import it into FrontPage. That way, you can adjust the picture size, specify custom save options, and perform other edits, such as tweaking the graphic's colors or cropping out a portion of the picture.

tip

You can browse and download scads more clips from the Microsoft Web site by clicking the Clips Online button at the top of the Clip Gallery window. When you download clips, you may see a dialog box asking whether you want to save the clips or open them. Contrary to what you probably expect, you must choose the option that opens the graphic. Otherwise, the graphics don't get dumped into the right folder on your computer. To access your new clips, click the Downloaded Clips category icon on the first screen of the Clip Gallery.

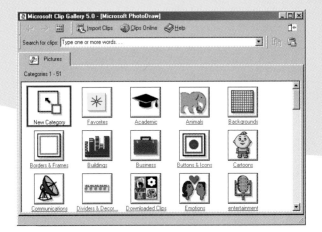

Figure 8-12
Click an icon to see all clips in that category.

Back

Forward

All Categories

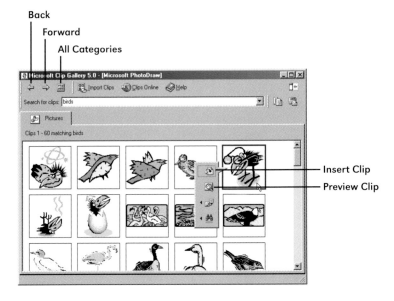

Figure 8-13
Click a thumbnail, and then click the Preview Clip button to get a closer look at the graphic.

Insert Clip

Preview Clip

tip

The Designer Clip Art folder, which is inside the PhotoDraw Clipart folder, contains many simple black-and-white sketches that you can fill and stroke as you see fit. You can launch a wizard that guides you through the process of using Designer Clip Art by clicking the Templates visual menu and then clicking Designer Clip Art.

Color Effects

Plug-ins

Distort

3-D

Text   Crop Size

Show For Help, press F1

photography

for
THE WEB

All you need to know about . . .

- ■ **Taking better photos for your Web site**

- ■ **Retouching photos**

- ■ **Selecting the area you want to edit**

- ■ **Cropping away the edges of a picture**

- ■ **Making areas transparent**

- ■ **Adjusting colors and sharpening focus**

- ■ **Combining photos**

- ■ **Saving pictures in the GIF and JPEG formats**

note

As in Chapter 8, the steps in this chapter feature Microsoft PhotoDraw 2000 Version 2, but the general concepts apply no matter what software you use. In fact, the actual implementation of many tools is much the same in all entry-level image editing programs. If you can't figure out one of your tools, check your software's help system for more information.

About 20 years ago, I traveled to New Orleans with a new camera in hand. I was working as an editor for a travel magazine at the time, and I wanted some shots to accompany an article for the next issue. Just before sunset, I spotted a saxophone player leaning against a streetlight in the French Quarter, backlit by the rose-streaked sky. What a find! I put eye to viewfinder and snapped a series of great images. Or so I thought. As I began packing up my camera gear, already daydreaming about the how the magazine's art director would gush over these wonderful photos, I realized that I had taken every single picture without removing the lens cap.

I regret to tell you that even with all the advances in photo editing software, no one has yet come up with a fix for this bonehead mistake, which every photographer makes at some point. The good news is that you can correct just about every *other* photographic flub, whether it's due to an error on your part or a camera malfunction. (Always blame the latter if you can get away with it.)

In this chapter, I'll introduce you to the basics of photo editing, from erasing portions of a picture to making focus and color adjustments. You'll also find picture-taking tips that will reduce the time you spend cleaning up your photos. In addition, I'll explain how to size and save your images in the JPEG and GIF formats for use on the Web.

Taking Better Web Pictures

Whether you're shooting pictures of your company's latest product or your family's newest kid, you can improve the photos that come out of your camera by remembering the following tips:

- **Press the shutter button correctly.** I know that sounds goofy. But if your camera offers autofocus, autoexposure, or both—as most point-and-shoot digital and film cameras do—you need to press the shutter button in a special way to enable those mechanisms to do their jobs. After you frame the picture, press and hold the shutter button *halfway* down. This tells the camera to read the scene and dial in the exposure and focus settings. Depending on the camera, you'll either hear a beep or see a light near the viewfinder change colors when the camera has done its thing. You can then press the shutter button the rest of the way down.

■ **Get the clutter out of the background.** Scan the scene you see in the viewfinder to look for distracting background objects. Make sure there aren't any lampshades or potted plants that appear to be growing out of your subject's head, for example. Don't shoot against busy wallpaper or some other backdrop that draws the eye away from your main subject. Sure, you may be able to remove troublesome background elements in a photo editing program, but why not opt for an ounce of prevention instead of a pound of cure?

■ **Use a tripod for better focus.** Even if you have very steady hands, use a tripod whenever possible. The slightest camera shake can result in a blurry image. Another trick to reduce the chance of camera movement is to shoot using your camera's self-timer mechanism. Press the shutter button to kick the timer into gear, and then take your hands off the camera so there's no chance that you'll jar it at the moment the image is captured.

■ **Zoom in for close-ups.** If your camera has a zoom lens, take your close-up shots by zooming in instead of moving the camera closer to the subject. Your subject will be the same size in the photo, but you'll get less background in the scene. (Try it to see for yourself.) If you don't zoom, check to see whether your camera has a *macro* focus mode, which adjusts the lens to get sharper close-up pictures. The camera manual should tell you how far away you need to place the camera for proper focus.

■ **Shoot or scan Web-only photos at minimal resolution.** As discussed in Chapter 2, Web pictures demand far fewer pixels than print pictures. Most printers produce the best output when given 300 pixels for each linear inch of the print. (For example, for a 2-by-2-inch print, you need 600 pixels horizontally and 600 pixels vertically.) But for Web images, you need only one image pixel for each screen pixel that you want to fill. For example, a 320-by-240-pixel image fills half the screen at a monitor resolution of 640 by 480 pixels.

tip

If you're planning on separating subject from background in the photo editing stage, you can simplify your editing work by shooting against a plain background that's significantly different in color from the subject. Most photo editing programs offer a tool that can automatically clip away the background if there's enough contrast between it and the subject. PhotoDraw offers two such tools, which you can read about in the upcoming sections "Drawing an outline between contrasting areas" and "Selecting areas by color."

see also │ For a thorough review of sizing pictures for the Web, see Chapter 3.

You can eliminate excess pixels in your image editing program, of course, but dumping a huge number of pixels can diminish quality. So don't use ultrahigh-resolution settings when shooting or scanning pictures that will be used only on your Web site. If you need both print and Web versions of an image, you may want to shoot or scan the picture twice, once at a high resolution and once at a Web-appropriate resolution.

Secrets for Shooting Shiny Stuff

Unless you have a full-fledged photography studio at your disposal, shooting metallic, glass, or porcelain product shots can be problematic. If you use a flash or bring the object into the sun, you can wind up with unwanted reflections where the light bounces off the object, as in the middle of the glass decanter on the left in Figure 9-1. But if you try to shoot in the shade or indoors without some artificial light source, the exposure is too dark, as in the right image in the figure.

Figure 9-1
Shooting with a flash created a flare in the center of the decanter (left), while shooting without any artificial light underexposed the image.

Flash, EV 0.0   No flash, EV 0.0

Here's how I solve the problem. First, the flash stays off. I do switch on a few artificial lights—the clamp-on shop lights sold in hardware stores work fine—but I position them so that they're not shining directly on the object. I also set up a "light tent," hanging a white sheet or curtain between the light source and the object to diffuse the light.

If the light level is reasonable but still not enough to get a proper exposure, I tweak my camera's *exposure value,* or *EV,* setting. This feature is found on many cameras today. It enables you to boost or decrease the settings chosen by the camera's autoexposure mechanism. If you raise the EV value above the default, 0.0, you get a brighter exposure than normal; lowering the value results in a darker picture. I used an EV setting of +0.7 to shoot the image shown on the left side of Figure 9-2; for the right image, I raised the value to +1.3. Notice that turning off the flash and raising the EV setting not only eliminated the reflection that plagues the flash example but also brought out the green in the glass.

No flash, EV +0.7   No flash, EV +1.3

Figure 9-2
Raising the EV setting enables you to turn off the flash and still get a good exposure.

If your camera offers a choice of exposure *metering modes,* you can also play with different modes to adjust the exposure. The metering mode determines what areas of the scene the camera considers when gauging the available light. By default, most cameras base exposure on average light levels throughout the scene, a metering mode sometimes called *matrix mode.* If you're shooting a dark object against a light backdrop, this mode may result in an exposure that's fine for the background but leaves the object in the shadows. To get a better image, try switching to *spot* metering mode, which sets exposure based on the light at the center of the frame, or *center-weighted* metering, which takes the entire scene into account but gives more importance to the center of the frame.

Fixing Photographic Flaws

Even if you follow the tips in the preceding sections religiously, you won't get perfect photographs from every exposure. Fortunately, image editing programs make it possible to correct many small image flaws—and even some pretty big ones. In the next several sections, you'll find some simple tricks for rescuing problem pictures.

Selecting the Area to Edit

As is the case when you're working with text or graphics in PhotoDraw, before you can use any photo editing tools you must select the area you want to adjust. If you want to change the entire photo, just click it to display the standard selection outline and handles.

To select a portion of a photo, use the Cut Out command, found on the Crop Size visual menu. The Cut Out command offers four different ways to create custom selection outlines, which I explain in the next sections. But regardless of which Cut Out method you use, keep the following points in mind:

■ Contrary to its name, Cut Out doesn't delete selected areas. Instead, it *duplicates* them. You can send the copy to the top of the object stack in the current picture, which enables you to apply color corrections, special effects, and other edits to the area without touching the rest of the picture. (Chapter 8 explains the Object List and the concept of object stacking.) Or you can send

note

Although the tools and effects I discuss in this chapter are designed primarily for digital photos, you can use them to alter simple graphics too. However, be aware that most of the special effects *rasterize* drawn objects (convert them from vector objects to pixels). So you may want to make a backup copy of your picture before you apply the effects, just in case you need the object in its original life form later. For more about pixels and vector objects, see Chapters 2 and 3.

the duplicated area to a brand-new picture or to the Clipboard. After sending the copy to the Clipboard, you can paste it into another open picture by clicking Paste on the Edit menu. To delete something from a photo, use the Erase command, discussed in the section "Making Areas Transparent."

■ Normally, any pixels inside the selection outline are selected. But if you select the Cut Out Opposite Area check box in the workpane, you reverse the selection outline. Pixels outside the outline become selected, and pixels inside the outline become deselected.

What's the point? Well, suppose you have a complex subject set against a plain background—an ornate church spire in a sea of blue sky, for example. Drawing a precise outline around the spire would be difficult. But you can use the By Color selection option, which selects pixels according to color, to quickly select the sky and then reverse the outline so that the spire is selected. See the upcoming section "Selecting areas by color" for more help with this approach.

■ If you want to select just certain areas of multiple photos or graphics—for example, to select just the blue cars in three different auto-racing images—first select the pictures by pressing Shift as you click each one. Then draw your selection outline using the Cut Out command. Now your edits affect only selected areas throughout the group. Note that even though you selected pixels from several objects, the duplicated pixels form a single object. Using the car example, you wind up with a single object consisting of all the blue cars.

Another way to select portions of multiple graphics is to use the Cut Out tool, accessible from the Formatting toolbar; the button looks like an arrow surrounded by a dotted outline. This tool does essentially the same thing as using the Cut Out command in the By Drawing mode, with the Square shape selected. (In fact, although the workpane disappears when you activate the tool, if you click the Show button, the Cut Out workpane reappears.) Just drag with the tool to create the outline. Hold down the Shift key and drag to create a square outline.

lingo

In some image editing programs, the command that swaps the selection outline is called Inverse. For that reason, photo-editing experts sometimes talk about *inversing the selection outline*. If you're using a program other than PhotoDraw, you may also find an Invert command, but that command typically has nothing to do with selection outlines. Instead, it reverses the colors in an image, just like PhotoDraw's Negative effect, discussed later in this chapter.

Selecting geometrically shaped areas

When you choose Cut Out from the Crop Size visual menu, the workpane offers four selection methods: By Shape, By Drawing, Edge Finder, and By Color, as shown in Figure 9-3. The first option draws selection outlines in simple geometric shapes.

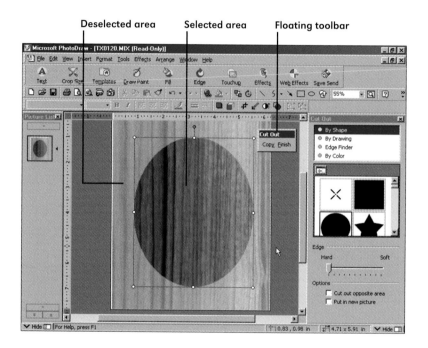

Figure 9-3
Use the By Shape option to create selection outlines based on simple shapes.

When you work with the By Shape tool, you can create a hard-edged outline or a soft, fuzzy outline, known officially as a *feathered* outline. With a hard edge, you'll wind up with a crisp border between edited and unedited areas, as in the left example in Figure 9-4; a soft edge results in a gradual transition, as in the right example. For both images, I started with a full-color picture of wood. Then I drew an elliptical selection outline in the center of the picture and sent the copied pixels to the top of the object stack. Next I selected the bottom object—that full-color wood image—and used the Grayscale filter, discussed later in this chapter, to drain it of all color. The copied pixels on the top layer remain untouched by the edit. Finally, I added the two text objects on top of the two wood layers.

Hard edge   **Soft edge**

Figure 9-4
*A hard-edged selection outline
creates a distinct boundary
between edited and unedited
areas; a soft edge creates a
gradual transition.*

To draw a shape-based selection outline, take the following steps:

1   After selecting the photo (or group of objects) you want to edit, choose
    Cut Out from the Crop Size visual menu to display the Cut Out workpane.

2   Click By Shape at the top of the workpane, and then choose a shape from
    the list. PhotoDraw covers your photo with a translucent coating, as
    shown in Figure 9-3.

3   Drag in your picture to create the selection outline. PhotoDraw punches
    a hole in the translucent coating in the shape you chose, as shown in
    Figure 9-3. Anything visible through the hole will be selected, assum-
    ing that you don't select the Cut Out Opposite Area check box in the
    workpane. If you do, everything outside the hole will be selected.

    The hole itself is surrounded by a standard selection outline, and
    you can drag the selection handles to adjust the size, shape, and
    rotation of the hole just as you do to alter a text or graphic object. (See
    Chapter 8 for details.) To move the outline, drag inside it.

4   Drag the Edge slider to adjust the softness of the selection outline. To
    create a hard-edged outline like the one I used for the left example in
    Figure 9-4, drag the slider all the way to the left. For a feathered edge,
    drag the slider to the right.

5   To copy the selection to a new picture, select the Put In New Picture
    check box at the bottom of the workpane. Otherwise, clear the check box.

tip

A feathered outline makes
photo retouching less
obvious because you don't
see a distinct boundary
between retouched and
unretouched areas.

tip

Anytime before you click
Copy or Finish, you can
cancel the selection
operation by pressing the
Esc key on your keyboard.

6 To copy the selection to the Clipboard, click Copy in the floating toolbar, labeled in Figure 9-3 on page 200. Click Finish instead if you want to send the selection to a new picture or to the top layer in the current picture's object stack.

Drawing a custom outline

You also can draw a free-form selection outline, as shown in Figure 9-5. As always, the first step is to select the photo or objects that you want to edit. Then click By Drawing at the top of the Cut Out workpane, click Draw in the floating toolbar if it's not already selected, and drag to create the outline. The dashed line that appears represents the outline.

Figure 9-5
Choose the By Drawing option in the Cut Out workpane to draw a freehand selection outline.

Start point

Selection outline

tip

To automatically create a
straight segment when
creating a selection outline
using the By Drawing option,
let up on the mouse button,
move the mouse to where you
want the segment to end,
and click.

If you're not happy with your last click or drag, click Undo Last in the floating toolbar and try again. To erase the entire outline and start over, click Reset and then click Draw on the floating toolbar.

When you reach the start of the outline, marked by a big yellow diamond, put your cursor over the diamond and click. You can also double-click at any point to automatically create a segment that closes the outline.

After you complete the selection outline, you can adjust it by dragging the line segments that make up the outline. Here's how it works. As you pass your cursor over the outline, the segment under the cursor turns pink. Place the cursor at the spot where two segments meet, and both turn pink. If you drag at the intersection of the two segments, both lines move in tandem with your cursor. But if you drag on a single line segment, you split the segment in two, and the two *new* segments move with your cursor. Also experiment with the Path Smoothness slider in the workpane. Move the slider to the right to smooth out sharp angles all along the outline.

When you're happy with the outline, use the Cut Out Opposite Area and Put In New Picture check boxes to specify how you want PhotoDraw to proceed, as discussed earlier in the bulleted list in "Selecting the Area to Edit." Then click Finish in the floating toolbar.

Drawing an outline between contrasting areas

When the edges of the area you want to select bump up against contrasting pixels, like the butterfly in Figure 9-6, use the Edge Finder tool. As you drag with this tool, PhotoDraw automatically places the selection outline along the border between contrasting pixels.

note

The photo in Figure 9-5, by the way, provides a classic example of the plant-on-the-head syndrome I mentioned in the photography tips section at the start of this chapter. This poor girl looks like she's about to be attacked by some moplike creature from outer space. Fortunately, I was able to draw a selection outline around her and send her to an office where the working conditions are less menacing.

Selection rectangle   Start point

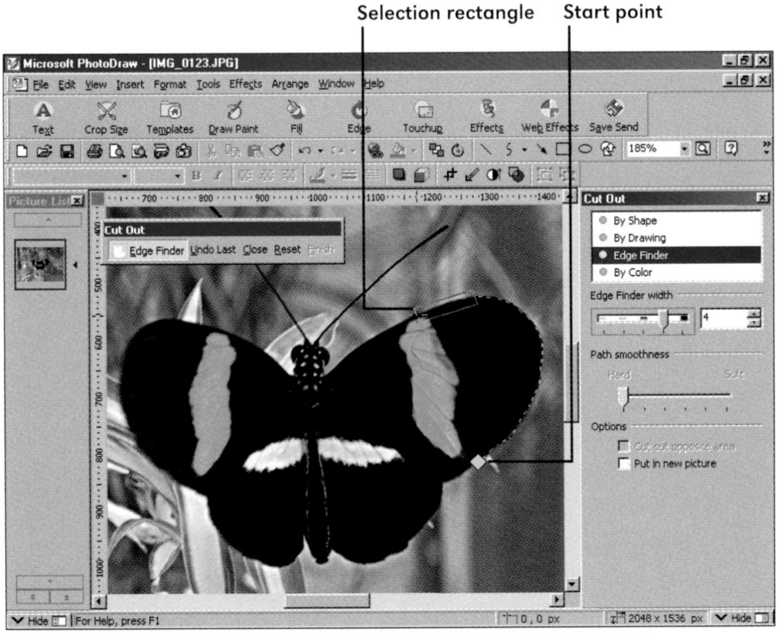

Figure 9-6
As you drag with the Edge Finder tool, PhotoDraw lays down a selection outline along the border between contrasting pixels.

tip

Adjust the Edge Finder slider in the Cut Out workpane to make the rectangle cursor larger or smaller. A larger rectangle enables PhotoDraw to roam further from your cursor when looking for the contrasting pixels. A medium value typically works best. (I used a higher value in the figure so that the rectangle would be easier to see.)

To give the Edge Finder a whirl, take these steps:

1 Select the photo (or objects) you want to edit. Then click Edge Finder at the top of the Cut Out workpane.

2 Click to start the outline. You see a small rectangle emanating from your cursor. The rectangle defines the region in which PhotoDraw will search for areas of contrast. Move your mouse so that the cursor is smack-dab over the border between the pixels you want to select and the neighboring pixels, and then click. After you click, PhotoDraw searches for the edge between the two areas and creates the first segment in your outline.

3 Keep moving the cursor and clicking to create additional segments. Click Undo Last in the floating toolbar to remove the segment you just drew, or click Reset and then click Edge Finder to start over.

4 To finish the outline, click the big yellow diamond that marks the beginning of the outline. You also can click Close in the floating toolbar to automatically create a final segment between the start point and the point of your last click.

5 If necessary, adjust the finished outline by dragging the Path Smoothness slider or tugging the outline's edges. When you drag a part of the outline, you see the same rectangle extending from your cursor as when you first drew the selection. Reposition the rectangle and then release the mouse to redraw the outline.

6 Select or clear the check boxes in the Options section of the workpane according to how you want PhotoDraw to treat the selection outline. (See the bulleted list in the earlier section "Selecting the Area to Edit" for more about these options.)

7 Click Finish in the floating toolbar.

Selecting areas by color

PhotoDraw, like most photo editing programs, offers a tool that selects pixels based on color. You simply click in your image, and PhotoDraw selects similarly colored areas.

The upcoming steps provide details of selecting by color. But first, I need to explain the Search Mode option in the workpane, which determines what pixels PhotoDraw considers in its color assessment. If you choose

Local, the selection outline stops where the program encounters differently colored pixels. For example, the left image in Figure 9-7 shows my original photo of some jewelry shot against a black velvet background. In the right image, a duplicate of the original, I clicked at the spot marked by the crosshair cursor. The black pixels inside the strand of pearls weren't selected because the white pearl pixels come between them and the clicked pixel. If you set the search mode to Global, all similarly colored pixels throughout the photo get grabbed, regardless of whether differently colored pixels fall between them and the pixel you click.

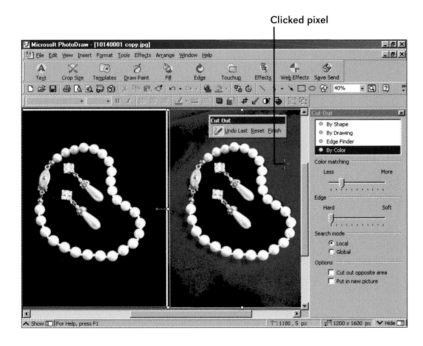

Figure 9-7
Click a color in the photo to select pixels with a similar color.

With that introduction out of the way, take these steps to select by color:

1. After selecting the photo (or objects), click By Color at the top of the Cut Out workpane, and then select a Search Mode option.

2. Click the area that you want to use as the basis for the selection. PhotoDraw covers the selected pixels with a hot-pink overlay, as shown in Figure 9-7.

3. If PhotoDraw selected too many pixels, click Undo Last in the floating toolbar. Then drag the Color Matching slider toward Less, which tells

tip

I mentioned this tip earlier, but it bears repeating: If you want to select a complex object that's set against a plain background, such as the pearl jewelry in Figure 9-7, use the By Color tool to select the background and then select the Cut Out Opposite Area check box in the workpane. Now the background is deselected and the object is selected.

PhotoDraw to be more discriminating when it searches for matching pixels. If you want to include a broader range of colors, drag the slider toward More. Just keep clicking in the image to add more pixels to the selection.

4   From here on in, everything works as it does when you use the By Shape selection option except that you don't get a Copy button for sending the selected pixels to the Clipboard. Drag the Edge slider to adjust the outline, choose Cut Out Opposite Area to reverse the outline, and select Put In New Picture if you want to send the copied selection to a new picture. Click Finish to wrap things up.

Snipping Away Part of a Photo

To trim away the edges of a photo—called *cropping* in the official photo editor's handbook—click Crop By Shape on the Crop Size visual menu or click the Crop button, labeled in Figure 9-8. Either way, you see the Crop workpane, which provides a selection of cropping shapes. In most cases, you'll use the first two shapes (the rectangle and the circle), but the specialty shapes can lend some interest to a photo on occasion, as long as you don't overdo them. I used the Angled Corners crop shape for the house photo in the figure.

PhotoDraw's cropping feature, although easy to use, has a few quirks. Here's the deal:

1   As always, first select the photo you want to crop. Then click a crop shape in the workpane. A translucent coating appears over the entire photo, as when you use the By Drawing selection tool.

Undo: The Greatest Thing Since the Eraser

Like almost every other computer program, PhotoDraw enables you to undo your last action. Press Ctrl+Z, or click the Edit menu and then click Undo to go back a step in time. If the Standard toolbar is visible, you can accomplish the same thing by clicking the Undo button. (It's the curving arrow that points to the left.) Change your mind about that undo? Press Ctrl+Y, or click Redo on the Edit menu, or click the Redo button on the Standard toolbar, which is right next to the Undo button.

But PhotoDraw takes Undo to a higher level. You can undo or redo a whole series of actions by repeatedly choosing Undo or Redo. Or click the arrow next to the Undo or Redo button to display a menu of actions you can reverse, and then click the edit point where you went wrong. PhotoDraw can keep track of about 20 edits, depending on your system's memory resources. Of course, after you save your image, you lose the chance to undo or redo changes made prior to the save.

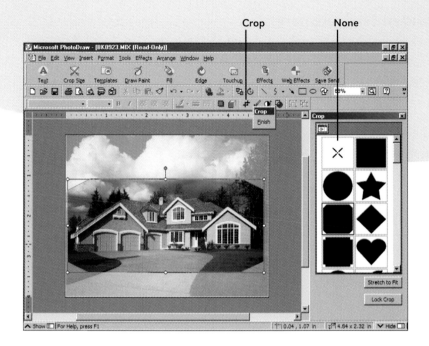

Figure 9-8
You can trim away the outer portions of a photo using a variety of crop designs.

2 Drag in your image to reveal the area you want to *keep*. Anything under the coating will get clipped away. Use the selection and rotate handles as usual to reshape and reorient the crop boundary; drag inside the boundary to move it.

3 Click Finish in the floating toolbar. PhotoDraw crops the photo, as expected. But at any time, you can go back and restore the original image by clicking the None icon in the Crop workpane, labeled in Figure 9-8. You can even restore the image *after* you save it to disk, as long as you save in the PhotoDraw format (.mix).

To permanently crop the image, click the Lock Crop button in the workpane. This time, you really and truly get rid of everything outside the crop boundary.

tip

To automatically enlarge the crop boundary so that as much of the photo as possible will be retained within the crop shape, click the Stretch To Fit button in the workpane.

note

Unlike other programs, which crop all layers in a picture simultaneously, PhotoDraw applies the crop only to the selected photo or object. You can crop multiple objects by selecting them before you crop. (Just press Shift as you click each object.) But in the process of applying the crop, PhotoDraw automatically groups the objects, as if you'd used the Group command on the Arrange menu. If you later ungroup the objects, the cropped areas return, even if you chose Lock Crop when applying the crop. For more about grouping, see Chapter 8.

Making Areas Transparent

PhotoDraw offers two tools for making pixels transparent. The Erase *command,* found on the Crop Size visual menu, completely erases pixels. The Erase *tool,* accessed via the Touchup visual menu, enables you to make pixels either fully or partially transparent.

No matter which transparency option you choose, if another object lies beneath the photo in the object stack, that object becomes visible through the transparent areas. (See Chapter 8 for more about object stacking.) Otherwise, you see the picture canvas.

To make a portion of your picture completely transparent, choose Erase from the Crop Size visual menu to display the Erase workpane, shown in Figure 9-9. Your next task is to draw a boundary around the area you want to make transparent. You do this using the same techniques you use to select an area using the Cut Out command, explained earlier. However, unlike the Cut Out command, the Erase command doesn't have a Put In New Picture check box, and the Copy button is disabled.

Figure 9-9
The top frame shape serves as a guide for drawing a custom outline in preparation for erasing the portion of the shirt that hangs outside the frame.

In Figure 9-9, I'm working on the woman's photo that appears in the Martin Realty Web page. (See Figure 4-2 in Chapter 4.) My goal was to erase the shirt areas that overhang the top abstract shape in the frame. So that I could see exactly where to erase, I moved the photo to the middle of the stacking order, underneath the top shape. Then I lowered the opacity of the top shape (using the Transparency effect on the Effects visual menu) so that I could see the woman's photo through the shape. Then I selected the photo, selected By Drawing from the Erase workpane, and drew my outline, using the edge of the shape as my guideline. After erasing the area, I made the shape fully opaque again and slipped it behind the photo.

The Erase tool on the Touchup visual menu enables you to erase pixels as if you were rubbing over them with a pencil eraser. In this case, your eraser is really a brush that "paints" transparency onto the pixels it touches. Choose a brush size and shape from the Touchup workpane, and then drag over the pixels you want to rub out, as shown in Figure 9-10. If you set the Amount slider to 100, you get full transparency, just as if you used the Erase command. At anything less than 100, you get partially opaque pixels.

note

Remember that the Erase command and tool don't delete pixels from the picture—they merely lower the pixel opacity. All pixels, even completely transparent ones, add to the size of the image file, so always crop your picture as tightly as possible before you save it for the Web. See the upcoming section "Saving Pictures for the Web" for more about how transparent pixels behave on a Web page.

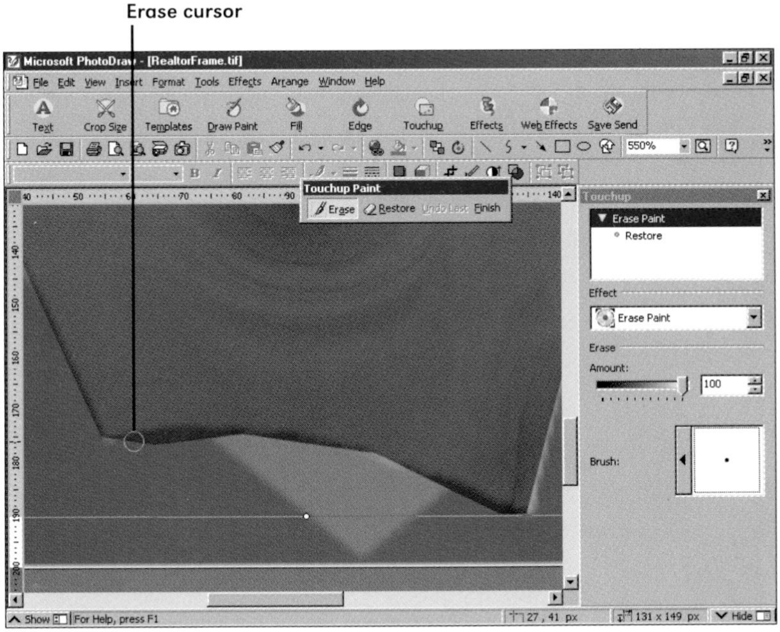

Erase cursor

Figure 9-10
Choose Erase from the Touchup visual menu, and then drag to lower the opacity of the pixels under your cursor.

tip

The Erase tool is perfect for getting rid of stray pixels that you miss when using the Erase command. In Figure 9-10, for example, I'm erasing the little remnants of the woman's shirt that I failed to include in the outline I drew in Figure 9-9. You can also use the Erase tool to touch up errant strokes of the painting tools, covered in Chapter 8.

lingo

If you want to sound like an image editing pro, refer to color and correction effects as *filters*.

To bring erased pixels back into view, click the Restore button on the floating toolbar and then drag over them. You can drag the Amount slider to adjust the amount of transparency. At 100 percent, the erased pixels are restored to full opacity. Use a lower setting to partially restore the pixels. Click Finish on the floating toolbar when you finish erasing.

Adjusting Colors, Brightness, and Contrast

Of all the photo editing tools, you'll likely get the most use out of the color filters. Using these tools, you can fix photos with color-balance problems—meaning that they're overly blue, red, or green—increase or decrease brightness, and perform other tricks related to color, exposure, and contrast.

On the Effects visual menu, click Color Effects to display the Color workpane, shown in Figure 9-11. Then select the filter you want to use from the Effect drop-down list. If you're not sure what a filter does, the upcoming sections explain each one.

Figure 9-11

Choose Correct By Painting to adjust your photo by dragging over the pixels you want to change.

Brush cursor

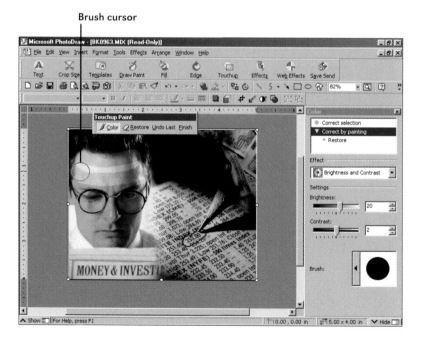

If you choose Correct Selection at the top of the Color workpane, your changes affect whatever portion of your picture is selected. (See the preceding sections in this chapter to find out how to select stuff.) Some filters offer an Automatic button when you work in this mode; click the button to ask PhotoDraw to assess the picture and make whatever change it deems necessary. If you don't like the results, press Ctrl+Z to undo the edit.

For all filters except Negative and Grayscale, you also can apply selective changes by dragging over the pixels you want to adjust. To go this route, choose Correct By Painting at the top of the Color workpane, choose a brush size from the workpane menu, and drag over the areas you want to change. Click Undo Last in the floating toolbar to undo your last edit. You can also click Restore in the toolbar and drag over altered pixels to bring back their original colors. Click Finish when you're done correcting.

Although the Correct By Painting option allows you to correct on the fly, achieving the results you want can be difficult because the effects of your drags are cumulative. For example, in Figure 9-11, I chose the Brightness And Contrast filter, adjusted the filter settings as shown in the workpane, and swiped from left to right across the top of the man's forehead. Then I moved the brush down and dragged in the other direction, winding up at the position marked by the brush cursor in the figure. Where my two strokes overlap, the pixels are twice as bright as the other altered pixels.

Unless you're making very subtle changes to a small area, you can usually get better results in less time by using the Cut Out tools to select the area you want to change and then applying your edit to the entire selection instead of trying to paint on the change.

Tweaking exposure and contrast

Choose the Brightness And Contrast filter from the Effect drop-down list in the Color workpane, and then drag the Brightness slider, shown in Figure 9-11, to correct underexposed or overexposed pictures. Drag the Contrast slider past the midpoint mark to boost contrast, making dark pixels darker and light pixels lighter. You can also click the Automatic button to have PhotoDraw assess brightness and contrast levels and adjust them for you. If you don't like the program's decisions, press Ctrl+Z to undo the change.

note

When you're adjusting picture brightness, keep in mind that pictures typically look lighter when viewed on a Macintosh computer than on a computer running Microsoft Windows. If your picture already borders on being too light on a Windows machine, tone it down a little to make sure that it's not unacceptably light on a Macintosh system.

Removing or adding a tint

As its name implies, the Tint filter adds a particular color to your photo. But it can also subtract a color from the image. Drag the Hue slider in the workpane to set the tint color, and then enter a positive Amount value to add more of the color. Enter a negative Amount value to subtract the color. In Figure 9-12, the left example is the original image; the right example shows the picture after I added a bright turquoise tint at the maximum Amount value, 100.

Figure 9-12
The Tint filter infuses all pixels with a specific color.

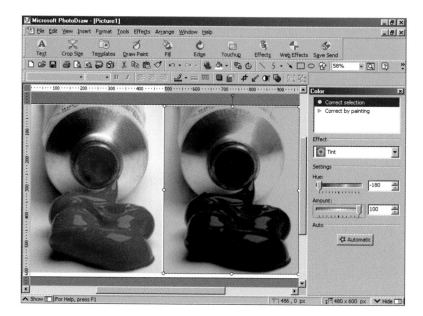

In Correct Selection mode, the Automatic button is supposed to automatically remove any unwanted color cast—for example, the greenish cast that often appears in pictures taken in fluorescent light. If PhotoDraw doesn't make this call correctly, press Ctrl+Z to undo the change and then remove the cast using the Tint filter's manual controls or those of its more sophisticated color-correction cousin, Color Balance.

Shifting all colors simultaneously

The Hue portion of the Hue And Saturation filter spins all selected pixels around the color wheel, which is a circular graph that plots out the entire spectrum of colors. Red occupies the 0-degree point on the wheel;

green sits at 120 degrees; and blue hangs out at 240 degrees. So if you raise the Hue slider to, say, 120, all pixels move 120 degrees clockwise around the wheel. Red pixels become green, green pixels become blue, and blue pixels become red. Pure gray, white, and black pixels don't change at all.

For a look at this color spinning in action, see Figure 9-13. The left image is the original. Raising the Hue value to 120 degrees sent the red paint pixels from their initial position on the color wheel, 0 degrees, to the 120-degree mark, which is green. Notice, too, the dark region around the upper-left rim of the paint tube. The original pixels have just a touch of blue in them. Moving those blue pixels 120 degrees takes them from 240 degrees to 360 degrees—or 0, depending on how you want to look at it—which is why they have a reddish cast in the image on the right.

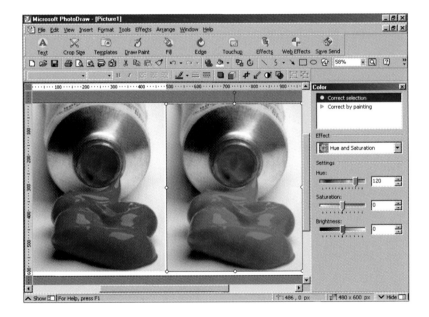

Figure 9-13
Use the Hue slider to spin colors around the color wheel.

tip

If doing all this color math seems intimidating, just remember this: If you find a photo that's perfect in all respects except color, play around with the Hue slider to see whether you can shift the colors to a palette that's more to your liking. Remember that you can select a portion of the image first to confine the change to a particular area.

Making your colors bolder

The other important slider offered by the Hue And Saturation filter, Saturation, increases or decreases color intensity. Raise the Saturation value to give dull colors a bit more life; lower it to suck some color out of the photo.

As for that Brightness command beneath the Saturation slider, I don't think you'll find much use for it. Unlike its Brightness And Contrast filter counterpart, which adjusts the brightness of pixels, this Brightness slider merely adds white to all pixels if you drag it to the right of the midpoint and adds black if you drag to the left of the midpoint. Any absolute black or white pixels remain untouched.

Colorizing a photo

Like Tint, the Colorize filter douses a photo with a single color. But while Tint mixes the new color with the existing colors, Colorize overrides the hue of the current pixels but retains their original brightness values, so you don't lose the photo's natural shadows and highlights. Also, you can choose to leave either white or black pixels untouched. The end result? Colorize leaves you with a single hue and is typically more subtle and natural than Tint.

To better understand the difference between Colorize and Tint, compare the image on the right side of Figure 9-14 with the Tint example in Figure 9-12 on page 212. In both cases, I used the same color—bright turquoise—and set the Amount slider to 100.

Figure 9-14

Colorize replaces all colors with the hue you choose in the workpane but retains the original highlights and shadows.

After picking a color for the Colorize filter, drag the Amount slider to adjust the intensity of the effect. To completely eliminate the original hues, set the Amount value to 100 or −100. A positive Amount value keeps white areas white; a negative value leaves black untouched instead.

Adjusting color balance

You can remove unwanted color casts using Tint, but you'll probably be happier working with the Color Balance filter instead. Color Balance enables you to add more of one color while subtracting another color and to work with three different pairs of colors. This is the professional's method for correcting out-of-whack colors.

The Color Balance workpane contains three color sliders representing the three primary colors in the RGB color model (red, green, and blue) and their direct opposites on the color wheel. Drag toward a color to add more of it and subtract its opposite by the same amount. In Figure 9-15, the image on the left contains a little too much yellow and green. I fixed the problem by setting the Magenta/Green slider to −8 and the Yellow/Blue slider to +10.

tip

Colorize is the perfect filter for giving a full-color photo that faded antique photograph effect. Select a brownish yellow for the effect color, and use an Amount value of −100. (I use a negative value because the white areas in an antique photo are more likely to shift color over the years than black areas.)

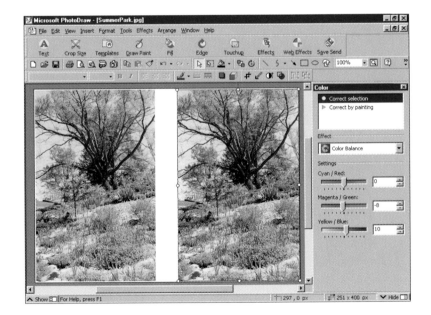

Figure 9-15
The Color Balance filter gives you more sophisticated color-correction controls than Tint.

Inverting and removing colors

The Negative and Grayscale filters are both one-shot, automatic filters. You can apply them only to an entire selection; you can't apply them by dragging as you can the other filters.

Negative inverts your colors, which creates a photo-negative effect. Grayscale sucks all color out of your image, leaving you only with shades of gray. Figure 9-16 shows examples of both effects. After duplicating the original image, shown at the top of the figure, I applied the Negative effect to the left half of the copy and applied Grayscale to the right half.

Figure 9-16
These autumn leaves (top) change colors the digital way, thanks to an application of the Negative filter (lower left) and the Grayscale filter (lower right)

note

A true grayscale image contains just 256 colors. The PhotoDraw Grayscale effect doesn't reduce your photo to 256 colors—it just makes all colors shades of gray. You can continue to use any color you want when you draw, paint, or add text. As an example, see Figure 9-4 on page 201, which includes one grayscale object (the wood background) and three full-color objects (the wood in the center of the frame and the two text objects).

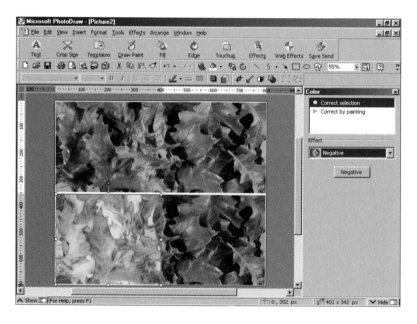

Restoring original colors

One of the really cool things about PhotoDraw's color filters is that as long as you save the picture in the PhotoDraw file format, you can get your original colors back at any time. The key is the Restore filter.

Like the other color effects, Restore offers two application modes, Correct Selection and Correct By Painting. To restore colors, you must use the same mode that you used to change them in the first place. If you applied your color effects using Correct Selection, click Correct Selection in the Color workpane, choose Restore from the Effect drop-down list, and click the Restore button. All original colors in the selection are restored. If you applied color effects using Correct By Painting, click

Correct By Painting in the workpane, choose Restore from the Effect drop-down list, choose a brush from the Brush list, and drag over the pixels you want to restore. Set the Amount slider to 100 percent to get all original colors back; lower the Amount value to lessen the impact of the tool, which leaves you with partially restored colors. Click Finish in the floating toolbar when you're done restoring.

tip

Anytime you're working with an effect in the Correct By Painting mode, you can access the Restore tool by clicking Restore on the floating toolbar.

Sharpening Focus

PhotoDraw, like most entry-level image editing programs, offers a Sharpen filter, which attempts to sharpen the focus of slightly blurry images. Choose Blur And Sharpen from the Touchup visual menu to reveal the single Blur/Sharpen slider. Drag the slider to the right to sharpen the image; drag to the left to blur it.

Exploring Other Photo Editing Options

The preceding sections introduce you to just some of the PhotoDraw photo touchup and effects tools. I don't have room to explore each and every photo editing feature here, but I want to provide you with a few last tips to help you explore the rest of the tools on your own. You can find more information about all the tools by clicking Contents And Index on the Help menu.

caution

Sharpening filters can't really restore focus to blurry pictures. What they do is create the illusion of sharper focus by increasing the contrast between neighboring pixels. Be careful not to oversharpen your pictures, or they'll appear grainy.

- Perhaps the most useful of the remaining tools is the Clone tool. With this tool, you copy pixels from one area and then drag to "paint" the copied pixels onto another region. Cloning is a great way to cover up tiny image flaws. For example, you can cover up a scratch in a scanned image by cloning neighboring pixels over the scratch.

- The Touchup visual menu offers automated filters for removing red eye, dust, and scratches from your pictures. Like most automated filters, these usually produce less satisfactory results than you get if you make manual corrections. To fix red-eye problems, just clone some correctly colored eye pixels over the red ones. Or dab some dark paint over the red pixels using the paint tools discussed in Chapter 8. You also can clone or paint away dust and scratches. Applying a slight blur to the area can also make dust and scratches less visible.

- You can apply shadows, artistic effects, and all the other special effects discussed in earlier chapters to photos as well as to text and graphics. Also play with the Distort filter on the Effects menu to create funhouse effects. To add a simple frame around a photo, use the options on the Edge visual menu.

- To move, copy, rotate, align, or otherwise rearrange photos, follow the same steps provided for manipulating graphics in Chapter 8. However, resizing photos involves some special considerations, which the next section covers.

- To combine several photos into a collage, open the first picture and then use the techniques described in Chapter 8 to insert additional photos. You can merge photos, graphics, and text into a single picture, as I did to create the image in Figure 9-17. The "film" background is just a black rectangle to which I added a row of white rounded rectangles at the top and bottom to form the sprocket holes. I inserted the three photographs and then added the text labels beneath each picture.

lingo

After creating a composite picture like the one in Figure 9-17, you can turn it into an *image map*, which just means to format it so that elements in the image serve as links. Chapter 10 explains how to assign links to images in Microsoft FrontPage 2000.

Figure 9-17
This image consists of a drawn graphic (the film), three photos, and text labels.

Resizing Pictures

When sizing photos—or any graphic, for that matter—for screen display, you work in terms of pixels, not inches or pixels per inch. Each image pixel equates to one monitor pixel, so you simply set the number of horizontal and vertical pixels in your image according to how much of the screen you want the image to consume. I cover this topic thoroughly in

Chapter 3, so I won't repeat that discussion here. But do remember these pertinent facts:

- Adding pixels does not improve on-screen image quality. It merely makes your picture display at a larger size and, more important, can degrade image quality.

- Removing pixels usually does less damage, but you may notice some quality loss if you dump a large percentage of original pixels.

With those warnings out of the way, you set the final number of pixels in your picture as follows:

1 First, save a backup copy of your image in case you ever need your original pixels back.

2 Click the photo to select it.

3 On the Crop Size visual menu, click Resize.

4 If the photo is the only object in the picture—you don't have any text, graphics, or additional photos—click Resize Picture at the top of the Resize Picture workpane and set the Units value to pixels. Make sure that the Maintain Proportions check box is selected so that you don't distort the photo. Then enter the new dimension in the Width or Height box.

  If the photo is one of several objects in the picture, click Resize Picture and set the Units value to pixels. Then click Resize Object and enter the new photo dimensions. (Double-check this step—it's important that you select Resize *Object* here. Resize Picture enlarges all objects.)

You also can drag the handles that appear around a selected photo to change its size. You'll see the pixel numbers change in the Resize Workpane as you drag the handles.

Note that PhotoDraw doesn't really add or delete pixels until you save your picture in some format other than the PhotoDraw format. Instead, it simply enlarges or reduces the existing pixels to display the picture at the size you specify. That means that you can play around with the photo size in PhotoDraw without worrying that each time you change the size, you're doing more harm to the image by continually adding or subtracting pixels. When you save the picture to GIF or JPEG (or any other file format except the PhotoDraw format, for that matter), the program makes the official change to the pixel count.

lingo

Adding or deleting pixels from an image is known as *resampling*.

tip

Many Web design programs enable you to resample photos after placing them in your Web page. But I recommend that you do this work in your image editing program instead. After you resample an image, you can sometimes improve its appearance by applying a small amount of sharpening or tweaking contrast, which requires your image editor. In addition, the image processing engines in imaging software typically are more sophisticated than in programs that aren't geared primarily toward this task.

lingo

GIF stands for Graphics Interchange Format. GIF is pronounced either "jiff" or "gif" (with a hard *g*), depending on who you ask. If you ask me, it's a hard *g*, as in *graphics*.) JPEG, pronounced *jay-peg*, stands for Joint Photographic Experts Group, which is the name of the organization that developed the format. PNG, pronounced *ping*, stands for Portable Network Graphics.

Saving Pictures for the Web

When preparing graphics for the Web, you can pick from two file formats: GIF and JPEG. You may hear about other formats, such as PNG, but they aren't supported widely enough to make them a good choice at present.

If you're working with a photo, JPEG is the way to go; for simple graphics and text objects that feature large areas of solid color, go GIF. You also must use GIF if you want your Web page to show through transparent areas of the picture or to apply animation effects, explored in the next chapter. (However, see the tip at the end of the "Saving Photos as JPEG Images" section to find out a way to fake GIF transparency and still use the JPEG format.)

In either case, the first step is to save your picture in the PhotoDraw native format, .mix. All other formats *flatten* the picture, which means that they merge all picture objects and you can no longer manipulate the individual objects as you can when they lived separate lives.

The rest of this chapter details how to save pictures in all three formats as well as how to retain transparent areas when you save in the GIF format.

Saving in the PhotoDraw Format

Always save a copy of your picture in the PhotoDraw format, .mix, when you close the picture after editing it or before you save it in some other format. Also save frequently while you're working on the picture so that if your system freezes or the power goes out, you don't lose all your edits.

Saving in PhotoDraw works pretty much like it does in other programs. You do have a few unique options, however. Here's the lowdown:

- To save the entire picture for the first time, click the File menu, click Save As, give the picture a name, and then select the PhotoDraw format from the Save As Type drop-down list. Select a storage location, and click Save or press Enter.

- When you save using the PhotoDraw format, you can choose to merge all objects. Click the Options button in the Save As dialog box to display a tiny dialog box. Select the Save Picture As One Object check box, and click OK to return to the Save As dialog box.

    Why would you want to do this? Because PhotoDraw can move faster when working with a smaller group of independent objects. Flattening a picture can also reduce file size, another factor in how quickly PhotoDraw does your bidding. However, be sure that you're really done editing the individual elements before you save them as one.

- To resave an open picture in the same format you previously used, press Ctrl+S or click the Save button on the Standard toolbar.

- To resave the picture in some other format or under another name, click the File menu and then click Save As.

- To save just the selected object, click the File menu and then click Save Selection.

Saving GIF Images

GIF is the format of choice when you're saving simple graphics with broad areas of flat color, like those featured in Chapter 8. GIF does have a major drawback—it can save a maximum of 256 colors, which can make photos and graphics with lots of subtle color changes look terrible. Figure 9-18 shows you the difference between a full-color photo and one that's been reduced to 256 colors.

Figure 9-18
A full-color image (top) takes a turn for the ugly when saved in the GIF format (bottom) because GIF can save only 256 colors.

But GIF also offers some important advantages. First, files are usually smaller than JPEG images because of the 256-color limit. Second, you can apply special GIF effects that make the image appear to move on the Web page, as explored in the next chapter. But more important, you can save a picture in a way that enables the Web page background to show through empty parts of the picture canvas.

Figure 9-19 shows a section of the Coho Winery Web site featured in Chapter 1. In the left example, I took advantage of the transparency option, so the empty canvas areas around the wine glasses are invisible. In the right image, saved without transparency, you see the canvas, which is white in this case.

Figure 9-19
Here you see examples of graphics saved with GIF's transparency option (left) and without (right).

The one fly in the GIF transparency soup is that a thin fringe of canvas pixels may be left behind along the edges of opaque areas. If you place the image on a Web page that uses a dark background, the stray pixels create a white halo like the one that surrounds the left strawberry in Figure 9-20. (This assumes that your picture canvas was white, as by default.) When you save your image using the Save For Use In Wizard explained in the upcoming steps, you can tell PhotoDraw to tint those canvas remnants with a color that will blend into your page background. In the right

Figure 9-20
Stray canvas pixels create a white halo (left); filling the renegade pixels with blue eliminates the problem (right).

example in the figure, I specified the same blue that I used for the picture background.

PhotoDraw goes about this business of creating a GIF with transparency a little differently than most other photo editors. In most programs, you can make a single color transparent when you save to GIF. You choose the color, and then the photo editor makes all pixels that are that color transparent throughout the image. PhotoDraw does have a tool for specifying a transparent color, which you access by clicking the Set Transparent Color button on the Formatting toolbar. But all this really does is bring up the Erase workpane with the By Color option selected. You click the color you want to make transparent, and PhotoDraw erases similarly colored pixels, as explained earlier in this chapter. If you prefer this approach, go ahead and use it, but still fill your canvas with a background-blending color to reduce the possibility of haloing.

Now that you've got a grip on GIF, the next two sections explain how to save a picture with and without transparency. In both cases, I show you how to do the job using the Save For Use In Wizard, which I think is the easiest route to glory.

Creating a GIF image with a see-through canvas

If any portion of your canvas is empty, PhotoDraw gives you two options when you save to the GIF format. You can leave the empty areas transparent, so the Web page background is visible through them, or you can fill them with a solid color. Take these steps to go the first route:

1 On the File menu, click Save For Use In to open the Save For Use In Wizard. You also can choose Save For Use In from the Save Send visual menu.

2 Click On The Web and then click Next. Figure 9-21 shows the screen that appears.

3 Assuming that you want to save the picture at its current size, click the As A Picture option. If you want to create a thumbnail version that you can use as a link to the picture at its original size, click the As A Thumbnail option instead. Chapter 10 explains how to link the two pictures together.

Figure 9-21
Click As A Picture to save the picture at its actual size; choose As A Thumbnail to create a tiny preview version of the image.

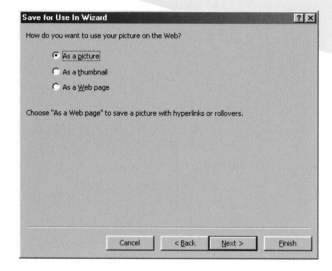

4   Click Next to display the screen shown in Figure 9-22. Select Let The Web Page Background Show Through, as shown in the figure.

Figure 9-22
To retain the transparency of empty canvas areas, choose the first option on this screen.

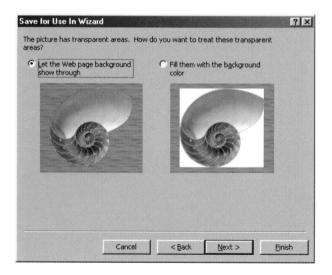

5   Click Next to display the screen shown in Figure 9-23. Select the top option, My Web Page's Background Is The Following Solid Color, and choose the color of your Web page background. PhotoDraw uses this color to tint any fringe canvas pixels at the edges of your transparent areas.

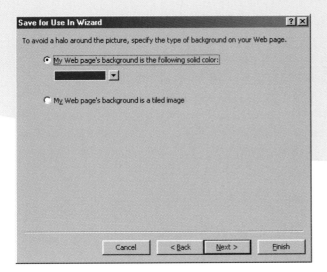

Figure 9-23
These options determine how PhotoDraw colors any fringe canvas pixels to make them blend with the Web page background.

If your background is a patterned image, you may get better results if you select the My Web Page's Background Is A Tiled Image option. This option doesn't take the color of the Web page background into account and has the effect of adding a faint shadow around the visible image areas. If you're not happy with the look when you add the picture to your Web page, resave the picture and select the My Web Page's Background Is The Following Solid Color option instead.

6 Click Next to display a screen that sums up the choices you just made. Click the Save button to proceed to the standard Save As dialog box, where you can give the image file a name and choose its storage location as usual.

Filling transparent areas with a solid color

If you want to fill empty canvas areas with a solid color, you follow a different path through the Save For Use In Wizard:

1 Follow steps 1 through 3 in the preceding section, and then click Next to display the screen shown earlier in Figure 9-22.

2 Click the Fill Them With The Background Color option. Then click Next to display a screen where you can select the fill color.

3 Click Next to display the screen shown in Figure 9-24. This screen gives you access to one of the program's hidden jewels. Here you can see previews showing your picture will look saved as a GIF image and as a JPEG image saved at various levels of JPEG compression (explained in the upcoming section "Saving Photos as JPEG Images"). You can also see how long the file will take to download at various modem speeds. Note that the initial preview displays the upper-left corner of the image. You can drag inside the Uncompressed (Original) box to scroll the display so that you can see another area of the image.

Figure 9-24
This screen of the wizard enables you to see how your picture will look when saved as a GIF image and at several JPEG compression settings.

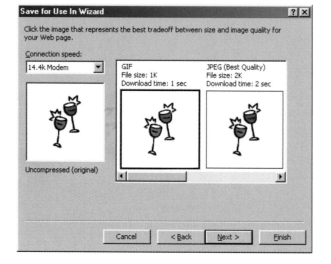

note

For some reason, the Save For Use In Wizard sometimes has problems with picture canvases that you fill with a solid color using the Format Background command, explained in Chapter 5. If you have trouble, remove the background by selecting No Color in the Format Background workpane. Then follow the preceding steps to fill the background with a solid color.

4 Click the GIF preview if it's not already selected, and then click Next or Finish. As far as I can tell, the two buttons do the same thing. That is, they display a summary screen that shows your final save settings.

5 Click Save to display the Save As dialog box, name your image file, set the storage location, and click Save.

Saving GIF images that have no transparent areas

If your picture doesn't have any transparent areas, you get to skip a few steps in the Save For Use In Wizard. Open the wizard by clicking Save For Use In on either the File menu or the Save Send visual menu. On the first screen, click On The Web and then click Next. Click As A Picture, and click Next again. Now you're whisked directly to the preview screen shown in Figure 9-24. Click the GIF preview image, click Next, and click Save.

Saving Photos as JPEG Images

As I explained a few sections ago, you should save photographs in the JPEG format. JPEG retains all your image colors rather than limiting you to 256 colors like GIF.

JPEG also enables you to compress images to shrink file sizes. Be aware, though, that JPEG uses *lossy compression,* which means that it dumps image data in order to achieve smaller files. Too much lossy compression can wreck an image, as shown in Figure 9-25.

tip

If your Web page uses a solid-color background, you can create the appearance that a JPEG image has a transparent canvas by filling the canvas with the same color as the page background before you save.

Figure 9-25
The more compression you apply, the more image data you lose, and the worse your picture looks.

Best quality   **High quality**

Medium quality   **Low quality**

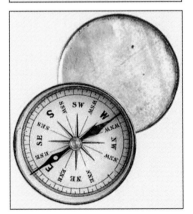 

To save your picture in this format, follow the same procedure I explained in the preceding section. In the screen shown in Figure 9-24 on page 226, select the image preview that provides the best trade-off between image quality and file size and then proceed with the save as usual.

Uncovering PhotoDraw's Sophisticated Save Options

If you're new to digital imaging or Web graphics, stick with the PhotoDraw Save For Use In Wizard to save your pictures. But if you're familiar with GIF and JPEG and all their associated options, you may want to bypass the wizard and do a "manual" save by clicking Save As on the File menu.

After you select GIF or JPEG as your file format in the Save As dialog box, click the Options button to display the Export Options dialog box, which contains advanced GIF and JPEG options. The figure below shows the GIF settings available in the dialog box. For this format, you can choose to convert the image to a grayscale image, save the image using a custom color palette, and even set a threshold to determine what level of opacity PhotoDraw should use when deciding which pixels should be transparent and which should be left alone. Note that the program automatically applies LZW Compression to GIF images; this is a *lossless* compression scheme that does no damage to your image quality.

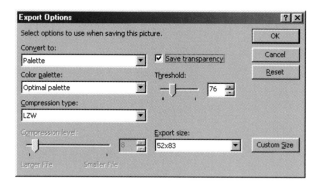

For JPEG, you can choose to convert the image to grayscale as well as to specify how much JPEG compression you want to apply. The option in the Export Options dialog box gives you a higher degree of control over the exact amount of compression than you get when you use the Save For Use In Wizard.

For all file formats, clicking the Custom Size button displays a dialog box that enables you to set print resolution, pixel dimensions, and print size. These options have no place in your Web-graphics preparation, but they're mighty handy for print projects.

If you want to explore these advanced options further, search the PhotoDraw help system, which is accessible from the Help menu. Or click the Question Mark button in the upper-right corner of the Export Options dialog box, and click an option to see what it does.

10

HTML

INTO THE PICTURE

All you need to know about . . .

- Adding graphics in FrontPage

- Tweaking pictures using FrontPage tools

- Positioning graphics

- Formatting a graphic as a link

- Turning a graphic into an image map

- Creating thumbnails that link to larger images

- Adding alternative text to graphics

- Using advanced Web technologies to create rollovers and animated GIFs

You may find it odd that I've spent nine chapters showing you how to create Web graphics but I haven't yet explained how to actually add a picture to a Web page. The truth is, though, that understanding the stuff I've presented in all the preceding chapters makes this final bit of business go much more smoothly, for reasons that will become clear as you work your way through this chapter.

In addition to finding out how to get your graphics into Microsoft FrontPage 2000, you'll learn how to use graphics as links, create thumbnail images that link to full-size pictures, and specify alternative text labels for graphics. I'll even show you how to venture a little beyond basic HTML to create animations and rollover effects.

Preparing Your Picture

Before you place a picture onto your Web page, you need to complete a few preparatory steps:

- **Set the picture size in pixels.** Chapters 8 and 9 show you how to size pictures in Microsoft PhotoDraw 2000. If you don't understand how to work with pixels as your unit of measurement, review Chapter 3. Remember that each image pixel translates to one screen pixel, so just set the image size according to how many screen pixels you want the picture to consume. More image pixels do *not* improve the picture quality of an on-screen image; they merely make the picture display larger.

- **Save a copy of the picture in the GIF or JPEG format.** I explain both options in Chapter 9. If you want empty areas of the picture canvas to be transparent on the Web page, you must use GIF. But for photos, use JPEG. Both formats result in some data loss, so always save a backup copy of the picture in a format that retains all image information, such as the PhotoDraw native format, .mix. (In case you're not using PhotoDraw, other safe formats include TIFF, BMP, PNG, PICT, and the Adobe Photoshop native format, PSD.)

- **Check the picture's file size.** Each byte of data in the file adds to the picture's download time, so strive for the smallest possible files. You can shrink file size by dumping pixels, which also reduces the on-screen size of the picture. If you save to the JPEG format, you can apply image compression to reduce file size as well, but remember that too much compression results in a poor picture.

tip

The PhotoDraw Save For Use In Wizard offers previews that help you find the right balance between image quality and file size when setting JPEG compression levels. (See Chapter 9 for help.) The preview also lets you compare how your image will look if saved to the GIF format instead of JPEG, a move that can result in smaller files in some cases but limits your picture to 256 colors.

Importing Pictures into FrontPage

On the surface, adding a picture to a Web page in FrontPage is a simple matter. The process is essentially the same one you use to put a picture into a document in Microsoft Word, Microsoft Publisher, and other Microsoft Office programs. But there are a few important differences, so here's a step-by-step guide:

1 Click at the location where you want to insert the picture.

2 On the Insert menu, point to Picture and then click From File. The Picture dialog box appears, as shown in Figure 10-1. If you've already added graphics to the Web, their filenames appear in the list box on the left. Click a file to see a preview in the box to the right. To insert one of these images into your page, click its filename and click OK.

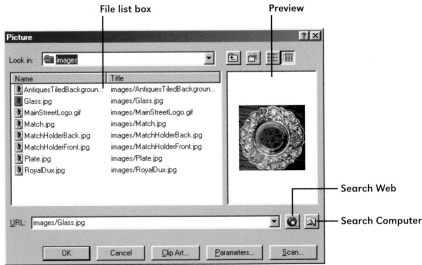

Figure 10-1
Click a filename in the list box to see a preview of the graphic.

tip

If the Pictures toolbar is visible, clicking the leftmost button, labeled Insert Picture in the upcoming Figure 10-3, opens the Picture dialog box. The next section discusses the toolbar.

If you are creating a new stand-alone page that is not part of a Web and you haven't saved yet, the Select File dialog box opens automatically; move on to step 3 to locate the picture file.

caution

Remember that every picture increases download time. After you insert a picture, check the page download estimate, shown on the status bar in the lower-right corner of the FrontPage window. (You can right-click the estimate to choose the modem speed on which you want FrontPage to base the estimate; I suggest 28.8.) There's no hard-and-fast rule for how long is too long, but in my opinion, if your page takes more than a minute to download, you risk losing your audience. Depending on your audience and page content, many people may not even wait that long. To find out how to reduce the file size of your images, see Chapter 9.

3 To select a file from outside the current Web, use these options:

- If you stored the picture in the default Webs folder—My Documents\ My Webs in Microsoft Windows 95, Microsoft Windows 98, or Windows Me—choose that folder from the Look In drop-down list at the top of the Picture dialog box. You then see a list of subfolders and files in the file list box. Double-click a folder to display a list of the files within. Just click a picture file and click OK to insert the picture.

- To track down a file located elsewhere on your computer, you need to open the Select File dialog box. As mentioned earlier, this dialog box might open automatically. You can also open the dialog box by clicking the button labeled Search Computer in Figure 10-1. After you find the file, click OK.

- You can click the Clip Art button at the bottom of the Picture dialog box to insert a graphic from the Microsoft Clip Gallery or click the Scan button to scan a picture directly into FrontPage. The Scan button also enables you to download a picture from a digital camera. However, I don't recommend these options. FrontPage isn't designed for picture editing, so its controls for sizing, editing, and saving the graphic to the GIF or JPEG format aren't as sophisticated as those in PhotoDraw and other dedicated graphics programs. So open the picture initially in your graphics software, prepare it as described in the preceding section, and then insert the finished image into FrontPage.

- Clicking the button labeled Search Web in Figure 10-1 enables you to launch Microsoft Internet Explorer and track down a file on the Internet. This feature is a little tricky, however, and doesn't always work correctly. An easier option is to close the Picture dialog box, load the page in your browser, right-click the image, and then save the picture to your hard drive. Then import the image into FrontPage as just described.

4 After you place your picture on the page, you need to save it as part of the current Web. Click the File menu, and then click Save to do so.

If you previously saved your Web, you see the Save Embedded Files dialog box, shown in Figure 10-2. Otherwise, FrontPage first presents the regulation-issue Save As dialog box and asks you to save the Web. The Save Embedded Files dialog box appears after you click the Save button.

tip

Despite its name, the URL box at the bottom of the Picture dialog box works just like the File Name box in the standard Open dialog boxes used in most Office programs. You can simply type the graphic file's pathname in the box and click OK to insert the picture into your Web page. (A pathname contains the filename plus the name of the drive and folder in which the file is stored—for example, C:\My Documents\ My Pictures\SkyImage.jpg.)

note

When you save your image as part of a Web, FrontPage makes a *copy* of the image file and puts the copy in the Web. Your original image file remains in its original location.

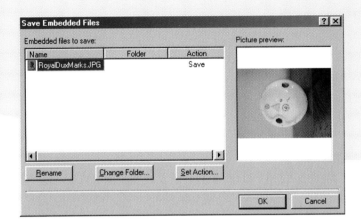

Figure 10-2

After inserting a picture, save it via this dialog box to make it an official part of your Web.

However you get to the Save Embedded Files dialog box, you have the option to choose the location where you want to store the image. You can just click OK and accept the default, which places the image inside your Web's main folder, or click the Change Folder button to choose a subfolder inside the main folder. I store all my graphics in the Images folder that FrontPage creates for each Web. That way I can easily find the picture later if I want to use it again in the current Web or in another Web.

5 After specifying the folder, click OK.

Are Web Pictures Yours for the Taking?

The inclusion of a button to search the Web in the Picture dialog box may lead you to believe that it's okay to download and use any picture that you find on the Web. Most Web browsers reinforce that notion by providing a specific command that saves a picture to your computer's hard drive. A few Web sites even offer to scour the Internet for pictures related to a specified subject and then download the images for you. However, unless you have specific permission to use someone else's images, doing so could land you in serious legal hot water for violating copyright laws. Note that the laws apply whether or not you see a copyright statement on the Web site.

On the flip side of this issue, you need to think about ways to prevent other people from illegally using *your* images. Companies such as Digimarc (*www.digimarc.com*) offer software that embeds security technology into your digital photos and services that search the Web looking for sites that are using your photos without permission. For good background information about the whole issue of copyright law, you may want to visit the Web site of the United States Copyright Office (*www.lcweb.loc.gov/copyright/*).

Deleting a Graphic from a Web Page

To delete a graphic from a Web page in FrontPage, just click it to select it and then press Delete. This deletes the picture from only the current page, however; the image file remains part of your Web if you saved the Web since you imported the picture. To remove the file from your Web, first display the Folder List, which shows folders and files associated with your Web. (Click the View menu, and then click Folder List to display the list if it's not visible.) Then click the graphic filename, and press Delete. FrontPage then displays a dialog box asking you to confirm the deletion; click Yes to do so.

Doing Minor Alterations in FrontPage

FrontPage provides a few basic graphics editing tools, which you access via the Pictures toolbar, shown in Figure 10-3. (Click the View menu, point to Toolbars, and then click Pictures to show and hide the toolbar.) I recommend that you do your picture editing work in your graphics program, not FrontPage, because you'll have access to more sophisticated tools. But if you need to make minor adjustments and you're short on time, the upcoming list introduces you to some of the quick fixes you can do with the FrontPage tools.

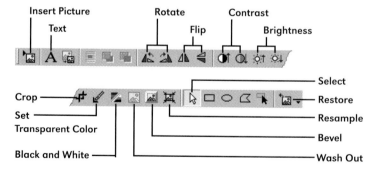

Figure 10-3
When a picture is selected, you can make simple adjustments by using the buttons on the Pictures toolbar.

note

If you're using an image as your page background and nothing on your page is selected, your picture edits affect the background image.

■ **Select**   Whenever this button is selected—as it is automatically most of the time—clicking on a graphic selects the graphic. This is the first step to making changes to a graphic in FrontPage. Your edits affect only the selected graphic.

- **Text**   The text button enables you to add labels to a selected graphic. You can also set up the text to link to another area of the Web. I suggest that you do all your text work in PhotoDraw when creating your graphic, however, because the implementation of the FrontPage text tool is a little confusing for most people. In addition, PhotoDraw offers a text anti-aliasing feature not found in FrontPage.

- **Rotate and Flip**   These buttons spin your picture 90 degrees counterclockwise or clockwise or flip it horizontally or vertically.

- **Contrast and Brightness**   The first two buttons raise and lower image contrast, respectively. The second pair of buttons adjusts brightness.

- **Crop**   This button enables you to clip away pixels at the edge of the picture. Click the button to display a rectangular crop boundary on the graphic. Drag the handles around the edge of the boundary to adjust it. Then click the Crop button again to lose everything outside the boundary.

- **Set Transparent Color**   This button enables you to make all pixels of a certain color transparent and reveal the Web page background behind the graphic. Click the button, and then click the color in your graphic that you want to make transparent.

  Be aware that this feature converts your image to the GIF format, which is the only Web format that supports transparency. The downside to GIF is that it reduces your image to a maximum of 256 colors, which can make some pictures look blotchy. For more about GIF, see the end of Chapter 9.

- **Black and White, Wash Out, and Bevel**   These three buttons apply special effects. The first converts all colors in your picture to shades of gray, the second desaturates and lightens the picture to give it a faded appearance, and the third applies a simple 3-D effect around the edge of the picture to make your graphic look like a raised button. Collectively, I give these three a big "eh, okay, whatever." They're not altogether useless and they're not harmful to your image, but they don't offer the same kind of flexibility and control as their counterparts in PhotoDraw.

caution

Unlike the PhotoDraw crop tool, which enables you to crop your picture temporarily and then retrieve cropped areas later, the FrontPage crop tool applies a permanent crop. You can always click Undo to undo the crop, of course, but after you save the Web, you can no longer get cropped pixels back.

caution

All edits that you apply via the Pictures toolbar affect only the copied picture file that FrontPage saves with the Web page. The original image file remains unaltered. So if you want to use the edited image in another Web or page, you must import the copied image file from the Web folder instead of importing the original image file.

Also, if you place the same picture multiple times in a Web, *all* copies respond to your edits. That's because FrontPage doesn't create a new picture file every time you place the image in the Web; rather, it uses the same file for all the copies. This reduces the download time of your Web because only one image file is required.

■ **Restore**   Ah, now here's a button that can really come in handy. Click this button to return your picture to the way it looked before you started messing around with it. As long as you haven't saved the Web page since you began your editing, you're cool. Otherwise, you have to delete the picture and reimport the original image file if you want to go back to square one.

Setting Size Attributes in FrontPage

When you import an image into FrontPage, the picture appears at the exact pixel dimensions you specified when preparing it in your image editor. (If you need help with this part of the process, see Chapters 3 and 9.) FrontPage does offer some controls for resizing pictures, but all are dangerous except one. Here's what you need to know:

■ After adding a picture to your Web page, right-click the graphic and choose Picture Properties to open the Picture Properties dialog box. Then click the Appearance tab, shown in Figure 10-4, and select the Specify Size check box, as shown in the figure. This control tells FrontPage to include the picture dimensions in the HTML instructions that define your Web page. This information enables the Web browser to correctly position page elements before the pictures have completely downloaded, which translates to a page that displays properly faster.

■ When you select the Specify Size box, the Width and Height boxes become available. *Don't mess with these values!* Changing them does not change the number of horizontal or vertical pixels in the image; it merely sets the *display size* of the picture—that is, you're magnifying or reducing the image display, just as if you were zooming in or out on the picture in PhotoDraw. That sounds innocuous enough, but it's not a good idea.

tip

To add a simple black border to a graphic, right-click the picture and choose Picture Properties from the shortcut menu. Inside the Picture Properties dialog box, click the Appearance tab and then set the border size by adjusting the Border Thickness value. The border size is measured in pixels. If you later assign a link to the graphic, the border color changes to match your link color settings in the Page Properties dialog box.

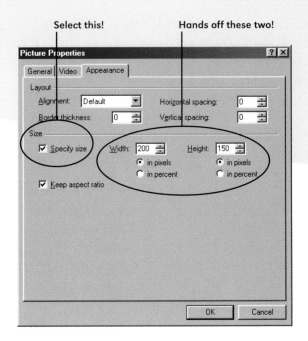

Select this! Hands off these two!

Figure 10-4
*Always select the Specify Size
check box, but* don't *change the
Width and Height values.*

If you increase the display size, you lower picture quality, as
illustrated in Chapter 3. And if you reduce the display size, you
wind up with a download time that's longer than it needs to be.
If you want the picture to be displayed at a smaller size, delete
pixels in your image editor and reimport the image into FrontPage.
That way, your file doesn't contain any meaningless pixels, and
the image download time is shorter.

■ Dragging the square handles that surround a selected graphic in
FrontPage does the same thing as changing the Width and Height
values in the Picture Properties dialog box. In case you dozed off
during the last bullet point, this is a Bad Thing.

tip

Although you should always try to precisely size your pictures before putting them into FrontPage, if you *do* wind up with a picture too large or too small, you can play with the size in FrontPage to find out what dimensions you really need. When the graphic size looks right, head for the Picture Properties dialog box and jot down the Width and Height values on the Appearance tab. Then delete the graphic, open and resize the original in your image editor, and reimport the resized picture into FrontPage. (If you saved your Web after inserting the first graphic, display the Folder List and delete the original graphic file from the Web folder before you insert the resized picture.)

■ The Pictures toolbar contains a Resample button; it's labeled in Figure 10-3. If you ignore my sage advice and change the display size of your graphic in FrontPage, clicking this button resamples your picture to match the new display size—that is, it adds or deletes pixels from the image so that you actually have exactly the number of pixels shown in the Width and Height boxes in the Picture Properties dialog box.

I recommend that you avoid the Resample button, for reasons I've discussed in earlier chapters. Adding pixels won't correct the quality loss caused by increasing the display size, but it *will* increase your image file size and download time. Deleting pixels is less detrimental—you might not notice much change in image quality, and you will decrease file size and download time. But do this chore in your image editing program. All resampling engines aren't created equal, and your image editing program is probably more capable of the task than your Web building program. Also, you may be able to improve the appearance of a resampled picture by using your image editor's sharpening filter.

Positioning Pictures

You can adjust the position of a selected graphic as follows:

■ Use the Alignment drop-down list on the Appearance tab of the Picture Properties dialog box, shown in Figure 10-4, to align text with respect to surrounding text. (To open the dialog box, right-click the graphic and choose Picture Properties from the shortcut menu.) Figure 10-5 shows the results of a few of the positioning options. In all cases, I inserted the graphic and then typed the text. I put each example in a table cell, so FrontPage aligned the contents with respect to the cell borders. Notice that the Default and Bottom alignment options do the same thing.

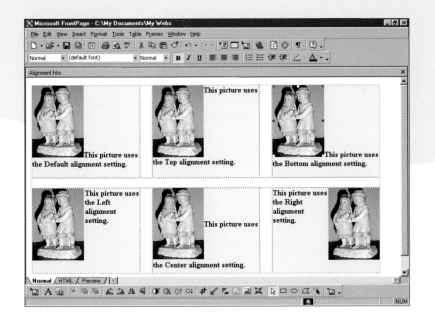

Figure 10-5
The Alignment setting in the Picture Properties dialog box controls the placement of a graphic with respect to the adjacent text.

- If there is no text on the same line as the graphic, choosing the Center option from the Alignment menu moves the picture to the center of the line.

- Normally, pictures bump right up against the neighboring text. You can put more space around a picture by raising the Horizontal and Vertical spacing values found on the Appearance tab of the Picture Properties dialog box. (See Figure 10-4.)

tip

If you applied a border to a picture using the Border Thickness option in the Picture Properties dialog box, the border may appear to change when you adjust the Horizontal and Vertical spacing values. When you look at the graphic in Page view in FrontPage, the border may look like a thin double-line border instead of a single-line border. Don't worry—the border will appear correctly in the Web browser.

caution

FrontPage offers what it calls Absolute Positioning, which enables you to drag and drop pictures around the page to position them and also to stack pictures and text on top of each other. Absolute Positioning also gives you more options for how text wraps around graphics. You access these features by choosing Position from the Format menu and by using the buttons on the Positioning toolbar. (Click the View menu, point to Toolbars, and then click Positioning to show or hide the Positioning toolbar.) The Pictures toolbar also contains a few positioning buttons.

However, Absolute Positioning features rely on advanced HTML technologies not supported by all browsers, so I suggest that you avoid them. Otherwise, your page layout will go haywire if the page is loaded into a browser that doesn't support Absolute Positioning. To turn off these features, choose Page Options from the Tools menu, click the Compatibility tab in the Page Options dialog box, and clear the CSS 2.0 (Positioning) check box. (The check box is cleared by default when you choose certain browsers or browser versions from the menus on the Compatibility tab.) I turned off the option when shooting the screen shots for this chapter, which is why the positioning buttons on the Pictures toolbar appear grayed out.

lingo

Using Graphics as Links

A picture on your Web page can do more than sit there looking pretty. You can format it as a link to another area of your site. The next few sections explain your options for using pictures in this way.

Creating a Simple Graphical Link

You can turn any picture into a graphical link in FrontPage by using the same process you use to create a text link:

1 Click the picture to select it.

2 Press Ctrl+K or choose Hyperlink from the Insert menu to display the Create Hyperlink dialog box, shown in Figure 10-6. You can also click the Hyperlink button on the Formatting toolbar to access the dialog box.

Figure 10-6
Open the Create Hyperlink dialog box to select the destination that you want to link to your graphic.

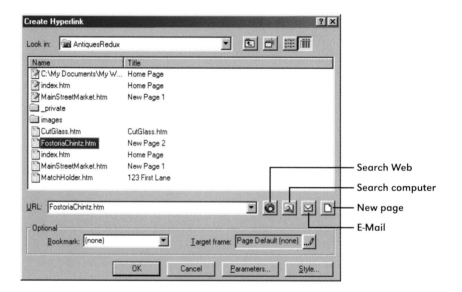

3 The next step is to specify what page you want the browser to display when someone clicks the graphic.

■ To link to a page in the current Web, click the page name in the list at the top of the dialog box. You can switch to a different Web by selecting it from the Look In drop-down list.

■ To link to a page stored in a folder not available via the Look In drop-down list, type the page address in the URL box or select from a list of previously assigned links by clicking the arrow at the right end of the box.

■ You also can click the buttons labeled Search Web or Search computer in Figure 10-6 to track down a page that's on an active Web site or stored on your computer.

4 Click OK to assign the link and close the Create Hyperlink dialog box.

That's the basic process. But you can create a few variations on the theme by using other controls in the Create Hyperlink dialog box, as follows:

■ **Create a link that opens an e-mail message window**. Click the button labeled E-Mail in Figure 10-6, and then type your e-mail address in the resulting dialog box. When the link is clicked, the browser launches the user's e-mail program and opens a new message window that has your address already entered as the destination address.

■ **Link to a new page**. Click the button labeled New page in Figure 10-6. FrontPage launches the New dialog box, and you can create your new page as usual.

■ **Link to another area on the same page**. If your Web page is very long, you might want to create a link that jumps from one part of the page to another. The first step is to insert a bookmark at the spot where people will end up if they click the graphic. To do so, select the text or graphic at the destination spot, choose Bookmark from the Insert menu, type a simple name for the bookmark in the Bookmark dialog box, and click OK. Next select the graphic that will serve as the link, press Ctrl+K to open the Create Hyperlink dialog box, select the bookmark name from the Bookmark drop-down list, and click OK.

To change the link information, right-click the graphic and choose Hyperlink Properties from the shortcut menu. FrontPage displays the Edit Hyperlink dialog box, which is just the Create Hyperlink dialog box under an assumed name. Enter the new link information and click OK.

Breaking a Link

To remove a link and return your graphic to a plain old picture, right-click the graphic and choose Hyperlink Properties to open the Edit Hyperlink dialog box. Double-click the URL box to highlight all text therein, and then press Delete so that the box is empty. Then click OK to close the dialog box.

Creating Image Maps

Image map is geekspeak for a graphic that's set up to link to different pages depending on which area of the graphic gets clicked. In the example shown in Figure 10-7, I linked the leftmost photo in the graphic to a page that offers more information about portrait photography options, the middle photo to a page that describes wedding and event photography, and the third photo to a page detailing school photo packages.

Figure 10-7

To create an image map, drag with one of the Hotspot tools to define the boundaries of the hot spot regions.

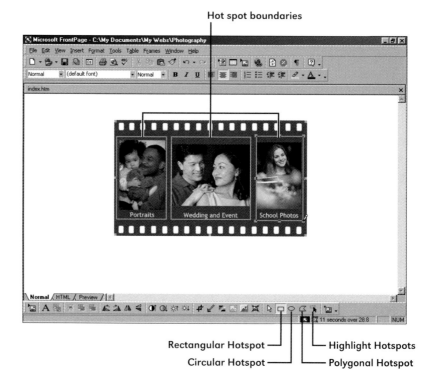

Hot spot boundaries

Rectangular Hotspot — Highlight Hotspots

Circular Hotspot — Polygonal Hotspot

To create an image map in FrontPage, you draw outlines to define areas of the image that will be clickable, known as *hot spots*. You can see the three hot spot outlines I drew for the photography image map in Figure 10-7. Follow these steps to draw your hot spot outlines and assign the respective links:

1 Click the graphic to select it.

2 If the Pictures toolbar isn't displayed, click the View menu, point to Toolbars, and then click Pictures to bring it to life.

3 Click one of the three hot spot buttons, labeled in Figure 10-7, depending on the shape of the hot spot you want to create. Click the first button to draw a rectangular outline, the second button to draw a round outline, and the third button to draw a polygonal outline.

   With the first two options, you just drag in your image to draw the outline, as you do with the simple shape tools in PhotoDraw. The polygonal tool works a little differently: Drag to create the first line, click to set the endpoint of the line, and drag again to create the next segment. When you reach the beginning of the boundary, click to close the shape.

4 After you draw an outline, the Create Hyperlink dialog box appears. Enter the link information as described in the preceding section, and click OK.

5 Repeat steps 3 and 4 to define the rest of your image map hot spots.

   After you create a hot spot, you can edit it as follows:

■ To resize a hot spot, click the area to redisplay the outline and then drag the handles that appear around the outline.

tip

Leave a gap between the edges of the hot spot outlines so that people don't "miss" the hot spot they want and trigger the adjoining one if they're not dead-on with their mouse pointer.

tip

If you have trouble distinguishing the hot spot boundaries, click the Highlight Hotspots button on the Pictures toolbar, labeled in Figure 10-7. Your graphic disappears temporarily, and the hot spot boundaries appear as simple black outlines. The selected hot spot is filled with black. Click the Highlight Hotspots button again to switch back to the regular image and boundary display.

note

Sometimes, you may be able to reduce your overall page download time by creating a "faux" image map. Instead of combining separate graphics into one image and then mapping out hot spots, as in Figure 10-7, import each piece separately into FrontPage and assign individual links via the normal process. If you insert the graphics right next to each other, they appear to form one seamless image, just like an image map. (Creating a table to hold each piece can make arranging the picture pieces easier.)

Why would this approach affect download time? Because you may be able to save one or more of the individual graphics in a way that results in a smaller total file size than if you combine them all into one. For example, perhaps you could apply a higher degree of JPEG compression to one of the graphics than is possible for the others. Try both methods to see which one gives you the shorter download time.

- ■ To move a hot spot, drag inside the outline.
- ■ To change the link information, right-click the hot spot, choose Picture Hotspot Properties from the shortcut menu, and then enter the new information in the Edit Hyperlink dialog box.
- ■ To delete a hot spot altogether, click the area to display the hot spot boundary, and then press Delete.

Creating Thumbnail Links

If your image contains lots of product shots, you may want to include a thumbnail-size version of each image and then link the thumbnail to a full-size image. You can then add text to your page that invites people to click a thumbnail to view the larger version of the image. This saves people time when browsing because thumbnails are small in size and can be downloaded quickly. People can download the larger images if they want a closer look at a particular product.

The next two sections show you how to create a thumbnail link by using an automated FrontPage feature and how to do the job on your own, which gives you some additional flexibility.

Using the FrontPage Auto Thumbnail feature

FrontPage can create a thumbnail version of any image in your Web and then swap it for the original image on the Web page. When someone clicks the thumbnail, the browser displays the larger image all by its lonesome. In most browsers, you then have to click the Back button to return to the page that holds the thumbnail image.

To create this type of thumbnail, click the image to select it and then click the Auto Thumbnail button on the Pictures toolbar, labeled in Figure 10-8. FrontPage creates the thumbnail, substitutes it for the original, and adds the appropriate link information.

tip

You can customize the size of your thumbnails and give them borders or beveled edges by choosing Page Options from the Tools menu and then adjusting the settings on the Auto Thumbnail tab of the resulting dialog box. Your changes affect the next thumbnails you create.

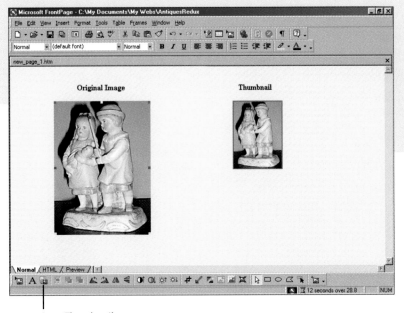

Auto Thumbnail

Be sure to save your Web after you create the thumbnail; you'll see the same Save Embedded Files dialog box you get when you save the first time after inserting any new graphic. For more about the Save Embedded Files dialog box, see the section "Importing Pictures into FrontPage" at the beginning of this chapter.

To edit the thumbnail link, use the same techniques discussed earlier, in the section "Creating a Simple Graphical Link." To delete the thumbnail, click it and press Delete.

Linking a thumbnail to another Web page

In some cases, you may want to link a thumbnail to a larger image that you put on a regular page in your Web. For example, I linked the thumbnail version of the match striker on the home page of the antiques Web site, shown at the top of Figure 10-9, to a separate product page, shown at the bottom of the figure.

note

If you saved the Web before deleting the thumbnail, both the thumbnail image file and the original image file remain in the Web's folder, just as when you delete a regular graphic after saving the Web. Display the Folder List (by clicking Folder List on the View menu), click the image file, and press Delete to get rid of the file completely. If you want to bring back the original image to the page, just insert it again by clicking the Insert menu, pointing to Picture, and then clicking From File, as discussed at the start of this chapter.

Thumbnail link

Figure 10-9
The thumbnail image of the match striker links to a product page that offers larger views and more information about the object.

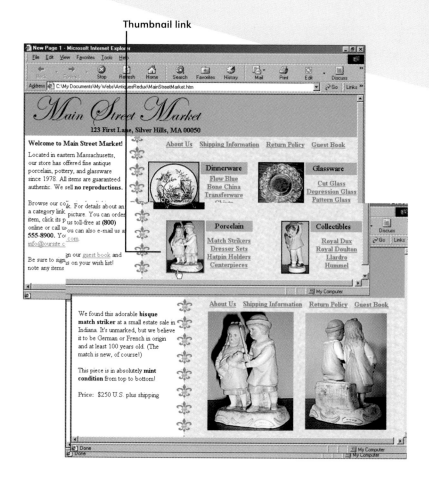

To set up this structure, I created both my original and thumbnail images in PhotoDraw and inserted each into their respective pages in the Web. Then I clicked the thumbnail image and assigned a regular hyperlink using the process outlined earlier in this chapter, in the section "Creating a Simple Graphical Link."

tip

If you previously used the Auto Thumbnail feature to create your thumbnail, you don't have to start all over to link the thumbnail to another Web page as I did. Just insert the original image into the product page, and add any accompanying text or graphics that you want to appear on the page. Then switch back to the page that contains the thumbnail, right-click the thumbnail, choose Hyperlink Properties from the shortcut menu, and change the link information to point to the product page.

Providing Alternative Text for Graphics

As much as we graphics folks love to admire our work, the harsh reality is that some people who visit our Web sites will never see our graphics. Most browsers enable the user to view pages without any graphics at all, and people who have slow Internet connections or just want the fastest possible download times take advantage of the no-images option. In fact, I sometimes surf graphics-free when I'm in a rush to find information. Hey, I said I like looking at my *own* graphics—I'm willing to forgo other people's images at times.

So how do you account for the possibility of people turning off your graphics? Add a brief text label that is displayed in place of the graphic. The text message can serve two purposes. It can indicate the content of the graphic—for example, *Spring bouquet in cachepot*—so that people can decide whether they want to view the actual image. Or it can state the action triggered by the graphic—for example, *Click here to order*.

In some browsers, alternative text comes into play even when graphics are displayed. It appears in place of the graphic until the picture is fully downloaded. And whenever the mouse cursor passes over the image, a small label containing the text appears.

You specify alternative text for a graphic as follows:

1 Right-click the graphic, and choose Picture Properties from the shortcut menu. You see the Picture Properties dialog box.

2 Click the General tab if it's not already at the forefront of the dialog box as shown in Figure 10-10.

note

FrontPage doesn't provide an automated method for specifying alternative text for the individual hot spots in an image map, just the entire image map. But you can add it manually to the HTML code that defines the image map. First, click any hot spot to display and select its outline. Then click the HTML tab at the bottom of the program window to display the HTML code for the page. The code related to the overall image map should be highlighted. Just before that code, you should see separate lines of code for each of the hot spots. These lines begin with an open bracket symbol plus the words *area href* and an equals sign, like this: <*area href*=. Right after that, you'll see the address or name of the page that's linked to the hot spot, followed by the shape, the coordinates for the hot spot, and then a close bracket symbol (>). Click right before the close bracket symbol, press the Spacebar once, and type *alt= "your text"*, substituting the label text that you want to appear for *your text*. Be sure to include the quotation marks around the text. Here's an example of how a finished line would look:

```
<area href= "Portraits.htm" shape="rect" coords="296, 43, 390, 189" alt= "Portraits">
```

3 Type your alternative text in the Text box, and click OK.

Figure 10-10
*In the Text box, type the text that
you want people to see if they
display your pages with graphics
turned off.*

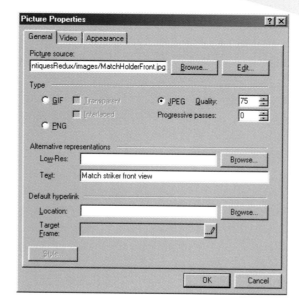

tip

To preview your alternative
text with graphics display
turned off in Internet
Explorer, save your Web and
then choose Preview In
Browser from the File menu
in FrontPage. Choose
Internet Explorer in the list,
and then click Preview. When
your page loads, choose
Internet Options from the
Tools menu. Click the
Advanced tab, and scroll
down to the Multimedia
section in the list of options.
Clear the Show Pictures check
box, and click OK. Then click
the Refresh button to view the
text-only version of your page.

Creating Special Web Effects

Throughout this book, I've focused on simple design changes that rely
solely on HTML features that enjoy widespread browser support. But I'm
going to finish by showing you how to create two special effects that
require advanced HTML technologies: animated GIF images and rollover
buttons. With the help of these effects, you can create graphics that blink,
spin, and perform other gyrations.

A Word About "Low-Res" Alternative Images
Directly above the Text box
in the Picture Properties dialog box, you see an option titled Low-Res. Because of its name, people naturally
assume that this option has to do with image resolution. It doesn't. Remember, *resolution*—pixels per inch—
is *irrelevant* on the Web. For more on this shocking statement, see Chapter 3. The Low-Res option deals with
color depth—the number of colors in an image. You can create two versions of an image, one in full color
and one with a reduced color palette, and then tell the browser to display the reduced-color image as a
placeholder until the full-color version is downloaded. The image with the smaller color palette won't look
as good on-screen but will load faster because fewer colors mean a smaller file. The point is to give viewers
a quicker way to see what the image contains so they don't have to wait for the entire image to arrive before
they know whether the content interests them. However, not all browsers support this feature. You're also
adding to the page's overall download time because you're sending an additional image.

However, a couple words of caution before we begin: First, animations and rollover buttons may cause problems for people viewing your
site with very outdated browsers, although both effects have been around
for a few years and so enjoy much wider browser support than some of
the newer multimedia features. I leave it to you to weigh the potential
risks against the benefits.

Second, *use these effects in moderation*. The more effects you add to
a page, the less impact each one has. A single flashing star placed next
to a special offer brings prominence to the promotion. Dozens of flashing
stars scattered all over the page overshadow whatever message you're trying
to communicate—unless, of course, your message is "I like flashing stars!"

Moving Pictures (Animated GIFs)

An *animated GIF* is a series of separate images that are displayed one after
the other to create the appearance of movement. All the images that make
up the animation are stored in a single GIF file, which also contains
instructions that tell the browser the order in which the images should
load, the position where each image should appear, and how long each
image should appear on-screen.

PhotoDraw offers a wizard that you can use to create a GIF animation
based on your custom graphic. Try it out:

1 Create the graphic you want to animate. Set the graphic size, and save
  it in the PhotoDraw format, as discussed at the end of Chapter 9.

2 Click Animated GIF on the Web Effects visual menu. The workpane
  displays thumbnails representing all the available animation effects,
  as shown in Figure 10-11. Click a thumbnail to see a preview of the
  effect on a sample graphic; click Preview In Browser to see your actual
  graphic in an animated state in Internet Explorer.

3 After you decide on an effect, click Finish at the bottom of the workpane
  to launch the Save Animated GIF Wizard. On the first screen, you see the
  current size of your graphic in the Export Size drop-down list. Click Next
  to move to the next screen of the wizard, shown in Figure 10-12.

Figure 10-11

PhotoDraw offers a wizard that can turn a simple graphic into an animated GIF.

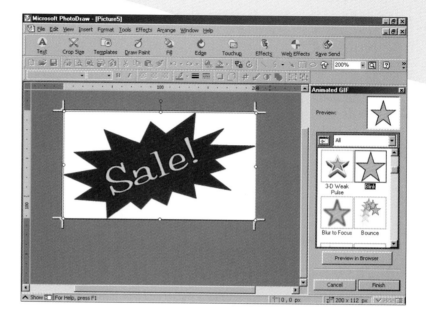

Figure 10-12

If your graphic contains only Web-safe colors, choose the second palette option.

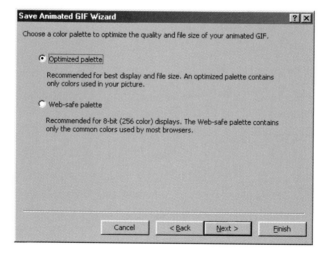

4 This screen enables you to specify the 256-color palette that you want your GIF image to follow. (Remember, a GIF image has a limit of 256 colors.) If you created your graphic using only Web-safe colors, as discussed in Chapter 3, choose the second option. But if some colors might be outside that palette, choose the Optimized Palette option. This option customizes the 256-color palette based on the actual colors in your picture. Mind you, you still may not wind up with all your original

colors, but you'll probably get closer than with the Web-safe palette option. Click Next to proceed to the next screen of the wizard.

see also

You can specify a custom palette for any GIF image that you save in PhotoDraw, animated or not, by bypassing the Save For Use In Wizard and using the regular old Save As command on the File menu instead. In the Save As dialog box, click the Options button to uncover the custom palette options. For more about saving files in the GIF format, see Chapter 9.

The next two screens are part of the normal Save For Use In Wizard that I discussed in Chapter 9. You can specify whether you want empty areas of the picture canvas to be transparent, so that the Web page background shows through, or to be filled with a solid color. Click Next after making your choices to advance to the screen shown in Figure 10-13.

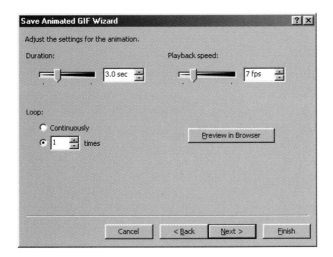

Figure 10-13
Here you can adjust the actual animation settings.

5 On this screen, you can specify the Duration value, which represents the total time that it takes to display all images in the animation once. The Playback Speed slider controls how quickly the animation will progress from one image to the next, measured in frames per second. A higher value creates a smoother effect.

If you choose the Continuously option, the animation keeps playing over and over (a surefire way to annoy people). Choose the other Loop option to tell the browser to play the animation a certain number of times—once is my vote—and then stop. You can click the Preview In Browser button to see the effect in Internet Explorer as you're tweaking these settings.

6 Click Next, and then click Save to display the Save Animated GIF dialog box. Give your graphic a name, and save the file.

Rollover Buttons

You've no doubt seen navigation buttons that change when you put your mouse cursor over them or click them. Some buttons appear to "push in," like a real push button, while others glow or change colors when you activate them.

Mouse-responsive buttons are called *rollovers*. You create rollovers by creating two or more versions of the button and then adding instructions into your HTML code that tell the browser to swap one picture for another in response to different *events*. An event, also known as a *state*, is an action that a browser can detect, such as a mouse click or movement. Many designers go for two rollover events, *onmouseout* for when the button is inactive and *onmousedown* for when the button is clicked. Some designers add a third event, *onmouseover*, which is triggered by a mouse cursor moving onto the button.

Figure 10-14 shows the graphics that make up a three-event button for a Web commerce site. From top to bottom, the graphics represent the *onmouseout*, *onmouseove*r, and *onmousedown* events.

Figure 10-14
The browser switches from the top button to the middle or bottom graphic, depending on the mouse action.

Submit Order —— *onmouseout* event

Submit Order —— *onmouseover* event

Submit Order —— *onmousedown* event

PhotoDraw provides a special effect that converts a graphic to a rollover button that has *onmouseout, onmouseover,* and *onmousedown* events. After applying the effect, you can send the button directly to FrontPage. Here's the drill:

1 Draw the graphic that you want to use as a button. Note that your entire picture will be used, but only the selected object will get the actual rollover effect. So if your button contains separate objects, group them before you move on. (Chapter 8 tells you how.)

2 Size your picture canvas so that it's about 10 percent bigger than the graphic. Some rollover effects add new pixels around the edge of your graphic, and if the canvas fits the original button exactly, the effect pixels get clipped when you save the button. To size the canvas, drag its handles, as discussed in Chapter 8. (Click the View menu, and then click Background Handles if you don't see them.)

3 Save your graphic in the PhotoDraw format (.mix) as outlined at the end of Chapter 9 so that you can access it again later if needed.

4 Select the graphic (or the object that you want to get the rollover effect), and choose Rollover from the Web Effects visual menu. You see the workpane options shown in Figure 10-15.

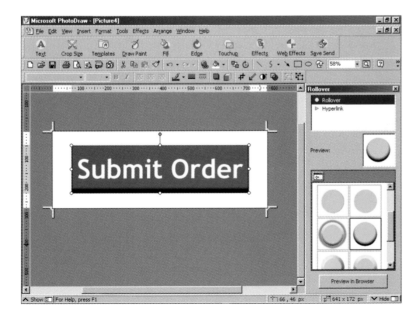

Figure 10-15
Click a thumbnail to preview the rollover effect in the workpane.

5 The thumbnails in the workpane represent different rollover effects. Click a thumbnail, and watch the Preview box in the workpane to get an idea of how the effect looks. PhotoDraw reformats your graphic to show the *onmouseout* appearance of the selected effect.

6 To see how your button will look when activated on the Web page, click the Preview In Browser button in the workpane. PhotoDraw launches Internet Explorer and displays your button in an empty browser window. Pass your mouse cursor over the button to see the *onmouseover* appearance; click the button to see the *onmousedown* appearance.

7 Switch back to PhotoDraw, and continue trying effects until you find one you like. (Pay attention to the canvas size—if any part of the button hangs off the canvas after the rollover is applied, resize the canvas to accommodate it.)

8 Click Hyperlink at the top of the workpane. Then specify what page the browser should load when the button is clicked.

9 Click Options at the top of the workpane to display an option where you can specify alternative text for the button, as discussed earlier in this chapter. You also can add text that will appear in the browser's status bar when the mouse hovers over the button. By default, the status bar shows the address of the linked page.

10 Your next step is to send all the button instructions and components to FrontPage. You can put the button at the top or bottom of the page that's currently open in FrontPage or create a new page to hold the button. (But don't worry, I'll show you how to relocate the button to some other position in a moment.) If you want to put the button on an existing Web page, switch to FrontPage, open the page, and then switch back to PhotoDraw.

On the File menu, point to Send To, and then click Microsoft FrontPage to display the dialog box shown in Figure 10-16. You can also get to this dialog box by clicking Send To Microsoft FrontPage on the Save Send visual menu. In the dialog box, click one of the three destination options I just mentioned.

Figure 10-16
PhotoDraw limits you to three destination options when you send a rollover button to FrontPage, but you can move the button after it's placed in FrontPage.

11 Click the Options button to display the dialog box shown in Figure 10-17. Here you can choose the file format and other file saving parameters for the button graphics. See the end of Chapter 9 for more information about saving Web graphics. Be sure to select the Slice Picture Into Separate Images option if it's not already selected.

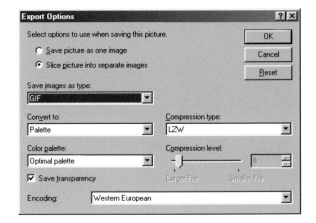

Figure 10-17
Select the Slice Picture Into Separate Images option when sending a rollover button to FrontPage.

tip

Although the GIF format is normally the right choice for simple graphics such as buttons, the JPEG format does a better job of retaining the subtle shadings in the shadows and glows applied by some rollover effects. Experiment with both options to see which one works best for the effect you choose. Of course, if you want the picture canvas to be transparent, you'll have to go with GIF.

12 Click OK twice to close the PhotoDraw dialog boxes and ship the rollover package to FrontPage. FrontPage comes to the forefront with your button at the location you chose in step 10. Your button appears inside a small table that's created automatically. Again, don't worry about the exact positioning of the button on the Web page yet; I'll explain how to relocate it momentarily.

13 In FrontPage, click the File menu and then click Save to save the rollover graphics and HTML instructions with the current Web page.

14 If you're happy with the position of the rollover button, you're done. But if not, click any cell in the table that contains the button, click the Table menu, point to Select, and then click Table to select the entire table. Next press Ctrl+X or click Cut on the Edit menu to move the table to the Clipboard temporarily. Then click at the location where you want to place the button, and press Ctrl+V or click Paste on the Edit menu to move the table from the Clipboard to your Web page.

note

A rollover that you create in PhotoDraw will include four graphics: one for each of the rollover states plus a spacer graphic. Be sure to keep all these graphics in your Web folder, or the rollover won't work.

see also | *To find out more about working with tables, see Chapter 4.*

Appendix

web-safe colors

As discussed in Chapter 3, you should select colors from the 216-color Web-safe palette when formatting text, choosing backgrounds, and creating basic graphics for your site. Sticking with this limited palette helps ensure that colors will display properly no matter what computer system, monitor settings, or Web browser people use to view your pages.

In this appendix, you'll find charts showing all the Web-safe colors along with their RBG values and hexadecimal codes. The colors are grouped in three categories: bright colors, neutral colors, and shades of gray. The table below lists the six hexadecimal pairs, and their RGB equivalents, that you can combine to create a Web-safe color. Remember that each hexadecimal code consists of three pairs of characters, the first pair representing the amount of red in the color, the second representing the amount of green, and the third representing the amount of blue.

See Chapter 3 for a complete explanation of color on the Web, including instructions on how to pick Web-safe colors in Microsoft FrontPage 2000, Microsoft PhotoDraw 2000, and Microsoft Word 2000.

Web-safe RGB values and their hexadecimal equivalents						
RGB value	0	51	102	153	204	255
Hexadecimal value	00	33	66	99	CC	FF

Examples of Web-safe RGB color values and their hexadecimal equivalents

RGB: 255,0,0	RGB: 255,255,0	RGB: 0,255,0	RGB: 0,255,255	RGB: 0,0,255	RGB: 255,0,255
Hex: #FF0000	Hex: #FFFF00	Hex: #00FF00	Hex: #00FFFF	Hex: #0000FF	Hex: #FF00FF

Bright Web-safe colors

				255, 0, 0 #FF0000	204, 0, 0 #CC0000	153, 0, 0 #990000	102, 0, 0 #660000	51, 0, 0 #330000
				255, 0, 51 #FF0033	204, 0, 51 #CC0033	153, 0, 51 #990033	102, 0, 51 #660033	51, 0, 51 #330033
			255, 51, 102 #FF3366	255, 0, 102 #FF0066	204, 0, 102 #CC0066	153, 0, 102 #990066	102, 0, 102 #660066	
		255, 102, 153 #FF6699	255, 51, 153 #FF3399	255, 0, 153 #FF0099	204, 0, 153 #CC0099	153, 0, 153 #990099		
	255, 153, 204 #FF99CC	255, 102, 204 #FF66CC	255, 51, 204 #FF33CC	255, 0, 204 #FF00CC	204, 0, 204 #CC00CC			
255, 204, 255 #FFCCFF	255, 153, 255 #FF99FF	255, 102, 255 #FF66FF	255, 51, 255 #FF33FF	255, 0, 255 #FF00FF				
204, 204, 255 #CCCCFF	204, 153, 255 #CC99FF	204, 102, 255 #CC66FF	204, 51, 255 #CC33FF	204, 0, 255 #CC00FF				
	153, 153, 255 #9999FF	153, 102, 255 #9966FF	153, 51, 255 #9933FF	153, 0, 255 #9900FF	153, 0, 204 #9900CC			
		102, 102, 255 #6666FF	102, 51, 255 #6633FF	102, 0, 255 #6600FF	102, 0, 204 #6600CC	102, 0, 153 #660099		
			51, 51, 255 #3333FF	51, 0, 255 #3300FF	51, 0, 204 #3300CC	51, 0, 153 #330099	51, 0, 102 #330066	
				0, 0, 255 #0000FF	0, 0, 204 #0000CC	0, 0, 153 #000099	0, 0, 102 #000066	0, 0, 51 #000033
				0, 51, 255 #0033FF	0, 51, 204 #0033CC	0, 51, 153 #003399	0, 51, 102 #003366	0, 51, 51 #003333
			51, 102, 255 #3366FF	0, 102, 255 #0066FF	0, 102, 204 #0066CC	0, 102, 153 #006699	0, 102, 102 #006666	
		102, 153, 255 #6699FF	51, 153, 255 #3399FF	0, 153, 255 #0099FF	0, 153, 204 #0099CC	0, 153, 153 #009999		
	153, 204, 255 #99CCFF	102, 204, 255 #66CCFF	51, 204, 255 #33CCFF	0, 204, 255 #00CCFF	0, 204, 204 #00CCCC			
244, 255, 255 #CCFFFF	153, 255, 255 #99FFFF	102, 255, 255 #66FFFF	51, 255, 255 #33FFFF	0, 255, 255 #00FFFF				
0, 255, 204 #CCFFCC	153, 255, 204 #99FFCC	102, 255, 204 #66FFCC	51, 255, 204 #33FFCC	0, 255, 204 #00FFCC				
	153, 255, 153 #99FF99	102, 255, 153 #66FF99	51, 255, 153 #33FF99	0, 255, 153 #00FF99	0, 204, 153 #00CC99			
		102, 255, 102 #66FF66	51, 255, 102 #33FF66	0, 255, 102 #00FF66	0, 204, 102 #00CC66	0, 153, 102 #009966		
			51, 255, 51 #33FF33	0, 255, 51 #00FF33	0, 204, 51 #00CC33	0, 153, 51 #009933	0, 102, 51 #006633	
				0, 255, 0 #00FF00	0, 204, 0 #00CC00	0, 153, 0 #009900	0, 102, 0 #006600	0, 51, 0 #003300
				51, 255, 0 #33FF00	51, 204, 0 #33CC00	51, 153, 0 #339900	51, 102, 0 #336600	51, 51, 0 #333300
			102, 255, 51 #66FF33	102, 255, 0 #66FF00	102, 204, 0 #66CC00	102, 153, 0 #669900	102, 102, 0 #666600	
		153, 255, 102 #99FF66	153, 255, 51 #99FF33	153, 255, 0 #99FF00	153, 204, 0 #99CC00	153, 153, 0 #999900		
	204, 255, 153 #CCFF99	204, 255, 102 #CCFF66	204, 255, 51 #CCFF33	204, 255, 0 #CCFF00	204, 204, 0 #CCCC00			
255, 255, 204 #FFFFCC	255, 255, 153 #FFFF99	255, 255, 102 #FFFF66	255, 255, 51 #FFFF33	255, 255, 0 #FFFF00				
255, 204, 204 #FFCCCC	255, 204, 153 #FFCC99	255, 204, 102 #FFCC66	255, 204, 51 #FFCC33	255, 204, 0 #FFCC00				
	255, 153, 153 #FF9999	255, 153, 102 #FF9966	255, 153, 51 #FF9933	255, 153, 0 #FF9900	204, 153, 0 #CC9900			
		255, 102, 102 #FF6666	255, 102, 51 #FF6633	255, 102, 0 #FF6600	204, 102, 0 #CC6600	153, 102, 0 #996600		
			255, 51, 51 #FF3333	255, 51, 0 #FF3300	204, 51, 0 #CC3300	153, 51, 0 #993300	102, 51, 0 #663300	

Key

255, 0, 0 — The first line shows the RGB values for each color in the chart. The format R, G, B is used.
#FF0000 — The second line shows the hexadecimal value for each color in the chart.

Neutral Web-safe colors

204, 153, 153 #CC9999	204, 102, 102 #CC6666	204, 51, 51 #CC3333	153, 102, 102 #996666	153, 51, 51 #993333	102, 51, 51 #663333
204, 102, 153 #CC6699	204, 51, 153 #CC3399	204, 51, 102 #CC3366		153, 51, 102 #993366	
204, 153, 204 #CC99CC	204, 102, 204 #CC66CC	204, 51, 204 #CC33CC	153, 102, 153 #996699	153, 51, 153 #993399	102, 51, 102 #663366
153, 102, 204 #9966CC	153, 51, 204 #9933CC	102, 51, 204 #6633CC		102, 51, 153 #663399	
153, 153, 204 #9999CC	102, 102, 204 #6666CC	51, 51, 204 #3333CC	102, 102, 153 #666699	51, 51, 153 #333399	51, 51, 102 #333366
102, 153, 204 #6699CC	51, 102, 204 #3366CC	51, 153, 204 #3399CC		51, 102, 153 #336699	
153, 204, 204 #99CCCC	102, 204, 204 #66CCCC	51, 204, 204 #33CCCC	102, 153, 153 #669999	51, 153, 153 #339999	51, 102, 102 #336666
102, 204, 153 #66CC99	51, 204, 153 #33CC99	51, 204, 102 #33CC66		51, 153, 102 #339966	
153, 204, 153 #99CC99	102, 204, 102 #66CC66	51, 204, 51 #33CC33	102, 153, 102 #669966	51, 153, 51 #339933	51, 102, 51 #336633
153, 204, 102 #99CC66	102, 204, 51 #66CC33	153, 204, 51 #99CC33		102, 153, 51 #669933	
204, 204, 153 #CCCC99	204, 204, 102 #CCCC66	204, 204, 51 #CCCC33	153, 153, 102 #999966	153, 153, 51 #999933	102, 102, 51 #666633
204, 153, 102 #CC9966	204, 153, 51 #CC9933	204, 102, 51 #CC6633		153, 102, 51 #996633	

Gray Web-safe colors

255, 255, 255 #FFFFFF	204, 204, 204 #CCCCCC	153, 153, 153 #999999	102, 102, 102 #666666	51, 51, 51 #333333	0, 0, 0 #000000

index

Note: Page numbers in italic refer to figures or tables.

Numbers and Symbols

Get on line, get the best deals, and get going!

U.S.A. **$19.99**
U.K. £14.99
Canada $28.99
ISBN: 0-7356-1110-6

Fly to Bali. Rent a room in a castle. Camp in a national park. No matter where in the world you want to go, ONLINE TRAVEL can help you plan and book your next trip like a pro! Consumer advocate and industry expert Ed Perkins shares five decades of travel experience—teaching you what to ask, where to ask, and how to ask for the best service and the lowest prices. You'll learn when using the Internet can save you hundreds of dollars—and when you can make a better deal over the phone. Whether you want to fly, cruise, or ride the rails, ONLINE TRAVEL shows you how to use what's available on line to save money—and have a great trip!

Microsoft Press® products are available worldwide wherever quality computer books are sold. For more information, contact your book or computer retailer, software reseller, or local Microsoft Sales Office, or visit our Web site at mspress.microsoft.com. To locate your nearest source for Microsoft Press products, or to order directly, call 1-800-MSPRESS in the United States. (in Canada, call 1-800-268-2222).

Prices and availability dates are subject to change.

Microsoft®
mspress.microsoft.com

If you can plug in a PC, you can build your own home network!

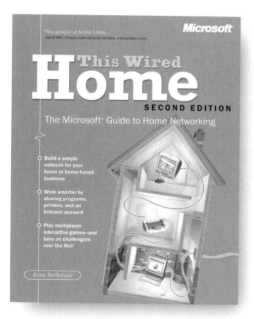

U.S.A. **$29.99**
U.K. £20.99
Canada $43.99
ISBN: 0-7356-1158-0

Are there two or more computers in your house—but only one printer? Do your kids want to play games on the Internet at the same time you want to check your e-mail? Is your entire household competing for the same dial tone? If you're running more than one PC under your roof, THIS WIRED HOME can show you how to build a simple network—and quickly multiply the computing power for your family or home office. Just follow the easy step-by-step instructions for creating a secure and reliable network that can grow as your family or business grows. This how-to guide is written in plain, non-technical language, so you can put the information to work right away.

Microsoft®

mspress.microsoft.com

Your *fast-facts*

guide

to *digital imaging* and *your PC*

Picture yourself creating amazing digital images for print, e-mail, and the Web with DIGITAL SCANNING AND PHOTOGRAPHY. Best-selling author Dan Gookin makes it easy to get started with the tools and how-tos for digital imaging on your home computer. Dan offers friendly, expert advice for matching the right scanner, digital camera, and software to your needs. And he shows you—with fun tips and easy-to-follow steps—how to take, scan, photo-edit, print, and e-mail digital pictures right now!

U.S.A.	**$12.99**
U.K.	£9.99
Canada	$18.99
ISBN: 0-7356-1012-6	

Microsoft®

mspress.microsoft.com

Target your
solution and fix it
yourself—**fast!**

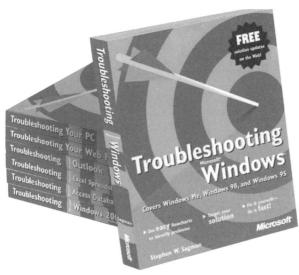

When you're stuck with a computer problem, you need answers right now. *Troubleshooting* books can help. They'll guide you to the source of the problem and show you how to solve it right away. Use easy diagnostic flowcharts to identify problems. Get ready solutions with clear, step-by-step instructions. Go to quick-access charts with *Top 20 Problems* and *Prevention Tips*. Find even more solutions with handy *Tips* and *Quick Fixes*. Walk through the remedy with plenty of screen shots to keep you on track. Find what you need fast with the extensive, easy-reference index. And keep trouble at bay with the Troubleshooting Web site—updated every month with new FREE problem-solving information. Get the answers you need to get back to business fast with *Troubleshooting* books.

Troubleshooting Microsoft® Access Databases
(Covers Access 97 and Access 2000)
ISBN 0-7356-1160-2
U.S.A. $19.99
U.K.   £14.99
Canada $28.99

Troubleshooting Microsoft Excel Spreadsheets
(Covers Excel 97 and Excel 2000)
ISBN 0-7356-1161-0
U.S.A. $19.99
U.K.   £14.99
Canada $28.99

Troubleshooting Microsoft® Outlook®
(Covers Microsoft Outlook 2000 and Outlook Express)
ISBN 0-7356-1162-9
U.S.A. $19.99
U.K.   £14.99
Canada $28.99

Troubleshooting Microsoft Windows®
(Covers Windows Me, Windows 98, and Windows 95)
ISBN 0-7356-1166-1
U.S.A. $19.99
U.K.   £14.99
Canada $28.99

Troubleshooting Microsoft Windows 2000 Professional
ISBN 0-7356-1165-3
U.S.A. $19.99
U.K.   £14.99
Canada $28.99

Troubleshooting Your Web Page
(Covers Microsoft FrontPage® 2000)
ISBN 0-7356-1164-5
U.S.A. $19.99
U.K.   £14.99
Canada $28.99

Troubleshooting Your PC
ISBN 0-7356-1163-7
U.S.A. $19.99
U.K.   £14.99
Canada $28.99

Microsoft Press® products are available worldwide wherever quality computer books are sold. For more information, contact your book or computer retailer, software reseller, or local Microsoft Sales Office, or visit our Web site at mspress.microsoft.com. To locate your nearest source for Microsoft Press products, or to order directly, call 1-800-MSPRESS in the U.S. (in Canada, call 1-800-268-2222).

Prices and availability dates are subject to change.

mspress.microsoft.com

Julie Adair King

Julie Adair King is the author of many popular books about digital photography and image editing, including *Digital Photography For Dummies, Adobe PhotoDeluxe For Dummies,* and *Microsoft PhotoDraw 2000 For Dummies*. In addition, she writes a weekly advice column about digital photography for Zing.com. She lives in Indianapolis, Indiana, where she runs her own company, Julie King Creative, Inc.

The manuscript for this book was prepared and galleyed using Microsoft Word 2000. Pages were composed using Adobe PageMaker 6.52 for Windows, with text in Garamond Light and display type in ITC Officina Sans. Composed pages were delivered to the printer as electronic prepress files.

COVER DESIGNER
Patrick Lanfear

COVER ILLUSTRATOR
Todd Daman

INTERIOR GRAPHIC DESIGNERS
Jeff Wincapaw

for Microsoft Press
Joel Panchot, James D. Kramer

PRINCIPAL COMPOSITOR
Elizabeth Hansford

PRINCIPAL GRAPHIC ARTIST
Rob Nance

MANUSCRIPT EDITOR
Shawn Peck

PRINCIPAL PROOFREADER
Lisa Pawlewicz

INDEXER
Liz Cunningham

OWNER REGISTRATION CARD   *Register Today!*   0-7356-1192-0

Return the bottom portion of this card to register today.

Easy Web Graphics

FIRST NAME   **MIDDLE INITIAL**   **LAST NAME**

INSTITUTION OR COMPANY NAME

ADDRESS

CITY   **STATE**   **ZIP**

(   )

E-MAIL ADDRESS   **PHONE NUMBER**

U.S. and Canada addresses only. Fill in information above and mail postage-free.
Please mail only the bottom half of this page.

For information about Microsoft Press®
products, visit our Web site at
mspress.microsoft.com

Microsoft®